Sociological Theory

Abhijit Kundu

Pearson

Associate Editor–Acquisitions: Qudsiya Ahmed
Associate Editor–Production: Barun Kumar Sarkar

ISBN: 978-81-317-6004-8

First Impression, 2012
Eighth Impression, 2022
Ninth Impression, 2025

Published by Pearson India Education Services Pvt. Ltd, CIN: U72200TN2005PTC057128.

Head Office: 1st Floor, Berger Tower, Plot No. C-001A/2, Sector 16B, Noida - 201 301, Uttar Pradesh, India.
Registered Office: Featherlite, 'The Address' 5th Floor, Survey No 203/10B, 200 Ft MMRD Road, Zamin Pallavaram, Chennai – 600 044.
Website: in.pearson.com, Email: companysecretary.india@pearson.com

Compositor: SNGT Publishing Services Pvt. Ltd
Printed in India by Pushp Print Services.

Contents

Preface

Simply understood, sociological theory offers us theory of society. Theory explains causalities, so sociological theory attempts to explain causal relations of society. As against popular notions of theory, we understand theory not just as speculations but as backed by empirical observations and facts. Sociological theory is different from social thinking. It is definitely rooted in the domain of historical social thought and philosophical worldview. Different sociological theories and thinkers represent different schools of philosophy and social thought. But more than just social inquiries, sociological thinkers indulge in rigorous methodological exercise to arrive at a systematic knowledge of society. Driven by different social and philosophical motivations and guided by specific epistemological thrust, sociological thinkers offer explanation for the principles of existence of society. The history of such explanation is as old as the discipline of sociology.

A textbook catering to the inquisitive student of sociology needs to trace the development of sociological theory from the classical to the modern period. The challenge of teaching sociological theory is to rescue the uninitiated student from a popular notion of theory as abstract and dry. By using original texts, students are being inspired to explore the intellectual worlds of the sociological thinkers. The seemingly disconnected thematic treatments are explained by relating them to the central task of a general theory of sociology—to seek explanatory statements on individual–societal relationships.

All the leading sociological thinkers are chronologically dealt in the textbook so that students can trace the continuity as well as the discontinuity of thoughts and themes. Every thinker is influenced by preceding thinkers and in turn impact succeeding thinkers. To appreciate all thinkers, this book tries to locate every theory in the social and personal background of its maker. A concise account of the formative background of every thinker is thought to entice the reader to take a deeper plunge into the theories. Such a treatment of sociological theory, in an elementary sense, can help in developing a perspective of sociology of knowledge.

Classical thinkers such as Karl Marx, Emile Durkheim, Max Weber and Vilfredo Pareto are all dealt as individual theorists. The salient themes of their thoughts are elaborated, whereas all the modern thinkers are seen through their respective schools of sociology. Obviously, the treatment of modern thinkers is restricted to their most significant contributions to sociology. An attempt has been made to make the thinkers intelligible and comprehensible to students of graduate and postgraduate levels. The introductory chapter tries to sketch the broad outlines of the occasion of classical sociological theories whereas the concluding chapter examines the thematic shifts and the running thread between all the theories—from the classical to the contemporary period. The book will enable students to make a curious and deeper entry into each of the sociological thinkers and their theories. As an aid, it addresses a wide base of social science students who choose to familiarize themselves with the wide range of sociological theories. Keeping this in mind, the key theoretical terms are specified in each chapter and adequate glossaries provided.

The book makes an attempt to embody the experience of long years of teaching sociological theory; using and explaining original texts as well as acquainting students with worthwhile commentaries on them. The publication of this textbook coincides with the uniform semesterization of degree courses in India at all levels of teaching. The shift to the new mode makes both teaching hours as well as the learning process dense. Without dispensing with the time-tested practice of reading the originals, the current pedagogical practice does require a book which would directly address the course syllabi and place the learning process in a comfort zone. By covering all the grand theories as well as the modern theories of more delimited scope, the book carries out an exercise—not to simplify the complex and at the same time not to complicate the simple.

The thrill of teaching and learning has kept me alert to read sociological thinkers every time afresh. I acknowledge my teachers at the Jawaharlal Nehru University, New Delhi; Emeritus professors Yogendra Singh and T. K. Oommen; and professors M. N. Panini and Dipankar Gupta—who all shaped my initial years of enchantment with sociology. My students with their active roles in classrooms have been a contributory factor in the present exercise. My pedagogical involvement with sociological theory was catalyzed by incisive guidance of Debjani to finally pen down this text. I thank her and, of course, Qudsiya Ahmed for her incessant editorial interventions. My publisher and all those who have assisted in the shaping of the book at various stages of its production deserve a special mention. I owe special thanks to Dr Hemalatha Reddy, my principal, who allowed me to enjoy the much needed leeway from institutional duties to indulge in quality time for writing the manuscript.

Abhijit Kundu

About the Author

Abhijit Kundu is Associate Professor, Department of Sociology, Sri Venkateswara College, University of Delhi. He completed his Ph.D. from Jawaharlal Nehru University, New Delhi. His area of specialization is sociological theory: its methods and perspectives.

Kundu has been a guest faculty at Aarhus University, Denmark, as part of a European Union-funded project of Contemporary India Study Centre, Aarhus, Denmark; and has acted as a resource person in the state-level orientation programme on Methodology (Social Sciences), organized by Kerala State Higher Education Council. He has co-authored *The Humanities: Methodology and Perspectives* (2009) and edited *The Social Sciences: Methodology and Perspectives* (2009). He has also published widely in national and international journals.

1

Introduction

Origins of Sociological Theory

Social life has always been subjected to inquiry and critical probing throughout history. It has been a human drive to push the boundaries of knowledge further, to come out of ignorance, the basic motivation being to explore the secrets of life. Much before the organization of knowledge in systemic form about social life, thinking human beings — from great sages and saints to social reformers have had incisive contemplation of their social environment. The advent of sociological theory is just a little more than a couple of centuries old. But it is preceded by a long history of sociological thinking. So we have a 'pre-history' of sociological theory contributed by the sharpest jural-religious thinkers to philosophers of great antiquity. The common thread of all such mostly speculative as well as incisive thinking is to seek answers to the organizing principles of social living. The twin concerns as to how a society holds meanings for its people and how to make such living better, have remained the core of every social thought and thinking.

FROM SPECULATIVE TO DEFINITIVE

Early social thinking, however profound, had very little to engage with in any empirical evidence. Sociology as a distinctive discipline developed out of all such social thoughts and ideas at a particular historical juncture of human civilization. The point of departure was marked by an age which sought the causes and the connections between things. Quite evidently, then, sociological theory is a product of the modern era. The rise of scientific thinking dominated human thought in the eighteenth and nineteenth centuries in the West. Sociological theory is a product of such a turn in human knowledge. It is the rise of science that changed the cognitive faculty of people vis-à-vis the conditions of their own lives. Science inculcated a spirit of observation and gathering of empirical knowledge. The objective was to settle with causal relationships that exist between events and occurrences of the social world. Sociological theory, then, is historically located at this fundamental turn of human history. As a theory it would always seek causal explanations which could be verified, tested and repeated with respect to the empirical reality.

Unlike the popular notion about 'theory' as removed from hard facts, it actually is based on facts. More appropriately speaking, both empirical data and theory work with each other in any scientific enterprise. Classical sociological theories were all grounded in the scientific tradition. Going a step further, one can say that sociological theory is grounded in the tradition of an assertion of social patterns which pre-exist and a belief that scientific study of such pattern/order could bring out general abstract 'laws' when based upon empirical study. The task of a theory is to come up with a statement that explains the meaningfulness between observed phenomena; the phenomena in turn being captured through concepts. Obviously, this marked a break from earlier philosophical and speculative thinking on society.

It is not that we all got to know about society only with the coming of sociological thinkers. We have had prior knowledge about society but sociological theory signalled the emergence of systematic knowledge about social life. It is based on an epistemology which held that the best knowledge was that which was premised on logic and evidence. The importance of logic and rational thought as well as of empirical evidence marks the new bent of human thought. All these were directed to think afresh and challenge 'beliefs' which dominated orthodox living and in turn, it often went against the most venerated traditions.

AGE OF ENLIGHTENMENT

To trace the origin and character of sociological theory we are led to acknowledge the impact of both the social and intellectual currents of Europe. It constituted the backdrop of the development of sociology as a distinctive intellectual activity. While the impact of the industrial and revolutionary democratic revolutions served as the social milieu, the Enlightenment thoughts at the turn of the eighteenth century provided the intellectual backdrop. At the level of ideas and worldview the Enlightenment signalled a dramatic break from age-old ideas and beliefs. The so-called medieval period of darkness and ignorance was replaced by a period of Enlightenment — an enlightened realization of reason and rationality as the key to all human and social progress.

The specific discoveries of the seventeenth century actually heralded the modern way of looking at the world. The root of sociology is easily traceable to the philosophers and scientists of the Age of Reason and of Rationality. Opposed to the hold of traditional and religious authority over knowledge, the thinkers of Enlightenment hailed the importance of critical reasoning and liberal individualism. An abiding faith in the power of human reason marked the age in Europe. Such ideas of progress and liberalism developed a new mode of looking at the world. A new attitude invited a new method of thought in every sphere of life. Existing beliefs and thoughts were put to scrutiny by various scholars across disciplines. French political philosopher, Charles de Montesquieu and the French writer, Voltaire led the way to liberate human thought from medieval ignorance and ignite the critical faculty in social inquiry.

It is also to be noted that sociology is claimed to inherit a dual tradition. According to Robert Nisbet (1967), while on one hand the radical–liberal ideas shaped the formative years of sociology, on the other, there were also conservative reactions to that. In terms of the central ideas of the discipline, Nisbet pointed out the distinctive character of sociology which treaded a dual path — that of radicalism as well as conservatism. Pointing to the five basic unit-ideas of sociology as community, authority, status, the sacred and alienation, he shows that nineteenth-century sociological thought worked on the conceptual opposites on each of these ideas.

Accordingly, the antithetical conceptual pairs of community-society, authority-power, status-class, sacred-secular and alienation-progress constituted the core of nineteenth century sociological thought.

> These ideas — community, authority, status, the sacred and alienation — taken together constitute a reorientation of European thought quite as momentous. I believe, as that very different, even opposite, re-orientation of thought that had marked the waning of the Middle-Ages three centuries earlier and the rise of the Age of Reason. Then it had been individualistic rationalism asserting itself against medieval corporatism and authority. Now, in the early nineteenth century, it is the reverse: the reaction of traditionalism against analytic reason; of communalism against individualism; and of the non-rational against the purely rational. (Nisbet 1967: 8)

As we note, Saint-Simon, Auguste Comte and Emile Durkheim's ideas of order, morality and community do echo the propositions of the conservative reaction against the liberal radical appeal of the Enlightenment, yet they all build their foundation on the scientific temper fostered by the same Age of Reason. The counteracting currents of liberalism, radicalism and conservatism continued to mark the nineteenth and early twentieth-century, which were reflected in the range of theories of the classical sociologists.

THE REVOLUTIONS

At the beginning of the nineteenth century, the European society was marked by the collapse of the old traditional authority; the resultant problem of order served as the social conditioning for the development of sociological theory. The political as well as the industrial revolutions overhauled the old order which rested on kinship, land, religion, local community and monarchy. Actually, the Age of Reason stimulated the questioning of the traditional order of society. The concepts of individual rights and democracy came to dominate social thinking. The American Revolution extolled the value of individual freedom and citizen's rights. The French Revolution of 1789 brought forward the principals of reason and justice, as the political rumblings sought for a new social order. The secular ideals of liberty and equality that stirred a whole range of French intellectuals also impacted upon other European societies. The whole scenario along with all the positive gains of a democratic revolution also put up the question of order and stability of a social structure. No wonder that we find in the writings of classical thinkers the concern with order and social change.

As the most significant product of the French Enlightenment, as well as a reaction to the French Revolution, Auguste Comte's (1798–1857) foundational efforts in developing a 'science of society' point to the social moment of early sociological theory. Published in 1839, in the fourth volume of *Cours de philosophie positive,* Comte first used the term *sociology*. Through a study of the history of the world ideas and thought, he proposed the law of three stages of human intellectual development. He surveyed the passage from theological thought to metaphysical and finally to a positive and scientific thought. Correspondingly he showed the social change from a militaristic to a legalistic type of society, ending with the modern industrial society. Comte's positivist insistence for a science of industrial society served as the formative ideas for all subsequent classical sociological thinking.

The French Revolution sparked off a series of political churnings which continued well into the nineteenth century in many parts of the world. Inevitably such reordering of society attracted sociological attention from incisive thinkers across the continent. The central problem that emerged from political upheavals was that of ensuring social stability. Re-thinking of individual–societal bonding(s) also figured as the dominant concern of classical sociological theory. The question of individual–societal relationship was further aggravated with the Industrial Revolution in the later eighteenth century with England as its epicentre. It spread across the Western societies and exhibited a culmination of a number of interrelated developments that transformed the very basis of economic production. The fundamental change of source of energy to machine from raw human and animal energy had a wide ramification in every society.

The social events that accompanied the Industrial Revolution were rapid urbanization, migration of rural people to cities, better communication, concentration of production activity, increased specialization and division of labour and so forth. The formation of an industrial working class and growing pauperization, the question of health and better working conditions and finally a growing antagonism between the newly formed social classes — all variously characterized a wide range of societies. The issues of modernization, equality and justice came to the fore in social philosophical deliberations. Quite evidently, thus, sociological thinking directed its attention to seek 'answers' to such intriguing issues of the changed social world. All such social issues and developments fundamentally prompted the thinkers to probe into the ties between an individual and the society. All classical sociological theories essentially were driven by this very problematic of resolving the issue of individual–societal relationship amidst overwhelming alterations of every aspect of social life. The search for regularities, patterns and processes of social change, whether in the name of 'social law' or otherwise, dominated classical sociological theory thereby. The methodological preference for a scientific mode of inquiry also was a direct fallout of the triumph of both the industrial as well as the political revolutions.

If Auguste Comte was a child of the French Revolution, Saint-Simon reacted directly to the grand societal changes occasioned by the Industrial Revolution. Claude–Henri Saint-Simon (1760–1825) was influenced by the Enlightenment thoughts prevalent in France. In 1807, he wrote *Introduction to the Scientific Studies of the 19th Century* to affirm the importance of observation in order to arrive at a science of social organization. Drawing upon organismic analogy, Saint-Simon held that the stable pattern of social order could be comprehended by deriving laws of social stability. Thereby, one could arrive at the broad historical trends of human society. The overall project to see for scientific laws was to gain control over the apparent gigantic changes that marked the post-Revolution European societies. In fact, Comte was highly influenced by Saint-Simon's treatise and ultimately recognized the fundamental ideas of Saint-Simon to propose the new discipline of Sociology in 1839.

ORGANIC ANALOGY AND EVOLUTIONISM

Apart from August Comte's pioneering effort to develop sociology as the abstract theoretical science of social phenomena and to formulate general laws of the variation of human thought process, the evolutionary perspective dominated the embryonic years of sociology. In fact Comte himself was influenced by physiology to effect the division of the study of society into two parts — *statics* and *dynamics*. Statics represented the aspects of order and stability of a society, while dynamics stood for the study of the laws of the succession of the stages of human development. In his concept of dynamics, Comte insisted on the idea of evolution and progress. Progressive development is evolutionary as Comte understood, but not a linear one. Accordingly, the course of social evolution is marked by a basic antagonism between the instincts of innovation and conservation. (Timasheff 1967)

The evolutionary scheme was furthered by Herbert Spencer (1820–1903), who readily incorporated Charles Darwin's ideas of the *Origins of Species* (1959) to reflect on the universal law of progression of human society. In the history of sociology, Spencerism is synonymous with evolutionism. He identified a parallelism between generalizations about living organisms and those involving societies. A general acceptance of the doctrine of evolution marked the several works of Spencer like *Social Statics, The Study of Sociology,* and *Principles of Sociology.* He held a close analogy between the biological organism and human society. Accordingly, the history of both the organic and the super-organic (social life) is a process of development and such a development involves an increase in both quantity and complexity. The ideas of natural selection and the survival of the fittest were present in Spencer's evolutionary scheme, but for him the idea of adaptation was purposive in case of social life. Subsequent classical thinkers of sociology were variously impacted upon by this elementary evolutionary scheme of Spencer. In many classical thoughts we find the traces of evolutionism in their conceptualizations of social development, progress and change.

BASIC IDEAS OF SOCIOLOGICAL THEORY

Ideas are a product of history and time, and not simply extensions of individual personalities. Any discipline is a product of a historical time. By locating the principal issues of a society we get a clue of the organizing concepts that govern the development of an intellectual activity striving to emerge as an organized system of knowledge. We have already seen the social events of the eighteenth and nineteenth century Europe as providing the milieu so necessary for the emergence of a new line of thinking among intellectuals. The focus on society as an organization, as an ensemble of social relationships and social action formed the backdrop of the development of classical sociological theory. The root ideas of sociology were located in the changes that marked the eighteenth and nineteenth century Europe. As commented upon by Calhoun and others (2002) the four most important social change to affect social life were:

i. The rise of individualism
ii. The rise of modern states
iii. The development of modern industry/large-scale markets, and
iv. The European expansion/colonization.

The ideas emerging from Reformation and Enlightenment fostered a new sense of self amongst the people. A qualitatively different notion of individualism that appeared was not an anathema of collective life or society. Rather a fresh and different way of understanding individual–societal relationship marked the 'new' society where more than communalties, associative and contractual ties were held at premium. The element of choice and freedom dominated social living in the new epoch.

Side by side there was a shift away from medieval aristocratic order marked by people's uprising to constitute democratic modern States. Attempts to create modern political institutions broke away from the notions of *Divine* order. People aspired to constitute nations and national governments which could cater to the aspirations of the people. The idea of nation-states developed as a bounded, internally organized population sharing similar culture and history. Such an idea of nation deeply influenced the new idea of society, which also entailed the idea of a civil society marked off from the State as a free zone of private interpersonal relationships.

Related to the constitution of a civil society was the spread of large-scale markets, which in turn were complementary to the development of industrial capitalism. The growth of impersonal sites of exchange of goods and services and an increasing emphasis on specialization of labour altered interpersonal relationships in society.

Finally, the expansion of the European power through exploration of the rest of the world resulted in the 'appearances' of hitherto 'unknown' people and society. Study of society and developing a theory of such got a fillip in the wake of such colonial exercises too. The recognition of 'other' cultures also prompted thinkers to compare and contrast human societies across the world. All of these events stimulated in a major way the birth of sociological theory to account for the organization and differences of human societies. The logic of society came to be the central concern as a result, which in other words has been the central purpose of sociological theory.

Key Words

- *Intellectual Background*
- *Scientific Theory*
- *Social Evolution*
- *Modernity*
- *Social Conditioning*

Glossary

Enlightenment: Essentially refers to the European Enlightenment of the eighteenth-century. The re-awakening to the thought of applicability of reason and science in order to understand and improve humankind.

Organic Analogy: Comparing with living organic beings. In sociology, understanding society like an organic body conforming to the scheme of evolution.

Civil Society: Marked off from the structures of the State and the Market, a space for voluntary social relationships and institutions. Classically speaking, a feature of modern society.

Theory: An explanatory statement on two or more phenomena on their meaningful relationships. While the phenomena are captured through concepts, the building blocks of any theory.

Discussion Points

- The bearings of Enlightenment Ideals on Sociology.
- The social background for the development of Sociology.
- The primary constitutive ideas of Sociology.

2

Karl Heinrich Marx (1818–83)

A theory is a product of its time as well as a product of the persona, the architect of such theory. It is quite interesting to note that all sociology courses dealing with classical sociological theories cannot but engage in great detail with Karl Marx's socio-philosophical writings, much of which has deep political intonations. The immediate image that Karl Marx brings to all practitioners of social sciences is that of a radical thinker, a revolutionary who proclaimed a ruthless struggle in favour of the proletariat class.

While it is true that much of the political activities of the twentieth-century had been shaped by Karl Marx's thoughts and application of his revolutionary ideas, scholars have intermittingly attempted to rediscover Marx, the sociological thinker. Hardly to be called as a sociologist, yet his wide range of writings on society and history serve as an unavoidable entry point to any theorization or understanding of society and its development.

Given the popular understanding of Karl Marx, the revolutionary social philosopher of nineteenth-century Germany, it would be interesting to note that in his doctoral thesis at Berlin University, awarded in 1841, there was hardly any focus on the class-struggle. The overriding emphasis on the proletarian revolution which students of Marx's writings draw with great enthusiasm scarcely figure in Marx's doctoral work which theorized on the fundamental self-centredness of the stoical philosophies of Democritus and Epicurus. A longing for unity with one's own self, a romantic revolt at that, actually marked Marx's journey into a fascinating discovery of the emergent modern society and its workings. Nevertheless, his thought process in the course of his life did go through the ebbs and tides of his time. The many variations in his thought process is quite expected, as we make a brief sketch of his eventful biography.

A BIOGRAPHICAL SKETCH

Born in 1818, Karl Marx spent his childhood in an atmosphere of prosperity, both material and cultural. More influenced by his father Heinrich Marx, he took an early interest in philosophy and history. The romantic poets, too, had their bearings on him, as he was drawn towards the German philosopher Georg Hegel.

After being awarded Doctor's degree from Berlin University, Marx joined the liberal paper *Rheinische Zeitung* in 1842 and became the editor-in-chief. He left the paper on the question of censorship and came closer to the French socialists, and started to collaborate with Frederick Engels. Engels turned out to be his closest associate and co-author in many of his subsequent works.

As Marx left Germany to seek a more liberal social condition of Paris he grappled with his early fascination with Hegelian idealism along with French socialist ideas. Side by side, he realized the importance of comprehending the English political economy. Such a combination of interests and his growing awareness of the wretched conditions of the industrial working class of the then European society were stimulated by Frederick Engels.

Because of his strings of radical writings, Marx was first expelled from France at the demand of the Prussian Government. He moved to Brussels by 1845, where he associated himself with the Communist League. Expounding the agenda for the international revolutionary movement, along with Engels, he brought out the Manifesto of the Communist Party in 1848. Possibly the most simple manual was written for the working class of the whole world to formulate its agenda and aspirations. It was the mid-nineteenth-century revolutionary sparks that touched not only France, but also Germany, Hungary and Austria. Marx was expelled from Brussels too in 1849. He was accused of incitement to armed rebellion, but was however acquitted by a jury. The counter-revolution declared him as a 'stateless' person. He moved to London and subsequently delved into his famous studies of the English working class conditions under industrial capitalism. He spent endless hours in the British Museum since 1852 to come up with rigorous research work on the working of capitalism. The outcome was the three volumes of *Capital*, of which only the first volume was published in his lifetime (1867).

It is instructive for us to realize that the failure of the political revolutions actually prompted Karl Marx not only to withdraw from active political activism, but also to engage in the scholarly research that gave us such a detailed understanding of industrial capitalism as a unique stage of society. Marx passed the last decade of his life in abject misery and weathered great personal loses. He did re-involve with the international movement of workers and emerged as the prominent leader of the *International* in later years, but its disintegration by 1876 and the failure of many revolutionary movements left him as a dejected scholar of great optimism.

Such a brief note of Karl Marx's eventful biography posits us to appreciate the intersection of the personal with the turbulent age of development of industry and technology. At the cross-section of the victory of capital and proletarian misery, Marx's writings can be historicized for our wholesome understanding of his seminal contribution to sociological theory.

MATERIALIST CONCEPTION OF HISTORY

Popularly, Karl Marx's materialist way of explaining historical development of human society is captured through the usage of the term 'historical materialism'. The essential question for Marx was how to explain the unfolding of the different stages of history. Is it because of the 'great' deeds of the 'great emperors' that history of mankind has undergone changes? Is it something mystical or accidental that such changes have come through? Marx contended that a comprehensive understanding of the historical development of human society needs to recognize mankind's productive activity in society as the most fundamental human activity. It is the most fundamental as it ensures the production and reproduction of human life and society. This is a materialist way of approaching one's society.

In his introduction to *Socialism: Utopian and Scientific* (1892), Frederick Engels expressed Marx's materialist conception as

> ... that view of the course of history which seeks the ultimate cause and the great moving power of all important historic events in the economic development of society, in the changes in the modes of production and exchange, in the consequent division of society into distinct classes, and in the struggle of these classes against one another. (Engels 1975: 23)

In our discussion of the topic, we shall return to the concepts of 'modes of production' and 'class' as mentioned in the above. At present we resolve that the historical march of society needs to be realized as not a function of any mystical or supernatural powers; it is not the ideas that moves history.

World philosophy primarily has had revolved around the two fundamentally opposing strands. The two opposing camps are based on the question of the relative importance/precedence of mind and matter. Broadly speaking, while the idealist philosophers underscore the primacy of ideas over matter, the materialist thinkers on the contrary ground matter as primary. In terms of theory of being (ontology), materialism considers that the natural world is prior to and causally independent of any form of mind/consciousness. While in terms of theory of knowledge (epistemology), the knowable world exists independent of our mind/consciousness. It is not that Marx invented materialism to propose a 'new' theory of society. Prior to him, in the German intellectual world, Feuerbach stood as the towering figure in materialist philosophy. Marx's application of the materialist philosophy is the most poignant in his *Thesis on Feuerbach* (1845), first published by F. Engels in 1888; and in *The German Ideology* (1845–46, co-authored with Engels). A new philosophy of history is proposed which denies any predestination of this word as there is no other-worldly causation of human society.

We have already noted that Marx had his predecessors in materialist philosophy. He responded to Feuerbach's notion of materialism. German philosopher Georg Hegel (1770–1831) shaped the early part of the nineteenth-century German thought to a large extent. After his death the Hegelian tradition got bifurcated into two streams: the 'old Hegelians' and the 'young Hegelians'. The 'young Hegelians' were critical of Hegel's tenets while still subscribing to the master's legacy. Ludwig Feuerbach (1804–1872) was among the 'new' group and he forwarded a materialist position challenging Hegel's excessive emphasis on consciousness and the spirit of society. We shall take up Hegelian philosophy subsequently, as we reach the seminal concept of *dialectics* as propounded by Marx.

As for Feuerbach, he argued by focusing on religion that we need to question Hegel's subjective idealism and we need to realize the material reality of real human beings instead of focusing on ideas. He debated that there is no spirit of society and that God is simply people's projection of their essence onto an impersonal force. In the process, all the positive attributes are projected onto God, while all the imperfectness stayed with the living people. According to Feuerbach, only a materialist philosophy could defeat such religion/God which would place the people and not their projections as the end in themselves. Marx shared the Feuerbachian rejection of the abstractness of Hegel's philosophy. Like Feuerbach, Marx too, was influenced by Hegel, but thought that Feuerbach was too one-sided on the question of materialism. It was just not a question of analysing the religious world; a materialist interpretation is also required for understanding the economy in particular and the entire social world in general.

AGAINST CRUDE MATERIALISM

Marx set out formulating his materialist conception of history by questioning the Feuerbachian materialist way of thinking. He was against a reductionist position; not inevitably all aspects of society could be reduced to matter in a linear simplified way. He did accept Feuerbach's criticism of Hegelian idealism. Feuerbach did set sensuous objects, really distinct from conceptual objects, but Marx realized that Feuerbach conceived to perceive human activity itself as objective reality. The chief defect was that such unqualified materialist philosophy conceived reality, sensuousness only in the form of the object, or of contemplation, human practice, and sensuous activity was left unattended. The active side of human sensuousness was ignored by the materialists, whereas the idealists only captured it abstractly. Idealism does not allow us to know the real, sensuous activity as such.

According to Marx, Feuerbach, while theorizing against abstract thinking of idealist philosophers like Hegel, did not conceive sensuousness as practical, human-sensuous activity. The bottom-line of *Theses on Feuerbach* is the eleventh thesis: '*The philosophers have only interpreted the world in various ways, the point, however, is to change it.*' For Marx, social life is essentially practical. All mysteries which mislead theory into mysticism find their rational solution in human practice and in the comprehension of this practice.

Marx essentially revolutionized the early materialist criticism of Hegel's idealist philosophy. He was careful to introduce the element of human creativity into the making of history. The following excerpt from *Theses on Feuerbach* illuminates this point:

> The materialist doctrine that men are products of circumstances and upbringing, and that, therefore, changed men are products of other circumstances and change upbringing, forgets that it is men who change circumstances and that the educator must himself be educated. Hence, this doctrine is bound to divide society into two parts, one of which is superior to society....
>
> The coincidence of the changing of circumstances and of human activity can be conceived and rationally understood only as revolutionizing practice. (Marx and Engels 1976: 7)

What was then the revolutionary twist to hitherto materialism effected by Marx? Simply put, he understood man not only as the object of history but also as its subject. Man is an object enjoying the capacity to become a subject: a subject who can intervene with the given circumstances and change their circumstances. A new philosophy of history is revolutionary to the extent that it proceeds from social reality and not from abstract categories or intellectual constructs. Here, the active role of man is emphasized as man is not just an object of history in a crude materialist way.

DIALECTICS

The one-sidedness in Feuerbach's materialism, according to Karl Marx, was due to his inability to appreciate the crucial notion of dialectic. For Marx, dialectic has been the most important of Hegel's contributions. The concept of dialectic images the world not as something fossilized or being made up of static structures. It underscores the aspects of dynamics, conflicts and contradictions as integral to the making and shaping up of the world around us. Thereby, it promotes a new way of looking at the world that stresses upon the 'to and fro' motions of its constituent elements — the processes and relationships of the world.

Hegel confined dialectics to the realm of ideas only. He propounded a kind of evolutionary theory of the world in idealistic categories. If Marx was fascinated by Hegel in his early years, it is due to the common thread that binds these two great enlightened figures. The shared awareness was all about the victory of the industrial revolution at the turn of the eighteenth century and its effect on human self — the increasing trend towards atomized individuals.

To reclaim the self, Hegel uses dialectics in explaining human history. As an idealist philosopher, Hegel proposed a superlative understanding of reality as absolute spirit, where the notion of dialectic is employed as a self-generating, self-differentiating and self-particularizing process of reason. He uses dialectics to explain human history. He considers that truth is the product of history and that it passed through various moments. His idealism considered history a product of the Spirit. Hence, truth is the whole and error lies in incompleteness. It is recognized from the contradictions it gives rise to. To remove this incompleteness, it needs to be incorporated in the whole, the fuller — the truth.

Hegel's pivot of 'absolute idealism' is that existence can be derived from essence. The essence is real and eternal. As an objective reality it is pre-fixed and the indeterminate being surpasses itself towards its essence. Ultimate realty is the Absolute Thought or Idea pregnant with the 'World of finite Spirits' and 'the world of Nature'. The Absolute is the 'Essence' of all essences, in the sense that it is comprehensive of all the finite essences or ideas, each of which stands for a definite set of concrete particular existents — living or non-living. Undoubtedly, the finite spirits stand nearer the Absolute Spirit than do other things, as they partake of the nature of the 'Absolute'. 'According to Hegel, the "Absolute Thought" or "Reason", being ultimate "Reality", is an absolutely independent principle and as such it freely transforms itself into "the world of spirits" and that of concrete existents — "the world of Nature". It is free by its very conception of self-explanatory and self-determined.' (Stace 1955: 59). That 'Absolute Thought' or 'Reason' is ultimate 'Reality'. Reality can be proved or disproved by reason alone. An absolutely self-determined principle, ultimate Reality negates itself within itself; and in so doing brings forth the world of particular concrete existents.

For Hegel, every idea is at once abstract and concrete. An idea is not purely a thought completely detached from concrete things, but it stands for a definite set of particulars and so far it is concrete. As purely abstract, an idea refers beyond itself to the concrete particulars it stands for only implicitly, while as concrete it does the same, but explicitly. Every idea therefore, contains within itself its opposite, thereby resulting in a contradiction therein; and this contradiction is resolved into a more concrete and more comprehensive idea and so on. The more concrete and comprehensive the ideas is, the greater the number of object it comprehends. That is to say, an idea, more concrete and comprehensive, contains within itself its opposite resulting in a further contradiction which is resolved into a still more concrete idea comprising a still greater number of objects of 'Nature'. And all such contradictions are finally resolved into the all-comprehensive absolute 'Idea'. Similarly, the 'Absolute Thought' or 'Reason', being essentially spiritual, is inclusive of all finite spirits. The 'Absolute' is in this sense comprehensive of all things and beings, actual and possible; and, being an independent principle. It freely manifests itself through finite things and spirits by rendering concrete the ideas or essences that constitute its content. In Hegel's own words:

> The Idea which is independent or for itself, when viewed on the point of its unity with itself, is Perception or Intuition, and the percipient Idea is Nature. But as Intuition the Idea is, through an external 'reflection', invested with the one-sided characteristic of immediacy or of negation. Enjoying, however, an absolute lib-

> erty, the idea does not merely pass over into life, or as finite cognition allow life to show in it. In its absolute truth it resolves to let the moment of its particularity, or of the first characterization and the other — being, the immediate idea, as its reflected image, go forth freely as Nature. (Wallace1892: 379)

In this process Hegel derives 'existence' from 'essence'. The essence is the inner world of being. Only when reason is complete, human consciousness realizes its full potential and thereby human subjects actually experience freedom. This is a condition of 'Absolute Spirit'. The process by which human strives to become more reasonable is understood as the dialectic.

However, Karl Marx wishes to correct the Hegelian dialectics of its idealistic trappings. Marx acknowledges Hegel's view that humankind is the product of the history that it has made for itself. In Hegelian dialectics, each historical development is conceived as the product of a previous less developed stage, whose necessary truth or completeness it is. But Marx's method of understanding development is not Hegelian. Throughout his life Marx remained critical as well as indebted to Hegel's dialectical framework. From the time of his *Grundrisse* (1857–58), Marx makes his attempt to strip the Hegelian dialectics of its mystified form very clear.

In Marx's own words:

> The mystification which the dialectic suffers in Hegel's hands by no means prevents him from being the first to present its general forms of motion in a comprehensive manner. With him it is standing on its head. It must be inverted to discover the rational kernel within the mystical shell. (Afterword to the 2nd edition, *Capital*, Vol. 1)

Marx concedes that Hegel has overcome the dualism between 'spirit' and 'matter'. But he has done so by conceptualizing material reality as if it is an embodiment of spirit. Marx critiques Hegel that he has explained history as if historical subjects live on a bloodless and mystical plane and, as if within the domain of human consciousness the displacement/replacement of one historical–cultural stage by another takes place.

Marx favours a materialist application of dialectics as he criticizes its idealist underpinnings in Hegel. For him, matter explains every aspect of existence. Matter is considered as the beginning and end of all reality. History is made as the result of practical human activity. The practical human activity is the principal one, which is a result of the human need to exercise technical-cognitive control over a variable natural environment.

In *The German Ideology* (1845–46), we do find Karl Marx's overall objection to philosophical idealism. Prior to Marx, Ludwig Feuerbach has indeed made a materialist critic of Hegel's idealism. We have noted in a previous section that the Feuerbachian position is that human consciousness is merely what we know in relation to some pre-existing and determining material reality. Such an external world as deterministic is not exactly given the ultimate and exclusive causal primacy by Marx. The creative aspect of human species is underscored by him, and that makes his position so different from a crude critic of ideation. So, unlike Feuerbach he talks about how the external pre-existing world is subjected to active intervention by human beings. The following quote from *The German* Ideology makes amply clear Marx's qualified view on idealism:

> In direct contrast to German Philosophy, which descends from heaven to earth, here we ascend from earth to heaven. That is to say, we do not set out from what men say, imagine, conceive, nor from men as narrated, thought of, imagined, conceived in order to arrive at men in the flesh. We set out from real, active men, and on the basis of their real life-process we demonstrate the development of the ideological reflexes and echoes of this life-process. (Karl Marx 1972 (1845–46): 47)

Human development involves an intricate involvement of active human beings with the external material world. The external world is apprehended through our senses. We shape this world with our active decisions. Thereby, the world is shaped by human beings and that human beings are not at the receiving end of history.

Marx concedes that Hegel was inspired by the spirit of the French Revolution but realized the significance of freedom and self-determination without adequately resolving the dualism between Spirit and Matter. From an abstract intellectual point of view Hegel has treated material reality as if it were the embodiment of 'Spirit'. So, Marx advances a dialectical method which sees history as constituted of acting human beings. History moves forward by a 'to and fro' dynamic relationship between real material life-processes and ideological conscious reflexes of such processes.

LAWS OF DIALECTICS

Frederick Engels, Marx's collaborator, actually advances and applies Marx's ideas to the study of nature as well. In his *Dialectics of Nature* (1883), dialectics is seen as the science of the general and abstract laws of the development of nature, society and thought.

> All nature, from the smallest thing to the biggest, from a grain of sand to the sun from the protista to man is in a constant state of coming into being and going out of being in a constant flux, in a ceaseless state of movement and change. (Engels 1883: 18)

Marx himself has talked about materialist conception of history which was later referred to as 'historical materialism' by Frederick Engels. Popularly, Dialectical Materialism is referred to as the Marxist method of studying social development. But the two terms 'Dialectics' and 'Materialism' were not coupled by Marx himself. Actually, it is a popular practice (indulged in by many Marxists) of realizing the combination of the dialectic of Hegel with the Materialism of Feuerbach. On its own understanding, dialectical materialism is cross-bred from the union of two philosophies: the mechanistic materialism of the Scientific Revolution (Feuerbachian) and Hegel's idealistic dialectics. The combination, rather, the cross-fertilization of materialism with dialectics transforms both. Popularly understood, the materialism of dialectical materialism is not, like its traditional ancestor, reductive. It does not reduce ideas to matter, asserting their ultimate identity. It holds, instead, that the material and the ideal are different, in fact are opposites. But this opposition is within a unity in which the material is basic or primary. Matter can exist without mind, but not vice versa, and mind is emergent historically from matter and remains dependent on it.

In simple words, dialectical materialism in opposed to the metaphysical way of thinking. The metaphysical way thinks of things as separable from one another ignoring their interrelationship. It takes a state of being as fixed, frozen and final ignoring their change and development. Essentially, the metaphysical way of thinking tries to ignore and discount opposites. Contrary to such an understanding, dialectical materialism not only holds that opposites are involved in every subject-matter but these opposites are inseparably connected with one another. Far from being exclusive, neither can they exist nor be understood except in relation to the other.

To put it concisely, dialectical materialism proposes that things come into being and continue to be so in a process of unending changes and development. As a methodological concept it attempts to explain progress in terms of contradictory, interacting forces. The development and progress of a state of being is not arbitrary but it follows certain laws, as enumerated by Engels. The gist of the laws is that the thesis and the anti-thesis culminate at a nodal point where one overwhelms over the other, giving rise to a synthesis. When this method is applied to the study of history of social development, it unlocks a revolutionary concept of change.

The aim of dialectics is to trace real changes and inter-connectedness in the world and to explain things in motion in its interconnection. The laws that such development follows are given by Engels in his *Dialectics of Nature*. The fundamental laws of dialectics are as follows:

i. *The law of the transformation of quantity into quality*: According to this law, gradual quantitative changes give rise to revolutionary qualitative changes
ii. *The law of unity of opposites*: This second law holds that the unity of any concrete reality is a unity of opposites or contradictions, and
iii. *The law of the negation of negation*: This unique third law claims that in the clash of the opposites, one opposite negates another and that in turn is negated by a higher level of historical development that retains something of both the negated terms.

In his *Capital*, Vol. 1, Karl Marx proclaims that merely quantitative differences, beyond a certain point, pass into qualitative changes. The most commonly cited example for the first law of dialectics is that of the change of water from a liquid state to a gas (steam), by increasing its temperature. When this law is applied to social history, one finds that it is best exemplified by the emergence of the classical capitalist system. Before the system of industrial capitalism comes into being, a process of accumulation of wealth in the form of money takes place in a few private hands. On the other side the formation of a propertyless proletariat class occurs. At a certain point of this social process, when enough money is accumulated to provide capital for industrial undertakings/re-investments and, on the other, when enough people are proletariarized to provide the required labour force (development of a labour market), a material condition matures up for the emergence of industrial capitalism. The new system is a qualitatively different system from its previous stage.

The second law of dialectics talks about the struggle of the opposites. The unity of the opposites entails a constant struggle between the opposites. We cannot invent an explanation with the help of dialectics, but the understanding of dialectics helps us to provide with the clue of where to search for the source of change. Contrary to the metaphysical notion of dialectics, the Marxian dialectics emphasizes that internal contradictions are inherent in all things and phenomena in nature.

The struggle between the opposites, between the old and the new constitutes the internal dynamics, or the internal content of the process of social development/transformation. The process of development from the lower to the higher stage takes place not as a harmonious unfolding of phenomena but as a disclosure of the contradictions inherent. We can exemplify such a dialectics of development from the orthodox unfolding of capitalism.

Popularly, we tend to understand class-conflict as the basis of contradiction, but the knowledge of dialectics informs us that class-conflict is merely a manifest form of a more basic contradiction. The two basic opposites under capitalism is the concentration of the means of production in large workshops/manufacturing factories and in the hands of a few capitalists. But the actual production is carried out socially. It is the mass of workers who set the means of production in motion. However, the actual producers do not own or possess the product, not even their own labour, which is all owned by the capitalists. The opposites are in actuality between the social nature of production versus the private nature of appropriation, which in turn is manifested in the contradiction between the two corresponding classes — the workers and the capitalists. In Marx's theme, this contradiction can only be resolved by the victory of the working class, whereby, the victorious working class sets up its dictatorship and initiates social ownership/appropriation to match a social production.

In this way, the laws of dialectics explains the capitalist system: as the principle of transformation from quantity to quality and that of the unity of struggle of the opposites are found to be at work. The third law, that is, the negation of negation essentially clarifies the unique character of negation in Marx's theory. If the first two laws describe the process of change and development, the last law makes clear the nature of such change; that every changed state of affairs is not something 'new', but a culmination of changes/evolution embodying aspects of the by-gone stages. In the stages of development all advancements of the past are always carried forward.

The third law talks about the negation of the negation. But negation here is not at all a case of simple no-saying. It has got its positive aspects as well. In order to negate, it is not that the original is restored back. For example, feudalism is a negation of the slave system, but feudalism also has its own negation and it has germinated within the ancient society state only. Similarly, in the social development of transition from capitalism to the project of socialism, what is new and rising in the economic life of capitalist society, i.e., the social nature of production contradicts the existing system of, private appropriation. The 'old' and that carried over from the past, i.e., private appropriation is negated by the new forces. The result is the working class waging a struggle against the capitalist class ensuring a stage for a classless society, i.e., a case of double negation results in a synthesis.

In other words, the third law is often expressed as a triadic interplay of thesis, anti-thesis and synthesis. The thesis is a justification of a state of being while anti-thesis is the opposition to it. Given the Marxian notion of dialectics, the result of this opposition is synthesis. The very term 'synthesis' signifies an advanced stage of development, carrying within it all the gains which are made in the preceding stages of development. The process of social development involves a struggle between the 'old' and 'new'. However, in the first place, the new stage could not have come about except for arising from and in opposition to the 'old'. The conditions for the 'new' arise and mature within the 'old'. So, the 'old' is not simply abolished totally, it only gives rise to the 'new' conditions.

Secondly, in the continuous process of development of various stages, an 'old' stage itself constitutes a stage of advance. First of all, in the course of development as a result of double negation, a later stage can repeat an earlier stage but is repeated only on a higher level of development. This is caused by advancement of division of labour and means of production. In this way, the dialectical laws provide us with a fascinating method to investigate the unfolding of the successive stages of history.

METAPHORS OF BASE AND SUPERSTRUCTURE

Popularly, the Marxian method is often employed with the help of two metaphors — the 'base' and the 'superstructure'. The 'base' stands for the basic structure (or infrastructure) of a society, which is held to be the economic structure or organization of the society under consideration. On the other hand, the 'superstructure' denotes the legal, cultural, political and ideological aspects of such a society. Following the dictum of 'being determines consciousness' it is being theorized that the 'economic base' gives rise to a society's cultural, ideological, political or legal face. The basic structure of a society is the way its production relations are organized and the Marxian method popularly implies that such economic organization determines a society's 'superstructural' elements. So, invoking the interplay between the 'base' and 'superstructure' the Marxian method attempts to explore the working of any society.

In fact, a synoptic account of the Marxian way to conceptualize the working of any society can be found in his *Preface to A Contribution to the Critique of Political Economy* (1859).

The following quote from Marx is possibly the most repeated one in the history of Marxian scholarship:

> In the social production of their life men enter into definite relations that are indispensable and independent of their will, relations of production which correspond to a definite stage of development of their material productive forces. The sum total of these relations or production constitutes the economic structure of society, the real foundation, on which rises a legal and political superstructure and to which correspond definite forms of social consciousness. The mode of production of material life conditions the social, political and intellectual life processes in general. It is not the consciousness of men that determines their being, but, on the contrary, it is their social being that determines their consciousness. (Marx 1968 (1859): 328)

If we follow the above quote, we learn that the general character of any society, its political and normative processes of life are all decided upon by its material life. The mode of production is the core of this material life. Or, in other words, the mode of production, or economic base of a society, is constituted of the productive forces and the social relations of production. It is the creative human beings who work on the means of production and give rise to social relations of production.

To appreciate the significance of the above seminal quote from Karl Marx, we need to make the distinctions between the concepts of means of production, forces of production, relations of production and mode of production.

Means of production refers to the land, capital, tools and techniques which are essential for any productive activity, in combinations or otherwise as required for the production of particular products. On their own they are just like any physical objects, or lifeless objects which cannot produce by themselves. They need to be put into 'life' by human labour power, i.e., active human beings need to act on/with them to transform the material world. When the means of production are enjoined by human labour, it is referred to as forces of production. That is,

Means of Production = Land, Capital, Tools/Techniques

Forces of Production = Means of Production + Human Labour

The next important concept to be disentangled is that of the social relations of production, or, simply the relations of production. The concept of relations of production refers to the nature of relationship that human labour has with the means of production; that is, whether the means of production are owned (including nature of such ownership in case they are being owned) or not by the actual producers (human labour). There can be a variety of such 'ownership relationship' and accordingly, at that level a production relationship is struck between the owners of the means of production (in case human labour is not owning the means of production) and the actual producers. Legally speaking, these relations of production are called property relations.

Every stage of human development is marked by a match between the forces of production and the relations of production. The synchronization between the two signifies a particular mode of production. In fact, in Marx's understanding of every stage of a society can be referred to as a particular mode of production. Hence,

Forces of Production + Relations of Production = Mode of Production

A particular mode of production signifies simultaneously a particular stage of social development and a particular match between the forces of production with the relations of production. To understand the dynamics of social development one needs to look into the dialectical relations between the forces of production and relations of production.

It is the unique species-characteristic of human beings to continuously work on the material world, since the beginning of human history human labour has been ceaselessly acting on/with the means of production and improving upon them through innovations and discoveries. With the ever amelioration of the means of production at every stage of their development, the forces of production tend to outgrow the existing relations of production. Only when the advancement and growth of the forces of production crosses a threshold, the existing relations of production no longer could 'match' the changed forces of production. The relations of production are then dialectically negated in favour of a new relation of production. This dialectical change signals a change in the mode of production. Overall speaking, this in turn signals a new style of society.

This dialectical understanding of unfolding of various stages of human development is expressed eloquently by Marx in *The Poverty of Philosophy* (1847):

> Social relations are closely bound up with productive forces. In acquiring new productive forces men change their mode of production; and in changing their mode of production, in changing the way of earning their living, they change all their social relations. The hand-mill gives you society with the feudal lord; the steam-mill, society with the industrial capitalist. (Karl Marx 1973 [1847]: 122)

The growth of productive forces is inherent in the nature of labour. It is not just meeting one's basic needs but human civilization moves forward by meeting ever refined needs. This is accomplished by the use of new tools, methods and knowledge. This is realized with a change of the forces of production. The division of labour, the growth of productive forces, the association of production and private appropriation inevitably give rise to social contradiction. Any given stage of development of the productive forces demands certain specific forms of property, specific relations between human beings engaged in the production process and relations of production. So, every level of the forces of production corresponds to particular forms of property and relations of production. It is a continuous process, where the ever developing forces of production enter into conflicts with the established relations of production. Such antagonistic interests dialectically push a particular stage of human development to its next stage.

In any society, be it pre-capitalist or capitalist, economic activity involves relations of production that make the labour power of some individuals the property of others. This relationship, according to Marx, is the essence of class exploitation. For example, in slave societies, the slave owner enjoys the total ownership of the slave's labour power. On the other hand, in the feudal societies the feudal lord has the exclusive ownership of the serf's labour power. The ownership pattern changes under capitalism, as the capitalist employer claims the ownership of his worker's labour power during the hours of employment. Overall, production in general is always a social enterprise.

STAGES OF HISTORY

According to Marx, all societies are marked by class divisions, except the stage of primitive communism. It is that elementary stage of human development where the division of labour was minimal. In the Marxian scheme, only with the specialization of division of labour, the class society has emerged out of undifferentiated original communal labour and property. The division of labour by identifying men with particular occupational specialization negates their range of capacities as 'universal producers'. We may recapitulate by saying that, the various stages of development in the division of labour are just so many different forms of ownership, i.e., the existing stage in the division of labour also determines the relations of individuals to one another with reference to the material, instruments and product of labour.

The Marxian scheme of progressive development of human society is marked by a progressive individuation of men accompanied by accelerated exchange of goods. It reaches its peak under a capitalist system of production. Throughout human history every stage of development unfolds into another state. Each stage has its own logic of development from which the successive stages appear.

It is important to note that Marx steadfastly is struck with historical materials, however fragmentary, to reconstruct the various stages of history. So, instead of speculating on the past, when he introduces the stage of history, he underlines the fact of 'written history'. The popular, often termed as a simplified version, scheme of historical stages shows a unilinear evolution of these stages. According to which the organization of human labour has undergone several dramatic changes in the course of human history. The stages which constitute the main course of history in Marx's materialist conception of history are:

A Pre-Class System or A Stage of Primitive Communism

Communal ownership of property is the defining feature of this stage of primitive communism. The earliest clans or tribes, which generally follow a migratory existence, have this kind of social organization. For Marx, the notion of private property does not derive from the state of nature but is an outcome of later social development. The stage of primitive communism should not be mistaken as a classless society but a pre-class society, as the very notion of 'class' is yet to develop.

Only at a certain stage of development, the nomadic became a stable agricultural community, signaling a settled community. As a consequence, development of tools and techniques (elementary) takes place. Along with the settlement of the community, due to less hazardous life patterns, the population increases. As a chain reaction the wants and needs keep increasing and such variously placed communities enter into increased contract with each other. Such contacts allow the basic idea of exchange to emerge for the first time in human history, i.e., the notion that one may not live on one's own; and that there could be meaningful exchange. An elementary notion of commodity and market emerges herein. This is inevitably marked by growth of specializati on as well as individuation.

Initially, the exchange system is that of a direct barter type, with further development of wider range of needs and commensurating commodities with an embryonic idea of market or exchange develops, which also marks interdependence of various groups.

Asiatic Societies

From the pre-class system, in a simpler unilinear evolution scheme the development of a specific type of ancient society (Germanic) is reconstructed, which in turn could give rise to an orthodox feudal system in Western Europe. Actually, this focus on a unilinear evolution, a chronological succession of epochs and the idea of social revolution as the overthrow of one system by a class exploited within the old system is somewhat a post-1859 concern of Marx and Engels. It is more attendant upon the overriding interest in the pre-capitalist stages of development as they explain the preconditions of capitalism. However, during 1857–58 while preparing notes and observations for *Capital*, Marx deals with a more complex scheme which talks of an *Asiatic Society*. Also, importantly Marx identifies Germanic, ancient and Slavonic forms of property and production as other alternate routes out of primitive communism.

The various forms, as we notice in such preparatory notes of Marx (which were compiled later and published as *Grundrisse*), actually indicates that the ever popular unilinear line of evolution may not be a historical certainty. In particular, Asiatic society does not create within itself the seeds of its own destruction (Hobsbaum 1964).

Asiatic societies have been understood as those not following the universal path of evolution of human societies. These are the societies of the Orient which are marked by despotism. Such oriental despotism is caused by the need for a centralized system of irrigation, e.g., as in China or India. They have powerful despotic leaders.

The static nature of these societies is termed as the Asiatic mode of production. It is being claimed that they are marked by an absence of private property particularly private ownership of and this leads to social stagnation. The static nature of Asiatic society results from the coherence of the ancient village community which puts up a face of self-sufficiency combining agriculture and handicrafts. The communities are stagnant also due to geographical and climatic reasons and are thereby dependent on irrigation which required a centralized administrative apparatus to develop large-scale irrigation system. The despotic state is experienced in public works and it corresponds to the self-sufficient, idyllic village communities.

The social immutability of the Asiatic mode of production is popularized as Oriental Despotism. Such a characterization of 'Asiatic' societies has been subjected to rigorous debates on the question of the unilinear view of history as suggested by Marx. But it would suffice to acknowledge that such an understanding of the Orient is mainly premised on Marx's journalist criticisms of the colonial British power in India, writing for *New York Daily Tribune*.

Ancient Society

Actually in Marx's scheme of the stages of human society, the emergence of the ancient society in Western Europe is of much importance. It follows the stage of primitive communism with the development for the fist time in human history of a class-divided society. The two distinct classes are the masters and the slaves.

Historically, classes come into existence when the surplus is privately appropriated. Because of privately appropriated wealth, it is sufficient for internally self-recruiting group to clearly set-off from the mass of the producers. Still, in ancient society, private property is overshadowed by public property, especially in Greece, although it is supposed to get abolished completely.

As a result of agreement as well as conquests, ancient societies are marked by a fusion of different tribes. Such societies finally give rise to sharply defined lines of social differentiation. The three factors responsible for such differentiation are:

i. Influence of landed property, especially in the Roman empire
ii. Concentration of landed property leading to extension and spread of slavery, and
iii. Aggressive colonization of other tribes.

The subsequent swelling of the ranks of slaves is matched by a handful of masters. The brunt of productive labour is borne by the slaves. The handful of masters has no intentions to innovate and improve the production from the existing resources. They lack interest even in commerce, trade and manufacturing activities. The slave system passes through different stages. They are found mainly around large cities such as Athens and Rome. The decay of the slave system leads to small-scale farming systems which are leased out. Expropriation of large number of peasants from the means of production is a consequence of the drive of the Roman Empire to accumulate wealth. This state is set thereby as a foundation for the emergence of the next stage, i.e., feudalism. According to Marx, such societies are destroyed by over-population and by their inability to find enough land for the ruling class, i.e., the masters.

The fall of the Roman Empire brings in a system of serfdom as the nobility is developed. A full-fledged serfdom experiences the shift from the master-slave relationship to nobility-serf relationship.

Feudal Society

The feudal stage develops in Europe after the collapse of the Roman Empire. The basis of feudal economy is the small-scale peasant agriculture involving the bonded serfs, and supplemented by domestic industry and handicraft production in town. Essentially, the feudal economy is a rural economy.

Under serfdom the producers surrender a certain amount of his produce to the lord. Interestingly, there is a low degree of alienation between the producer and the product. By and large, the serf is his own producer producing for the needs of his family and himself. The stage is marked by tranquility as the lord does not try to maximize profit from his estate, and rather leaves it for the serfs and tenants to produce. However, the serfs are tied to the lords by both economic as well as non-economic factors.

For an early development of capitalism, the disintegration of the feudal society is facilitated by growth of towns. The decayed urban centres which already exist develop as wealthy commercial centres. Progressive expropriation of small peasants from the means of production and control of production led them to fall back on their own labour and engage in trade/market activities. This, they accomplish by moving to those urban centres. Increase in market and trade activities in turn enhance the role of money and production of commodities. The importance of usury in the urban centres leads to the decline of fortunes of the landowning aristocracy. As a result, more and more serfs are freed from the control of the landlords. By the end of the fourteenth-century in England, the vast labouring population is made free peasant proprietor.

Historically, the chances of survival and revival of feudalism varies from society to society. The fate of feudalism is not the same everywhere as the scope of development of capitalism too is not uniform universally.

Capitalist Society

For classical development of capitalism, primary accumulation of capital is a must, i.e., surplus value generated needs to be ploughed back in the production forces. It is to be supplemented by full-fledged expropriation of the peasants from the means of production. All these are accompanied by a series of events marked with blood and fire.

The later half of the fifteenth-century is marked by a transformation of independent peasants into wage labourers. As a result of great feudal wars, the nobility lose resources. Hence, on one hand, there is an impoverished aristocracy and, on the other, there are a mass of free proletariat. Both are classically thrown into the market. The impoverished aristocracy increasingly gets involved in usury (exchange economy), and the free proletariat are disciplined through legislations to appear as full-fledged wage-labourers.

Many new factors like discovery of new land, large-scale maritime trade and development of mercantilism/manufacturing centres with improved manufacturing tools are stimulants for the development of capitalism. There are two distinct ways of subsequent development of capitalism. The first path is when a segment of the merchant class moves over from purely trading operations to take a direct hand in production. But Marx sees this particular way as fraught with enough obstacles to fully emerge as capitalism. Instead, the real revolutionary way is the one when individual producers themselves accumulate capital and move from production to expand their activity sphere. This way, much of the land is owned by capitalist farmers by employing wage labour and producing for commodity market. Land becomes a capital and production is organized along capitalist line. This classical way, because of the ever expanding market, stimulates greater division of labour. And simultaneously it creates technically more advanced means of production. Such enhanced mechanization of production leads to industrial revolution.

The essence of the capitalist stage of society is that the capitalists cannot exist without constantly revolutionizing the forces of production. On the contrary, the retention of the existing mode of production is the very first condition of existence of the system. The changes in the forces of production in turn revolutionize the relations of production. This is ramified in the society with uninterrupted disturbances, everlasting uncertainty and social strife. The accelerated unrest is a unique feature of the capitalist society. This distinguishes it from all the preceding stages. The subsequent stage germinates within these conditions, and under certain specific conditions a socialist stage emerges.

The emergence of such a socialist society and its further transcendence to a communist stage is projected by Marx as an inevitable future of a capitalist stage. The socialist stage works on the principle of social ownership of the means of production accompanied by a dictatorship of the working class. This stage has to finally ensure a total abolition of private property and thereby move beyond the dictatorship of the working class to a stage of communism. But the stages beyond capitalism are less analysed in Marx's own writings. Hence, they remain as future projections only.

With the application of the dialectical method we realize that in all the above types or stages of society the social regulation of labour is the foundation and base of the organization of human experience. This is a materialist way of looking at history. History, as the development of the human race, is determined by the nature of labour, division of labour and growth of productive forces. But, this fascinating theory is often fraught with the danger of mechanical oversimplification. In such mechanistic interpretations, the instruments of labour, not the men who use them are taken as the actual initiators and perpetrators of social change. This way, the forces of production are objectified. This vulgarization of Marx's theory equates the historical law with natural laws by identifying the two. It is true that Marx often talks about 'natural law of historical development', but a comprehensive reading of Marx's entire social philosophy should inform us that by social/historical law he sees law as having the characteristics of tendencies.

Beyond a mechanistic understanding of the relationship between 'base' and 'superstructure', we learn that it is the 'men who make history'. Whenever Marx analyses a concrete political situation (*The Class Struggles in France*), he makes it obvious that social being is more than just the sum of economic conditions. These conditions are affected by many elements of consciousness. Men, as embodiments of such consciousness, act on the material world. History proceeds from social reality and not from any abstract categories. It is constructed out of practice and not from any set of self-resolving ideas.

THEORY OF CAPITALISM

Adhering to his dialectical materialist interpretation of society, while dealing with his most influential treatise on the working of the capitalist system, Marx understands every economic category as an embodiment of real human relationships. No longer do the economic categories remain dry and lifeless at Marx's treatment of them, and hence, his examination of the capitalist economy is essentially an analysis of the economic aspects of capitalist social system.

Apart from the three volumes of *Capital*, Marx's analysis of industrial capitalist society is present in his *Value, Price and Profit* (1865), which is republished under the title *Wages, Price and Profit* in 1952, by Foreign Languages Publishing House, Moscow. The English version had to wait until the 1887 translation appeared. Marx tirelessly worked for more than two decades to 'lay bare the law of motion of capital', but Engels, his collaborator had to put together what Marx left behind in the form of notes and manuscripts to bring out Vol. 2 in 1885 and Vol. 3 in 1894.

In his 'Preface' to *Capital*, Marx has made it very clear that he has resorted to the force of abstractions, an abstract-deductive method, to analyse economic forms. As he claims this economic methodology which is based on abstraction is a unique tool with social scientists which helps them to move from the most abstract to the more concrete in a systemic step by step fashion. At every step simplifying assumptions are removed so that they have relevance to and explain more and more actual social reality. For Marx, the ultimate purpose is to 'lay bare the economic laws of motion' of modern capitalist society. Analysing capitalism as a historical system only allows him to theorize a future transcendence of the same system.

As a historical reality capitalism is explained as an economic system of transitory nature. While analysing the specific historical character of capitalism Marx recognizes the true interrelations between economic and non-economic factors in the totality of social existence.

COMMODITY

To understand Marx's theory of capitalist development, the single-most important analytical category is that of commodity. In fact, commodity has to be the entry point of any orthodox understanding of capitalism. A study of commodity is the study of economic relations of exchange. Commodity is anything that is produced for exchange rather than for the use of the producers. Marx sees the elementary stage of circulation as that of simple commodity production. This is marked by a situation where each producer has his own means of production and produces independently. Every producer satisfies his/her wants with direct exchange with other producers similarly placed.

Commodity production is an essential feature of capitalism but commodity production is not the universal and inevitable form of economic life. While it is true that we are all too familiarized with the form of economic life which dominates the modern period, it is still a historically conditioned form. It is not an intrinsic human nature to produce commodities. Commodity is a historical category. A product becomes a commodity when it is produced not just to meet human needs, but for exchange in the market. Like any other economic category, commodity also encompasses a relation between people. Thus, what interests Marx is not only the quantitative value that circumscribes commodity production, but the qualitative value problem. Also, between use-value and exchange-value, the latter is crucial for Marx to understand the relation between the commodity producers.

That a commodity satisfies some human wants, is a fact not so unique. This is the use-value of any commodity. In every age of human history a commodity has always remained an object of human desire. This relationship between the commodity and its consumer tells us only about the use-value of commodity. It does not express any social relationship, and hence, for Marx, it has only a limited scope in his analysis of capitalism.

Products have exchange-value only when exchange is a regular method of realizing the purpose of social production. Such a situation makes a product to qualify as a commodity. Commodities can be exchanged, but not products. When products are not exchanged they cannot have exchange-value. Through such an understanding of commodity and exchange-value, Marx arrives at the labour theory of value.

LABOUR THEORY OF VALUE

In simple terms, any two things could be exchanged only if both of them have something in common. For Marx, the exchange of commodity is nothing but a manifestation of a hidden social relation. The core element of all commodities is that they are all products of human labour. That common 'thing' is the common basic denominator which makes every commodity comparable and exchangeable. Therefore, the core element that is being exchanged is human labour.

Quantitative relations between things which we call 'exchange-value' is in reality an expressed form of social relation between commodity owners, or what come to be the same thing in simple commodity production, between producers. The analysis of commodity this way brings us to the labour theory of value, what is being exchanged is actually the embodied by each commodity. Value that lies behind a commodity is nothing but labour power that has gone into its making. By virtue of this unique property that commodities are exchanged is that, they are the products of labour. Thus they appear in the market as a bearer of social relations commodities. Understood from the standpoint of production, commodity is nothing but materialized human activity.

To appreciate labour as the substance of value, Marx brings in the notion of 'abstract labour'. Labour as 'abstract labour' signifies a general expenditure of human labour power. Since varieties of labour cannot be compared, the notion of abstract labour is invoked by him. It is labour in general without any differences and distinctions like skilled, semi-skilled, unskilled etc. Hence, Marx advances the labour theory of value with the help of the idea of abstract labour and talks of socially necessary labour time to produce a commodity as that which determines its value and which facilitates to compare them.

Marx makes it clear in *Capital*, Vol. 1, that,

> The labour, however, that forms the substance of value, is homogeneous human labour, expenditure of one uniform labour-power. The total labour-power of society which is embodied in the sum total of the values of all commodities produced by that society, counts here as one homogeneous mass of human labour-power, composed though it be of innumerable individual units. Each of these units is the same as any other, so far as it has the character of the average labour-power of society, and takes effect as such; that is, so far as it requires for producing a commodity, no more time than is needed on any average, no more than is socially necessary... The value of one commodity is to be the value of any other, as the labour-time necessary for the production of the one is to that necessary for the production of the other. (Karl Marx 1967: 39)

It clarifies that all special characteristics of labour which sets apart one from another kind of labour is ignored, so that all labour could be reduced to a common denominator. Hence, that the units of labour can be compared to each other, as each commodity absorbs a part of society's total labour force available. This unique characteristic of commodity makes 'commodity' the starting point and the central category to any Marxian understanding of capitalism.

COMMODITY FETISHISM

In the very first place, a commodity is a material object outside us. Its intrinsic property is to satisfy human wants and desires. The utility of a thing makes it a use-value, but for analysing capitalist economy, Marx has made it clear that it is the exchange-value which has made commodity a central category of the system. Capitalism is signaled by the transcendence of simple commodity production to a generalized commodity production.

The simple commodity production is explained by the notation of $C — M — C^1$, where the circulation process starts with a commodity C and the end is marked by a different commodity C^1. This circulation is facilitated by the intermediary money M. Here, the use-value of a commodity is at premium, whereas, the generalized commodity production starts with money and ends with money. Circulation is noted by $M — C — M^1$, where M denotes the initial money put in for a production process. The production process involves various commodities to come with a final product C, which again is sold of and realized in the market in the form of M^1. This M^1 has to be greater than the initial money M. This condition simply justifies the process of circulation. As we have seen earlier, exchange-value is solely important of any commodity in such a process of circulation. It is called generalized commodity production as every other aspect of social life attains the character of a commodity, that could be put in the market for buying and selling.

Commodities do not go to the market and make exchanges on their own. What is important to realize is that the owners of these commodities set the circulation in motion. Therefore, all the persons involved in the process of production act as and exist for one another merely as representatives of commodities. It becomes clear that the commodity essentially acts an alienating force. It alienates as the unique character of a community is that of concealing social relations. Instead, it takes up a fantastic reified image. Commodity production under capitalism leads to reification of all social relations. This is termed as 'commodity fetishism'. This is so as values of all commodities are definite masses of hidden labour time.

Commodity production at a large-scale is a necessary pre-condition for development of capitalism. What sets it apart from rest of commodity producing society is that here human labour power also becomes a commodity. Under capitalism, the ownership of means of production rests with one set of individuals while work is performed by another. Most interestingly, labour power as an important factor of production is also a commodity which is exchangeable. As a bearer of exchange-value labour is 'free', unlike the feudal or earlier stages, which could be put in the market and be owned by anyone who could buy it. This 'buying and selling' of labour is what Marx considers the *differentia specifica* of the capitalist stage. The final stage of growing commodification of the social world is reached under capitalism with human labour also attaining the character of a commodity.

SURPLUS VALUE

In Marx's scheme of generalized commodity production, noted by M — C — M^1, the justification is given by M^1 as greater than M. The specific historical form of capitalist production rests on the objective of ensuring the final money (M^1) as greater than the initial money (M). The task is therefore to analyse this increase in M, which would explain the origin of surplus value. As generating surplus value is the rationale of capitalists, we need to investigate the source of it. The clue is — of all the commodities which enter into the production process, which one has the unique capacity to create value over and above its own value? Marx holds that none else, except the commodity labour power has this capacity, and this becomes evident when we examine the way the value of commodity labour power is determined.

As in the case of any other commodity, the commodity labour power is also determined by the socially necessary labour-time required for its production and consequently for its reproduction. The minimum limit of the value of labour power is determined by the value of the commodities without the daily supply of which the labour cannot renew his vital energy; consequently by the value of these means of subsistence that are physically indispensable.

The capitalist buys the labour power as it values and pays in the form of wages, which is a sum correspondent to the value of the workers' means of subsistence. If we suppose this value is a product of 6 hours of labour, if a worker works beyond this sixth hour, all such labour adds on to the value which will appear in the final product. If the process were to break off at the end of the sixth hour, the capitalist would be able to sell the product for just enough to reimburse himself to his outlays. But the worker sells his labour power for the whole day (say, for 12 hours), as there is nothing in the nature of things that limits the working day to 6 hours or so. In such a scenario, the last 6 hours (out of the total 12 hours) value is created over and above that which is required to cover his means of subsistence. In short, a surplus-value is being generated for the capitalist. In a day's work, a worker is generating value more than the day's means of subsistence, which is the source of the all-important surplus-value under capitalism. Thus, the working hours could be divided into two parts: necessary labour and surplus labour. The products of necessary labour accrue to the workers in the form of wages, while the product of surplus labour is siphoned off by the capitalist in the form of surplus value. Generation of surplus varies according to varying circumstances.

The total value under capitalism can be expressed in terms of its three components as:

$$\textit{Total value} = C + V + S$$

where C = constant capital, the capital invested for procuring the means of production, i.e., tools, machines, land, technology etc.

V = variable capital, i.e., capital invested to pay wages to labour

It is unlike constant capital, as it varies and creates an extra value during a production process

S = surplus value, i.e., the surplus that is created in a process of production.

Total value = C + V + S, is the analytic base of Marx's theory of capitalism.

Using it, we can arrive at the notion of rate of surplus value and can also derive other important relation and rates. (Sweezy 1946)

$$\textit{Rate of surplus value } S^1 = S/V$$

Rate of profit P = S/C + V, is the ratio of surplus to the total capital outlay

Organic composition of capital $q = C/C + V$; it is the measure of relation between constant to variable capital in the total capital used in production. In non-technical language, q is the measure of the extent to which the labour is furnished with material instruments and machineries in the production process.

It is not the profit but the rate of profit P which is important for the capitalist to stay in the production process. The rate of surplus value (S^1) only explains the rate of exploitation in the capitalist form of production. Through a derivation from $P = S/C + V$, it can be shown that,

$$\textit{The rate of profit } P = S^1\,(1\text{-}q)$$

The magnitude of S^1 is directly determined by three factors:

i. The length of working day
ii. The quantity of commodity entering into the real wage, and
iii. Productiveness of labour.

The surplus value that workers produce can be increased by making them work for longer hours, known as 'absolute surplus value'. This can be achieved alternatively by improving the productive method, so that more is produced in the same time. This is called as the 'relative surplus value'. It is relative because it is not fixed like the first method. Increasing the working hours has a limit: one cannot stretch it beyond the fixed limit of a day, whereas improvisation of the productive method is a ceaseless process. A capitalist resorts to both the methods to face competition and being driven by a continuous desire to accumulate more. During the early stages of capitalism, the absolute surplus value is of importance but as capitalism develops, the importance of relative surplus value becomes more evident.

Any method of production which reduces the cost (technologies, discoveries, workers) will bring extra profit to those who introduce it quickly before the general price level has been forced down. Once the new method of production is generally adopted, competition will force prices down in line with the lower cost of production and wipe out any emerging high cost producers. Under capitalism, large-scale production is more important than small-scale production and competition forces capitalists to accumulate and re-invest to the maximum possible extent in order to produce on the large scale.

ACCUMULATION PROCESS

For a capitalist, the primary goal is ever expansion of capital. The two primary variables of capitalism are the rate of surplus value (S^1) and q (the organic composition of capital), discussed before. A capitalist gives effect to his primary goal by converting a major portion of surplus value into additional capital. His enhanced capital allows him to appropriate still more surplus value, which he again converts to capital. This is a typical accumulation process under capitalism. It is the driving force behind capitalism as $M — C — M^1$ is essentially a value expansion process. The value expansion is reflected in the subjective aim of the capitalist class. As long as he is the owner and representative of capital, a capitalist is important and measured accordingly in terms of power and prestige. Unless he is continuously expanding his capital, he cannot satisfy his urge to accumulate more and more. We have seen before that one who can implement the most improved technology/tools, methods for most efficient production, can also draw a higher surplus value. This renders absolute all means of production continuously. This has further ramification for the society, which we will consider later.

Given the desire for accumulation, a capitalist never consumes entirely the surplus value. To analyse the aspects of the accumulation process, Marx resorts to an expanded reproduction scheme to account for the three different parts into which the total surplus generated is channelized: (1) a part is consumed, (2) a part is added to variable capital, V, and (3) a part is added to constant capital.

Now, if variable capital is increased, it means more wages are given. The price of labour goes high in this case, which increases the demand for the same commodity, i.e., labour. This in turn means deviance of price of labour from its value. Under capitalism, for any other commodity except labour power, the equilibrating mechanism of demand and supply set these deviations right. But, labour power is no ordinary commodity, as there are no capitalists who can turn to producing labour power in case its price goes up. Obviously, this leads to a tendency of wages to go high under the impact of accumulation. We know, $S^1 = S/V$, and so any increase in V would lead to a fall in the rate of surplus value, which in turn will lead to a decrease in the rate of profit.

Given this entanglement, Marx says that capitalism works with a unique relative surplus of population, popularly termed as the *reserve army of labour*. For Marx the relative surplus population is the pivot upon which the law of demand and supply of labour works. The reserve army is recruited primarily from those who have been displaced by machinery; whether this takes the more striking form of retrenchment of labour already employed or the less evident but not less real form of the more difficult absorption of the additional labouring population through the usual channels.

Every capitalist tries to do the best he can do for himself by introducing machines and economizing on his wage bill. The net effect of all the capitalists operating in the same way creates a 'sac' of unemployed workers which in turn acts upon the wage level to keep it down. The reserve army of labour thereby effects a contracting pressure on the price of labour.

The enhanced mechanism of means of production indicates a growth of constant capital C at the expense of the variable capital V. The rate of accumulation and the introduction of labour saving machineries do not proceed on an even pace to preserve a nice equilibrium of wages ad surplus value. On the contrary, with accumulation and development of productiveness of labour that accompanies it the power of sudden expansion of capital also grows. A rapid burst of capita may result fro the opening of new market or a new industry. In such cases, the size of the reserve army of labour gets depleted and the check on the rise in wages is removed. So, surplus value may indeed be diminished in such cases.

Alongside of displacement of labour by machinery crisis and depressions take place as the specific capitalist mechanism of replenishing the reserve army of labour, whenever it gets reduced to a dangerously low level.

Out of the three parts of surplus, in the situation of conversion of large part of it to constant capital a very unique consequence follows. If more and more re-investment in additional constant capital is taken up, even if to make production more efficient (improving the tools and techniques), from the relationship rate of profit $P = S^1\ (1\text{-}q)$ it is evident that profit will fall down, as any increase in C leads to increase in q. We know from $q = C/C + V$, and as a consequence from $P = S^1\ (1\text{-}q)$, rate of profit falls down. According to Marx, this is a general tendency of rate of profit to fall because the change in the rate of surplus may be compensated or over-compensated by a change of organic composition of capital q.

Ultimately, such a tendency is avoided, so that capitalist production continues meaningfully. There are five direct ways to counteract on the falling tendency of rate of profit:

i. *Cheapening of the elements of the constant capital:* An increased use of machinery through raising the productivity of labour lowers the value by unit of constant capital

ii. *Raising the intensity of exploitation:* Speeding up or stretching out the working hours to ensure a higher rate of surplus value without affecting the amount of necessary labour

iii. *Pursuing an aggressive wage policy:* Depression of wages below their values, which is nothing but wage-cutting in practice, wherever possible

iv. *Activating the relative surplus population:* Increased machinery itself means more workers being set free from jobs, as a result of which the reserve army of labour swells in ranks. The existence of under labour is conducive to setting up of new industries with a relatively low organic composition of capital and hence a relative high rate of profit is made possible in new industries. Averaging with the old rate, the overall rate could be satisfying for capitalism to continue, and

v. *The existence of foreign trade:* Through foreign trades, necessities of life as well as raw materials for production could be produced, which would simultaneously cheapen the elements of constant capital as well as allow the variable capital to be kept low.

All the above methods are simultaneously or variously adopted by a capitalist to counter the falling tendency of rate of profit.

CRISIS OF CAPITALISM

Notwithstanding all the strategies and way outs that we have seen so far, throughout its history, capitalism is marked by periodic crises. These put the capitalist order on trial every time. According to Marx, crises are an integral and inevitable part of a capitalist order. It is out of the internal logic of capitalist development that such crises occur. For capitalism, production for profit is an end in itself. Growing accumulation leads to a blind chase for maximizing profit as a result of which crises and depressions are ingrained in the system itself. Marx is quite clear in admitting that real crisis can only be explained from the real movement of capital production, competition and credit.

However, we can analytically locate crisis in the circulation process itself. We know that capitalism is represented by $M — C — M^1$, as its process of circulation. The final M^1 has to be greater than the initial M, but the capitalist is not only interested to earn an absolute increase in M, but in a magnitude of increase in relation to the initial M.

When M^1 is less than M, it is known as depression, which is an extreme case. When profit is wiped out (even if $M^1 = M$), the production process will come to a stall. But as we have learnt earlier, for a capitalist just an absolute profit is not sufficient to continue in the production process. He is keen on a normal rate of profit, rather than an expected rate of profit. Unless that is accomplished, the capitalist will not re-invest but hold back his profit in the form of money or postpone reinvestment for a while. In the long run, he does join back when the situation becomes favourable or/and he reconciles with a new rate of profit.

Under unfavourable situation, a capitalist either postpones reinvestment or moves from one line of production to another. In the second choice also, there is a temporary interruption of the process of production. It is important for us to note that, a crisis can set in even if there is a positive surplus value.

Capitalist crises are explained as being of two types:

i. Falling tendency of rate of profit, and
ii. Problem of Realization, i.e., inability of capitalists to sell commodities at their values.

According to Marx,

> The barrier of capitalist made of production becomes apparent in the fact that the development of the productive power of labour creates in the falling rate of profit a law which turns into an antagonism of this mode of production at a certain point and requires for its defeat. (Karl Marx 1967: 349)

If we assume that accumulation of capital proceeds smoothly and labour saving technology and new techniques of production are available at right time and quantity, so that a stable reserve army of labour is protected which could prevent any undue upward pressure on wages — such a scenario would be highly unrealistic. Sharp fluctuations in the rate of accumulation partly caused by and partly leading to technical renovations, become more and more the rule. Now, if accumulation fluctuates, the reserve army of labour gets inflated. Subsequently, such accumulation leads to opening up of new market, new industries which in turn exhaust the reserve army. Once it is fully utilized, because of burst of accumulation, wages again go high. As a result, surplus value is cut; it will reach a point where surplus labour which nourishes capital will no longer be there. Profit will come down and automatically, capitalists would opt for contraction of investment. This is a crisis. Again as a reaction to such contraction once the reserve army of labour is filled up, it can restore the profitability of production and thereby sets a stage for resumption of accumulation process. However, the repetition of the whole process is a matter of time. The second type of capitalist crisis is that of the problem of realization. This may arise due to:

i. Disproportionality among various lines of production, and
ii. From under consumption of masses.

At times general crisis and over-production can arise from partial disturbances in the process of production and circulation. If all commodities are sold at their values then the relative proportion in which the various articles/objects are produced could be correct. There is no pre-plan according to which this proportion could be arrived at by the capitalist. Thus, on the one hand, if commodities are produced in excess then their prices go down and if commodities are produced inadequately, their prices rise up. It is only through a trial and error method that one can arrive at such proportion correctly, only if the other factors remain constant. But these factors (wage etc.) keep changing all the time. Therefore, to arrive at the correct proportion is not easy. Such disproportionality leads to crisis of realizing the value of commodities. This marks an anarchic nature of capitalist production. This unplannedness of capitalism is not amendable by any general law. The real price never confirms to an exactly fixed theoretical pattern by nature.

The second type of realization problem arises from under-consumption. When purchasing of the masses is not adequate enough, commodities are not converted to the form of money. This fails to satisfy the normal rate of profit. Paradoxically, this lack of purchasing power is self-created. As the capitalist production and accumulation process thrives on a reserve army of labour (unemployment) the commodities produced as a result of higher productivity cannot be fully purchased by masses (i.e., consumed). This is a case of under-consumption. Such unrealization of surplus value is inherent under capitalism as a result of under-consumption. This is a severe crisis faced by capitalism, which has prompted many post-Marx theorists to work on the theory of Imperialism and/or the third market.

Cumulatively, capitalism and its self-expansion appears as the starting point and the closing point of such a stage of society. As Marx thinks, the capitalists dig their own graves. Capitalists upgrade productive forces in their own selfish interests. The fundamental contradiction revolves on the issue of dislocation between productive forces and the social relations of production. The zeal for accumulation leads to increasing misery of the working class. Concentration of private appropriation reaches its peak under capitalism, while, production is social in character. The growing pauperization of the working class is indicated by Marx as the premise for a change of the system. A subjective realization of the exploitative nature of production under capitalism, is supposed to lead to heightened class consciousness on the part of the working class. This subjective awareness for an overthrow of the capitalist mode of production is likely to occur only when the objective conditions of the mode of production become ripe enough for such human intervention. An ensuing class struggle is all that is being suggested in Marx's various writings. However, in *Capital* we find a more scholarly treatise on the logic of capital development, with a reference to a transition to socialist stage. A socialist stage as a transitory one as we understand from Marx's scattered writings is necessary for a belief in mankind's final redemption in a Communist stage.

SUMMARY

The objective reality which we apprehend through our senses need not be just the object of contemplation. Marx's method of study primarily emphasizes this objective reality as sensuous human activity. This active side cannot be explained through abstract idealism when posited as a corrective to crude materialism. Instead, Marx effects a philosophy of practice to premise social reality as the interaction of objective and subjective factors. The

Marxist concept of dialectics helps us to realize social reality as a process, a movement and a change. Social reality is a dynamic of objective circumstances and creative human activity. Thereby, it offers us with a unique understanding of the unfolding of the various stages of history. Exhaustively researching on the capitalist society of this time, Marx offers a class analysis of human society. For him, all societies are class-divided societies with two main antagonistic classes: the ruling class owns the means of production and the ruled class works with the means of production. The exceptions are the stage of primitive communism and the one of matured communist society that Marx expects and projects as the 'final' stage beyond an intermediary socialist stage. In his model of society, the dominant economic class in any period is also the dominant class politically. In this scheme, it is the classes which are the agents of historical change, not individuals. Individuals engage in historical changes by virtue of being members of a social class. By diagnosing the logic of capital, and its inner contradictions, Marx promises an emancipatory image of society.

Key Words

- *Idealism*
- *Dialectics*
- *Capital*
- *Labour*
- *Fetishism*
- *Crisis*
- *Materialism*
- *Mode of Production*
- *Commodity*
- *Surplus Value*
- *Reserve Army of Labour*

Glossary

Class: All those that share similar positions in the relations of production.

Commodity: Anything and everything which has an exchange value, i.e. which can be bought and sold.

Forces of Production: Along with the means of production, when human labour power is added.

Historical Materialism: The materialist interpretation of the unfolding of historical stages of society. It explains society and its changes in terms of changing material forces of production.

Idealism: The philosophy which understands reality as constituted of only mental elements alone. It gives mind, beliefs, ideas, spirit and so forth the primacy in the existence of the world.

Means of Production: The tools, techniques, machines, raw materials, land — that enable human beings to act on the material world to transform and produce.

Mode of Production: A marker of any stage of society, an analytical combination of the productive forces and the relations of production.

Production Relation: Relations among individuals with respect to their ownership of productive forces.

Surplus Value: In a working day, the value created by workers over and above the value of their labour power (wages), which goes to the owners of the means of production to make profit in the market.

Discussion Points

- The philosophical underpinnings of Marx's social theory.
- The dialectical understanding of society.
- The logic of capitalism.
- The transcendence of capitalism.

3

Emile Durkheim (1858–1917)

Although August Comte is popularly held as the founding father of sociology, Emile Durkheim has to be credited with making sociology a standardized academic discipline. In fact, Durkheim is the pioneer in developing sociology into a social scientific discipline and thereby, establishing its legitimacy in the French academic world. He carried forward Comte's spirit of searching for a positivist method for studying society. In the world history of sociology, Durkheim remains as a leading figure in developing not only a distinctive conception of the subject matter of sociology but also as one who developed sociological theory in particular.

A BIOGRAPHICAL SKETCH

David Emile was the fourth child born to Melanie and Moise Durkheim on 15 April 1858. His birth place was the small town of Epinal, situated in the French Eastern-border province. Durkheim's father was a chief rabbi of that region and the last member of an unbroken line of eight generations of father–son rabbis.

As a descendant from a long line of rabbis, Emile Durkheim studied to be a rabbi and was destined to be the next one in the family. Interestingly, along with training in religions he attended secular schools too. However, ultimately he rejected the religious heritage. He was more in a mood for training in scientific methods as well in the moral principles needed to shape and govern social life.

Durkheim's childhood was spent in a family which was content and close-knit although not very wealthy. Coming from a healthy family, he was drawn in his youth towards a mystical form of Catholicism. Very soon he turned towards a more secular vocation, retaining his interests on moral order for social life. He even dropped his first name of David because of its Hebrew connotation. He left after his graduation from Epinal for higher studies in Paris. With rigorous preparation for admission to the elite Ecole Normale Superieure, he secured admission after three years. He studied in Ecole philosophy and history. Simultaneously, he was attracted to the sociological texts of August Comte and Herbert Spencer.

Durkheim obtained his doctorate degree from the University of Paris for the work which was published in 1893, entitled *De la division du travail social* in French. In English it translates as *The Division of Labor in Society*, which is considered as one of the fundamental classical texts in sociology. During the period 1882–87, he had to teach philosophy in some schools since sociology, as a discipline, was yet to develop in the academia. Only in 1887 he could secure a faculty position at the University of Bordeaux, France. This was actually facilitated by some substantial publications by him after his exposure to Germany. In Germany, Durkheim was introduced to the scientific psychology of Wilhelm Wundt.

It was to Durkheim's effort that for the first time in a French University a course on sociology could be introduced at Bordeaux. He was the chair of Social Science in the University from 1896 to 1902. Initially he was teaching courses in education to school teachers. His focus was essentially on imparting a moral education to young teachers so that it could be transmitted to students around. His concern was to arrest the perceived moral degradation around him at that time.

Finally, Durkheim was taken as a faculty member at the elite Sorbonne University, Paris. Due to sustained academic efforts he could secure the recognition of sociology at Sorbonne in 1913. Meanwhile Durkheim could entrench himself as a thorough professional of the discipline of sociology through consistent publication of some of the major texts in the history of the discipline. In 1893, as noted before, he published *The Division of Labor in Society*. Subsequent to this, in 1895 he brought out almost a manual for an appropriate sociological method in *The Rules of Sociological Method*. Immediately after that he applied this method to come out with the fundamental sociological treatise on *Suicide*, in 1897. Durkheim's study of aboriginal Australian society appeared in 1912 as *The Elementary Forms of Religious Life*.

Durkheim was instrumental in establishing sociology as an academic discipline and institutionalizing it in university departments subsequently. In 1896, he founded the journal *L'anee sociologique*. The impact of the setting up of a professional journal on the discipline was widespread. An intellectual circle could grow around the journal which impacted upon other humanities disciplines like linguistics, anthropology, psychology and history.

In sociology, Durkheim is seen as a bearer of a conservative traditionp — an inheritor of the Comtean tradition. However, during his time he was more in alignment with Liberal politics. His ideas attracted the then French government and it is being held that his liberal pro-republican views helped him to gain the confidence of the public as well as the government. But Durkheim refrained from taking any active role in political activities; this was with an exception. In 1894, Durkheim played an active public role in the defense of Captain Alfred Dreyfus, a French army official. Dreyfus was a Jew and was falsely convicted of treason through a court-martial by a conservative anti-semitic French military. Against the night-wing reactionary forces Durkheim defended Dreyfus with zeal and aided the liberal and socialist movement against it. From a deep sense of morality he struck to the grand task of contesting moral crisis and degeneration of the emergent modern society.

The influence of Durkheim's sociological concern among his students was so much that it permeated to other social science disciplines. During World War II, he actively wrote and campaigned for the French government. The killings of many of his favourite students during the War, including his son Andre' Durkheim, had a profound effect on Durkheim's mind. Grief-stricken he died at the age of fifty nine only, on 15 November 1917. Durkheim's contribution to sociology remains unsurpassed, with proposed writings on sociological methodology, sociology of modernity, education, religion and morality.

SOCIAL AND INTELLECTUAL INFLUENCES

Like all other classical thinkers on society, Emile Durkheim was greatly shaped by the rumblings of the emergent modern society of the nineteenth-century Europe. Despite his whole-hearted appreciation and application of the principle of science, rationality and strivings for social reformism, he is considered as a conservative intellectual. Paradoxically, he was politically liberal. The social milieu of his lifetime holds a clue to this.

The French society of Durkheim's time was marked by major socio-political events like Franco-Prussian War and its resultant recurrent political crises. Such a scenario was aggravated by persistent economic and political disturbances. The German occupation of his hometown Epinal and the wounds inflicted upon his Jewish community impaled upon Durkheim's young mind. The subsequent anti-semitic sentiments in France took him unaware as the indictment of Jewish citizens of France as responsible for the French defeat, was puzzling for him. More than anti-semiticism he understood the events as that of a lack of moral order of the day.

Rapid industrialization in France also resulted in repeated conflicts between the employers and the employees. The aggressive profiteering by the enterprises and the conflict with the working class marked the French society, which experienced a very short establishment of the Paris commune — an egalitarian republic in 1878. The ruthless action of the French government in crushing the Commune moved Durkheim, who opted for a need of a just moral order for France. He abhorred any violent actions from any side, and instead understood that since the French Revolution of 1789, the socio-political order gradually got enmeshed in divisions and disorder. What became of paramount interest for Durkheim when he was still a young student was to re-establish a moral fabric of the society in order to overcome the crisis. Thereafter, he dedicated himself to a study of society which could be reformative in its goal. He attempted to make sociology a discipline which could moralize the society. As he wrote:

> Although we set out primarily to study reality, it does not follow that we do not wish to improve it; we should judge our researches to have no worth at all if they were to have only a speculative interest. If we separate carefully the theoretical from the practical problems; it is not to the neglect of the latter; but on the contrary, to be in better position to solve them. (Durkheim 1964: 33)

As far as his intellectual shaping is concerned, Durkheim rejected his religions heritage in his teens and was also quite disinterested in his earlier years of education. The emphasis on the literary and the aesthetic was not to Durkheim's likings. On the whole, he was looking for a discipline guided by scientific methods to examine the moral crisis of the society. He was essentially into an intellectual frame of mind to reorganize the society on a firm moral ground.

Till Durkheim could introduce a course on social science the prestigious Ecole Normale did not have any course in sociology. Subjects like history and philosophy fell short of quenching Durkheim's thirst for developing a discipline which could understand and proceed from the general laws of society. Neither history nor philosophy used positivistic scientific techniques of investigating social phenomena. Nevertheless, Durkheim drew essential points from such traditional disciplines but stuck to his belief that one needed a positivist method to develop a science of society. He was of the view that, one needed an empirical perspective to study society, if one wished to develop general laws of society.

Before we note the particular intellectual figures with whom Durkheim came in touch and how they influenced his thinking, we need to acknowledge that Durkheim's sociological thinking was a synthesis of two opposite traditions of social thought. At the same time he was a product of the spirit of French Enlightenment, and a bearer of the conservative reaction against the Enlightenment thoughts.

From the philosophies of Jean-Jacques Rousseau, Voltaire and Diderot, Durkheim imbibed the spirit of liberty, democracy and rationality. Whereas, his penchant was for morality and organic social life, his insistence was on social order. As far as specific through influence is concerned, he was mainly drawn towards the German thinkers like Immanuel Kant, Herbert Spencer, Wilhelm Wundt and among the French were Henri de Saint-Simon and Auguste Comte.

Quite evidently, sociological ideas of Comte and Spencer were adopted and adapted by Durkheim. Comte's argument for a positive science of society was carried forward by him, although he was sceptical about Comte's grand idea of sociology becoming a new 'religion' of humanity. Also, on moral and scientific insights Durkheim was averse to Spencer's focus on utilitarianism as the basis of social evolution. Instead, he appreciated Spencer's thought on complexity, differentiation and integration as the basis of social evolution.

From the world of philosophy, Durkheim even recognized idealist philosopher Kant's idea about moral social existence. But Durkheim was keen to work on the nature of modern society. Unlike Kant's observation on morality in general, he was interested to diagnose the possibility of building up a moral order in the emergent industrial world. The clue was taken from Saint-Simon to vigorously examine the nature of intricate relationships that mark a modern industrial society.

The experimental psychology of the German psychologist Wilhelm Wundt inspired Durkheim to apply scientific experimental techniques to investigate social life as well. Although Wundt applied it at the level of individual psyche, Durkheim believed that the same could be extended to study human collective life. Charles Renouvier's position that a collective reality is as real as individual reality even at the psychological level had a profound effect on Durkheim's conception of collective conscience. Finally, it needs to be admitted that although Durkheim himself rejected the legacy of being rabbi's son and turned toward rational scientific thinking, his early years of vigorous disciplined life of a Jewish family had its bearing on him. Not that he was interested in religion per se, but the universal function of religion as a binding force and a moralizing agent remained a running thread in Durkheim's sociology.

METHOD OF STUDY

Emile Durkheim's primary task was to put sociology as a scientific discipline. For the purpose he worked towards developing a distinct subject matter of sociology. The idea was to work out a distinct conception of the subject matter of sociology and subjecting it to empirical study. Towards developing almost a manual for conducting sociological study, in 1895 he published *The Rules of Sociological Method*. Here, he argued and established that the specific matter of sociology is what he called *social facts*. Subsequently in 1897 Durkheim in his seminal work entitled, *Suicide* demonstrated the application of what he thought to be the appropriate method for a discipline like sociology — if sociology had to be considered as a science of society.

Methodologically speaking, Durkheim carried forward the positivist legacy left by August Comte. Considered to be the founding father of sociology, Comte advocated positivism as the philosophical backbone for sociology. He proposed a shift from social philosophy to social science. Drawing knowledge away from metaphysical and theological underpinnings positivism placed greater stress on immediate sensory experience and the data observed.

Positivism essentially imbibed the British empiricist tradition led by Francis Bacon. Positivism rests on a conviction that experience is the only reliable source of human knowledge. Comte in his *A General view of Positivism* (1898) illustrated the development of human society through the three different stages of knowledge. Accordingly, human society has moved from a stage of theological state to the final positive stage, through the intermediate metaphysical stage. It was the positive stage where all abstract and unproven ideas of the natural world were discarded. Instead, all natural phenomena were to be explained in terms of their material basis of inter-connectivity. The cause and effect relationship was held to be constant with a real basis.

To build a case for a new discipline like sociology as a science of society, Durkheim realized the effectiveness of the positivist school of thought. He opined that sociology remains largely a philosophical exercise dealing in a heterogeneous assortment of all embracing generalization, which rests more upon logical derivation from *a priori* precepts than upon systematic empirical study. Instead, Durkheim maintained that not everything and anything could be studied by sociology, but only a select group of social phenomena qualify to be its subject matter. They were to be termed as social facts, and the task of sociology was to seek the determining cause of a social fact in the social facts preceding it. Thereby, the laws of the causal relations of social phenomena could be achieved.

> We have seen that sociological explanation consists of exclusively in establishing relationships of causality, that a phenomenon must be joined to its cause, or, on the contrary, a cause to its useful effects. Moreover, since social phenomenon clearly rule out any control by the experimenter, the comparative method is the sole one suitable for sociology. (Durkheim 1982: 147)

Earlier Enlightenment thinkers conceived of society as a subjective and an artificial entity, so as to deny it as a part of nature. Arguing against such a conception of society, Durkheim proposed that society to could be studied like nature as an objective reality. Thereby, it could be studied scientifically. Like natural sciences the subject matter had to be open to empirical methods of investigation. What best could be studied empirically but social facts?

Durkheim asserted that the proper subject matter of sociology had to be only social facts.

> Here, then, is a category of facts which present very special characteristics: they consist of manners of acting, thinking and feeling external to the individual, which are invested with a coercive power by virtue of which they exercise control over him. Consequently, since they consist of representations and actions, they cannot be confused with organic phenomena, nor with psychical phenomena . . . they constitute a new species and to them must be exclusively assigned the term *social*. (Durkheim 1982: 52)

Social facts are defined by Durkheim as those emergent properties and realities of a connectivity that could not be understood in terms of the motives, inclinations, or actions of individuals. All are essentially shaped and governed by external social environments, and in twin are constrained by them. Social facts exist in their own right independently of individual manifestation. Thus, society is self generated (*sui generis*), which has its logic of existence irreducible to its components.

Just as physical and biological sciences have their own group of phenomena subject to their own methods of treatment, sociology too has its own exclusive subject matter, i.e., *the social facts*. However, not all facts are 'social'. They have distinct characteristics. Durkheim, therefore, defined social facts as ways of thinking, acting and feeling, external to the individual and endowed with a power of coercion by reason of which they impose upon him/her. He gave the example of the belief and practices of religious life inherited by an individual, as a *sui generis* entity that an individual is born into. They exist as a social phenomenon a priori.

The overriding interest of Durkheim was to formulate determinant social laws, which was possible once the subject matter attained the characteristics of objective 'social facts'. It is only then the social laws could study and explain the relationships between them. Hence, quite evidently Durkheim had to emphasize on the external, objective, measurable relationships among social facts. The three distinctive features of social facts according to him are that of *externality*, *constraining* and *generality*.

A thing like 'external' existence as a feature ensures that social facts do exist over and above the will or wishes of individual beings. As they exist a priori and independent of individual manifestation, they have an imposing character. In case of purely moral maxims, the public conscience exercises a check on every act of individuals, which is obtained by means of the surveillance it exercises over the conduct of individuals, aided by appropriate penalties at its disposal. Constraints are not always violent or explicit in day to day conduct, but only in moral maxims they are so. Durkheim also pointed out that social facts are not always backed by stable social organization; at times they may be backed by an element of social current in it. By social current he meant such temporary collective behaviour like crowd behaviour or spectator behaviour with which an individual gets swayed in only for a particular duration of time. Once the event gets over, the individual withdraws from the collective behaviour. Under conditions of such social currents, nobody instigates an individual to do so, yet one feels the urge to do certain things. Importantly, even if individuals spontaneously contribute to the production of the common emotion, the impression that is received would be markedly different from that if some individuals are left alone. However, Durkheim was clear that as for the forms that the collective state assume when refracted in the individuals, they become things of another sort.

The third important feature of social fact is that of *generality*. Durkheim held that sociological phenomena are not defined by their universality. Rather the connective aspects of beliefs and practices of a group characterize truly social phenomena. A social fact is a group condition repeated in individuals because it is imposed on them. It is found in each part because it exists in the whole. So, social phenomena are general because they collective, and not collective because they are general. Hence, society is supreme and individuals are all bound by the ascendancy of connectivity. This becomes evident if we consider the examples of the beliefs and practices that are transmitted to us ready made by previous generations. We receive and adopt them because they are being perpetuated as collective. In the same way, the very fact that they are treated as valid, indicate their authority and imposition. Thus, social facts being the special subject matter of sociology are distinguishable by characteristics of externality, constraining and generality.

RULES FOR SOCIOLOGICAL STUDY

In Chapter II of *The Rules of Sociological Method*, Durkheim put the first and most fundamental rule of sociological method as: *Consider social facts as things*. Social facts are not things, but Durkheim made a case for that. Social facts are to be considered as things. A thing is any object of knowledge which is not naturally penetrable by simple understanding. To treat facts of a certain order as things, we observe a certain attitude of mind towards them. We tend to treat them as exclusively knowable from outside.

Durkheim, in his attempt to assign sociology the stake of being a scientific discipline, stated the short comings of social theory:

> Instead of observing, describing, and comparing things, we are content to focus our consciousness upon, to analyze, and to combine our ideas. Instead of a science concerned with realities, we produce no more than an ideological analysis. To be sure, this analysis does not necessarily exclude all observation. One may appeal to the facts in order to confirm one's hypotheses or the final conclusions to which they lead. But in this case, facts intervene only secondarily as examples or confirmatory proofs; they are not the central subject of science. Such a science therefore proceeds from ideas to things, not from things to ideas. (Durkheim 1982: 14–15)

Durkheim pointed out that earlier social theorists, be it Comte or Spencer, had by and large failed to come up with the appropriate method to be used in analysing social phenomena. While it is true that Comte by stressing the necessity of the positivistic approach, had dealt with method but it was in too general terms. Spencer too tried to address the possibilities of scientific discipline in his *The Study of Sociology*, but fell short of developing a proper method which could be used by social theorists. Hence, Durkheim set out to formulate rules to help single out social facts. His methodology essentially rested on such formulation of rules. Having considered social facts as things, Durkheim suggested that certain rules need to be followed in order to study them objectively. In fact, those rules follow from the preceding basic rule:

i. In observing social facts, preconceptions must be set aside. According to Durkheim, sentiment is a subject for scientific study but not the criterion of scientific truth. For a true scientific exercise, social scientific method needs to free itself from all kinds of prejudices and preconceptions while observing social facts
ii. One must define social facts not as ideas, but in terms of their inherent properties. The subject matter of every sociological study should comprise a group of phenomena defined in advance by certain common external characteristics. All

phenomena, thus defined, must then be included in the group which is a precondition for classifying such facts, and

iii. Investigation of any order of social facts is to be conducted independent of their individual manifestation. This would ensure that all individual peculiarity could be ignored in favour of a general character.

EXPLANATION, CAUSALITY AND COMPARATIVE METHOD

According to Durkheim, when a social phenomena is to be explained, the primary task is to find out the efficient cause that produces it and, consequently the function if fulfils. As a social rationalist, Durkheim dismissed any notion that considers individual consciousness as the source of social evolution. Additionally, sociological laws do not follow from any general laws of psychology. In the nature of society itself lies the explanation of social life — society surpasses the individual in time and space, as a result of which it imposes upon individuals ways of acting and thinking.

> Now once the individual is ruled out, only society remains. It is therefore in the nature of society itself that we must seek the explanation of social life. We can conceive that, since it transcends infinitely the individual both in time and space, it is capable of imposing upon him the ways of acting and thinking that it has consecrated by its authority. This pressure, which is the distinctive sign of social facts, is that which all exert upon each individual. (Durkheim 1982: 128)

In the Durkhemian scheme, a whole is not a simple sum of its parts. By this principle, a society is not a mere sum of its individual members. Therefore, one needs to search for the immediate and determining causes of a social fact in the very nature of some other similar social facts. The determining causes of a social fact should be sought among social facts preceding it and not among states of the individual consciousness. As a consequence one also admits that the function of a social fact lies in relation to some social end only.

For Durkheim, sociological explanation consists exclusively in establishing relation of causality, i.e., connecting a phenomenon to its cause or rather a cause to its effects. Although he asserted that social facts are to be treated like things, yet when it comes to observing them, these facts are different from physical things. Hence, sociology has to take help of indirect means of observing social facts. To establish causation between social facts one needs suitable indicators to make comparisons between a prior and a subsequent state of phenomena. The indirect method of experiment is the comparative method. Comparative method is not meant for merely descriptive purpose. In fact, for Durkheim comparative sociology is de facto sociology.

Comparative method involves the use of social indicators which would serve for Durkheim as the means by which the abstract theoretical statements could be linked with operational definitions. This could only facilitate empirical studies. While it is true that *The Rules of Sociological Method* contains Durkheim's essential methodological statements, the application of the same is evident in all major sociological works. In his varied studies, Durkheim used three types of social indicators for making comparisons effective. He used them in combinations but one can see the predominance of *statistical comparisons* in his study of *Suicide* (1897). His first major work (thesis) *The Division of Labour in Society* (1893) is mainly based on *historical comparisons* using historical indicators. Whereas, the use of *ethnographic comparisons* dominates his study, *Elementary Forms of Religions Life* (1912). For Durkheim, the use of the comparative method is based on the assumption that 'a given effect has always a single corresponding cause'. In his study of suicide, he showed that since there were different causes of suicide, therefore, they were different types of suicides. He posited his methodology in the true tradition of the positivist thinking, the basic tenet of which is that Man and Nature belong to the same Universe and, further, the behaviour of both is governed by the material world. The relationship can be discovered and explained in terms of casual relationship, i.e., in terms of cause and effect relationship.

For all practical purposes, Durkheim basically advocated the method of concomitant variation to engage in comparative sociology. This was helpful as social phenomena cannot be compared under controlled situations, i.e., a direct experimental method is not possible. As he said:

> We have only one way of demonstrating that one phenomenon is the cause of another. This is to compare the cases where they are both simultaneously present or absent, so as to discover whether the variations they display in these different combinations of circumstances provide evidence that one depends upon the other. (Durkheim 1982: 147)

MECHANICAL AND ORGANIC SOLIDARITY

As a social theorist of the modern society, Durkheim was primarily interested in the changing nature of individual–societal ties as a society gets modernized. Given his social and intellectual bearings, Durkheim was interested to sociologically analyse the aspects of moral order of the society. He always thought morality as a binding force but at the same time he recognized the changing nature of that binding or regularity forces. His doctoral thesis published in 1893 was the result of such a concern. Essentially he was seeking an answer to a very basic question: how was that in the emergent modern society people were becoming more and more individualistic as well as independent but at the same time were becoming more solidaristic? Thus, a classic study on social solidarity one finds in *The Division of Labour in Society*. His famous concepts of mechanical and organic solidarity as markers of two different types of society — archaic and advanced respectively — are explained in his work. His doctoral thesis contended that growing individuation does not entail disintegration but under normal conditions promotes qualitatively better integration. Durkheim's comparative study of primitive and modern society in terms of what held society together is a central focus of his sociology.

The French title of Durkheim's doctoral thesis was *De la Division Du Travail Social.* Hence, it is not the economic growth of labour that he was interested in. By social division of labour he meant broadly social differentiation which entails interpersonal relationships, interdependence and complimentarity. As he classified,

> . . . the division of labour is not peculiar to the economic world; we can observe its growing influence in the most varied fields of society. The political, administrative, and judicial functions are growing more and more specialized. It is the same with the aesthetie and scientific functions. (Durkheim 1982: 38)

From a functional perspective Durkheim tried to examine the following areas:

i. What social needs are best satisfied by the division of labour
ii. The causes and conditions on which the division of labour rests, and
iii. The deviation from the normal conditions and the pathologic forms of division of labour.

Premising his understanding on an organismic analogy, Durkheim used the term function in the sense of how the different parts and movements of an organism are related to each other and fulfill the needs of the organism. Thus, the division of labour was examined as performing the crucial functions of the body society. On a psychological note, he even contended that attraction towards each other is not caused only as a result of likeliness or resemblances. Differences can also be a cause of mutual attraction. Not all differences, 'Only certain kinds of differences attract each other. They are those which, instead of opposing and excluding, complement each other' (Durkheim 1964: 55). Thus, he was basically focused on the needs satisfied by greater social differentiation in the society. For that, relying on historical indicators Durkheim attempted a reconstruction and comparison between two types of integration or solidarity — mechanical and organic.

Primarily interested to diagnose modern advanced societies, Durkheim used the historical data to show the extent of one type of solidarity against the other as evident of one type of solidarity against the other as evident in legal codes. In a positivistic quantitative manner he proceeded to say:

> But social solidarity is a completely moral phenomenon which, taken by itself, does not lead itself to exact observation not indeed to measurement. To proceed to this classification and this comparison, we must substitute for this internal fact which escapes us an external index which symbolizes it and study the former in the light of the latter. . . . This visible symbol is law. (Durkheim 1964: 64)

Making a comparative study of law/legal sanctions of two kinds of society, archaic and advanced, Durkheim arrived at two types of laws. The archaic societies are marked by repressive law, whereas the advanced societies are marked by more of restitutive laws.

Durkheim went on to argue that, the greater the degree of repressive laws in a society, the greater the indication of mechanical solidarity. On the other hand, the greater the extent of restitutive laws, the greater is the indication of organic solidarity. Generally understood, mechanical solidarity refers to solidarity out of similarities — a kind of communal collectivity. On the other hand, organic solidarity refers to solidarity out of differentiation. Here, differentiation emerges as a result of dissimilarities. The significant aspect of such differentiated, yet solidarity is that greater differentiation solicits greater reciprocal cooperation. Complementarity between differentiated parts is a hallmark of such solidarity, quite unlike that of mechanical solidarity where the totality leaves little scope for individuation or specialization.

By mechanical solidarity, Durkheim referred to in a general sense, solidarity which is premised on similarities. It is a collectivity marked by communal identities. On the other hand, by organic solidarity he meant such a solidarity which is arrived through differentiation. This differentiation is a result of dissimilarities. The dissimilar elements/aspects reciprocate with each other with a goal towards co-operation. Thereby, an organic solidarity is ultimately solidarity of complementary parts.

A society characterized by mechanical solidarity exhibits social integration which is based on a high level of shared beliefs, values, customs and ritual interactions. It is an integration of similarities. In such a society all individuals share the same conception of reality. This indicates a very weak development of individuality under mechanical solidarity.

> The totality of beliefs and sentiments common to average citizens of the same society forms a determinate system which has its own life; one may call it the collective or *common conscience*. No doubt, it has not a specific organ as a substratum; it is, by definition, diffuse in every reach of society. Nevertheless, it has specific characteristics which make it a distinct reality. It is in effect, independent of the particular conditions in which individuals are placed; they pass on and it remains. (Durkheim 1964: 79–80)

In contrast to mechanical solidarity, organic solidarity characterizes a society with individuals and groups who are engaged in highly different activities. Individuals here are different from each other in their uniqueness. Integration as a result is a matter of interdependence. Mutual obligation and reciprocity are imperative condition for social existence. Every individual who performs such specialized tasks brings in a new kind of integration. Specialized functions of differentiated parts ensure a society's continued survival. It is organic because the solidarity is not a result of similarities and likeness but an outcome of differences and complementarity.

> ... [T]he collective conscience leave[s] open a part of the individual conscience in order that special functions may be established there, functions which it cannot regulate. The more this region is extended, the stronger is the cohesion which results from this solidarity. In effect, on the one hand, each one depends as much more strictly on society as labour is more divided; and, on the other, the activity of each is as much more personal as it is more specialized. (Durkheim 1964: 131)

As against community life, Durkheim anticipated the rise of associative life in modern societies. Associative instead of an encompassing community life stands as a marker of modern social living. However, Durkheim was not in favour of a total and absolute replacement of communal bonding by differentiated individuals engaging in organic linkages. He, rather indicates the possibility and desirability of a measure of both, mechanical as well as organic solidarity in any normal modern society. This becomes evident when Durkheim writes, '...it is no necessity for choosing between them once for all nor of condemning one in the name of the other. What is necessary to give each, at each moment in history, the place that is fitting to it' (Durkheim 1964: 397–98).

Nevertheless, Durkheim had a consistent understanding of the features of division of social labour throughout his works. It was to understand the archaic societies primarily, not exclusively, in terms of similitude of their constituent elements. Similitude, here, signified homogeneity and communal identity to the exclusion of differentiation among roles in the groups or amongst groups in the layer social context. Although Durkheim conceptualized archaic primitive society as one of savage experience. Such an experience involves a total realization of the communal bond from which a modern society is free. The complex occupational specialization is typical of modern societies, accompanied by functionally specific norms. Unlike this complex yet organized structure the archaic societies were basically segmental societies.

CONSCIENCE COLLECTIVE: CRIME AND PUNISHMENT

Durkheim's concept of *conscience collective* stands as the axis of his explanation of social solidarity. Generally it is understood as an emergent characteristic of a society which is a result of a unified mental attitude to the events of the world. Interestingly it acts on the same (out of which it grows) and sustains it.

Every society is characterized by a particular set of collective representations — socially shared conceptions about reality. Such representations are shaped by collectively shared beliefs, values and norms of interacting individuals. Thus, such collective representations are generally shared by the members of society. According to Durkheim, collective conscience is formed by these collective representations. It then stands as a unified set of collective ways and rules of interpreting the world. Once it emerges out of the individuals' collective ways of acting, believing and thinking it attains a life of its own. It possesses an independent level of social reality onto itself. While it is realized only in individuals, essentially it is the psychic type of society. Thereby, collective conscience has its own conditions of existence and mode of development.

Collective conscience as a concept was of central importance for Durkheim in his examination of the changing nature of social solidarity. He, in fact, related this concept with the penal sanctions/legal system of a society. According to him, studying the nature of legal sanctions could serve as an entry point in the understanding of the nature of collective conscience of any society. In fact, sanctions/legal system could provide the appropriate indicators so necessary for making historical comparisons.

A repressive penal sanction is correlated with a strong collective conscience. For Durkheim, repressive penal sanction serves as the most objective index of mechanical solidarity. Repressive penal sanction features in such a society where the hold of the collective is overwhelming, which leave little room for individual initiatives. Repressive sanctions impose expiatory punishments upon the person who offends the collective conscience. The invincibility of the collective conscience, the strong nature of it leads to a strong reaction on behalf of the society, in case its collective sentiment is offended. Repressive law employs violent sanctions and aims to punish or destroy the one who violates the rule.

> There exists a social solidarity which comes from a certain number of states of conscience which are common to all the members of the same society. That is what repressive law materially represents, at least in so far as it is essential. The part that it plays in the general integration of society evidently depends upon the greater or lesser extent of the social life which the common conscience embraces and regulates. (Durkheim 1964: 109)

In contrast, restitutive sanction is seen by Durkheim as the feature of a different type of social solidarity — where the hold of the collective is less overwhelming. It is the organic solidarity which allows space for individuals to exercise discretion and choice. The hold of collective conscience is there still, but the nature undergoes a change. An improved division of labour allows individuality to grow and the hold of morality is less severe. Here, as Durkheim said, 'Society becomes more capable of collective movement, at the same time that each of its elements has more freedom of movement' (Durkheim 1964: 131). Thus, when the collective sentiment is hurt, the reaction is not expiatory but consists of a simple return to the state ante. Modern society marked by organic solidarity emphasizes on a legal system and not on punishment. 'Damage–interests have to penal character; they are only a means of reviewing the past in order to reinstate it, as for as possible, to its normal form' (111). This is so because an organic solidarity links individual conscience to the collective conscience not directly but through mediations — through the intermediary of special organs resulting from an advanced social division of labour. Contrasting the restitutive law with the repressive sanction Durkheim thus says, 'While repressive law tends to remain diffuse within society, restitutive law creates organs which are more and more specialized . . .' (113). The contractual nature of integration is seen as the principle reason behind such change in the nature of law.

Methodologically, it was important for Durkheim to study the nature of organized sanction in any society to comment on the nature of its solidarity. Crime is an act that disturbs the collective conscience of any society. Society acts as a reaction. Crime is a damage done to the moral order, so that the collective conscience reacts to restore the normal moral order. The sanctions are just the reactions against crime, and the sanctions are codified in the legal system of any society. The legal system or organized sanction serves as the relatively manifest component of any social structure. Substantively, it serves as an index of solidarity in the normal state of society. Thus, the study of crime and the nature of reaction against it, be it punishment or law was crucial for Durkheim to examine and analyse the nature of collective conscience and thereby, the social solidarity.

Durkheim theorized that when values are deeply rooted in the collective conscience, punishment might become an almost instinctive reaction. The emotion involved in the passionate response to crime is not pure affectivity. It is sentimental, structured by norms and symbols which interpose themselves between the stimulus (damage) and response (punishment). Here, punishment counters the unsettling threat of anxiety. In archaic societies the prevalence of passionate reactions against any damage to its collective moral order shows the lack of differentiation in social life. A common and essential foundation of all kinds of crime is that it violates the normalcy of the collective order. But interestingly, not all acts are considered to be criminal in all societies, which show that an act is a crime with respect to the nature of morality of a society. Durkheim also held that a certain rate of crime is inevitable and in fact, functionally crime provides the allocation for the dramatic display of social solidarity. The society comes into play the moment its collective conscience is threatened or being damaged. As a result, crime allows such occasions for a test and revival of the existing social institutions and relations. Again, the nature of reactions on such occasions indicates how far the society can absorb and show flexibility with respect to the acts of crime.

Since an act is criminal, it damages the collective conscience — such an understanding is inappropriate for Durkheim. Instead, only when it damages the collective conscience it becomes criminal. Thus, the collective conscience decides whether any act is a crime or not. Evidently, the reaction against such acts also differs from time to time, given the changing nature of the collective conscience. Durkheim studied the steady decline in repressive punishment since the nineteenth-century. He could see that the nature of law had undergone a change and the very emergency of restitutive sanction indicated to him that qualitatively social solidarity had undergone a change. The advanced modern societies to which the restitutive sanction correspond are no longer bound by totalistic ties. Instead, the contractual nature of ties between individuals facilitated by growing division of labour conforms to the general law of society. As understood by Durkheim,

> '[W]hen' men unite in a contract, it is because, through the divisions of labour, either simple or complex, they need each other. But in order for them to co-operate harmoniously, it is not enough that they enter into a relationship, nor even that

> they feel the state of mutual dependence in which they find themselves. It is still necessary that the conditions of this co-operation be fixed for the duration of their relations. (Durkheim 1964: 212)

ABNORMAL FORMS OF DIVISION OF LABOUR

Durkheim's foundational idea about the division of social labour is that it is a result of the struggle for existence. The struggle for existence is from within and acute as socialites become more voluminous and denser. The division of labour is a fall-out of the increase in the volume and density of societies, where the process is a continuous one. However, Durkheim was alert to the possibility of abnormal forms of the division of labour. He talked about three such forms:

i. Anomic division of labour
ii. Forced division of labour, and
iii. Inappropriate distribution of functions.

Drawing insights from the economic crises in France from 1845 to 1869, Durkheim indicated the case for the anomic division of labour. Industrial or commercial crises undermine organic solidarity and as a result social functions are ill-adjusted with one another. Even when industrial functions become more specialized, the conflict between capital and labour gives rise to normlessness. Finally, citing the seventeenth-century working class history, Durkheim pointed out that the birth of intensive large-scale industry had resulted in the absolute separation of workers from the employer signalling greater regimentation of workers. Resentment as a result of this also leads to anomie and the division of labour becomes a source of disintegration instead. However, these are historically exceptional and extraordinary situations.

Second, Durkheim talked about the forced division of labour which he thought was quite possible in society. It is so because unlike living organism where every anatomic part performs specific tasks automatically as a consequence of its nature and place in the organism, divisions in a society are quite subtle, delicate and liable to change. At times hereditary dispositions may deviate from actual aptitude for functions. For other reasons too, like institution of classes or castes, the distribution of social functions may deviate from distribution of natural talents. Such misfits cause forced division of labour which instead of strengthening solidarity ties create anxiety and antagonism. Forced division of labour does not mean the existence of pre-established rules on the basis of which different functions are assigned to different individuals. Regulations are not abnormal and thereby are not a cause of forced division of labour. It becomes forced when the division of labour lacks spontaneity. There should not be any obstacle, of whatever nature, to prevent an individual to choose a specialization and perform a function which is in tune with one's faculties, taste and aptitude. Thus, an idea of justice is mooted thereby by Durkheim at this point.

Finally, Durkheim talked about commercial industrial or other enterprise where the distribution of functions is inappropriate; inappropriate in the sense that, it does not offer adequate material for specialized individuals to perform effectively. As a result of this lack, integrated functional activity becomes less efficient. This insufficient work only makes solidarity imperfect. The incoherent integration is obvious as the different functions become discontinuous as the activity of each individual falls even lower than what it normally would be. It shows that normal division of labour does not only specifies the activity of an individual, but strengthens the substance of the specialization which makes such labour continuous. By adding more life, making individuals solidaristic, division of labour actually adds to the unity of the society.

SOCIOLOGY OF SUICIDE

Suicide (1897) is Durkheim's third major work but stands out as a monograph which bears the application of Durkheim's pronounced statements about appropriate sociological method. In this monograph he used government records containing suicide rate statistics for various segments of European population. For comparative purpose he studied suicide rate of ethnic groups, religious groups of different social strata, across time periods, and according to gender and marital status. His purpose was to establish suicide as a social fact and correlating it with nature and degree of social integration. With empirical evidence he showed that a sociological explanation could replace all prevalent notions of suicide as an individualistic act.

Precisely, Durkheim did not study suicide at the level of individual psychological dispositions. Instead, he was interested in the totality of suicides in a society; that is, for him the suicide rate is a phenomenon that qualifies as a social fact. Suicide rate, therefore, is a fact which is separate, distinct and amenable of study in its own terms. The data available to him allowed him to refute those theories which used to explain group variations in the amount of suicide on the basis of psychological, biological/racial genetic, climatic, or geographical factors. Instead, with social phenomenon such as the family, political and economic society and religious society he could establish a correlation. He contended by establishing the correlation that each society has a collective inclination towards suicide (a rate of self homicide) which is fairly constant for each society so long as the basic conditions of its existence continue to be the same.

Every social group has a distinct suicidal tendency which is a group phenomenon. Social cause of suicide can be located by analysing the conditions that each social group is exposed to. The root cause of suicide lies in the logic of existence of social groups. Durkheim found that there is no singular tendency to the act of self homicide. If there is a singular tendency, then we would have only one class of suicide. But if there are different tendencies, then, they are to be put into different classes. Durkheim methodologically left aside individual psychic condition to account for a group phenomenon like suicide rate. Suicide rate is irreversibly a group phenomenon because Durkheim's primary observation was that every society exhibits a particular suicide rate over a particular period of time. Additionally suicide rate varies amongst social groups exposed to varied conditions of social integration. It varies also across time. He held that, analytically it is not possible to observe individual manifestation for suicidal tendency. One cannot study the exact state of mind of any individual prior to the act of committing self-homicide. This absolute lack of data is more so because insanity-related suicide is far less in number than suicide committed by same people. However, no classification of suicide by same people can be made in terms of their morphological types. Hence, the process of classification is reversed by Durkheim. An indirect method of classification done by him rests on an etiological reasoning.

> Only in so far as the effective causes differ can there be different types of suicide. For each to have its own nature, it must also have special conditions of existence. The same antecedent or group of antecedents cannot sometimes produce one result and sometimes another, for if so, the difference of the second from the first would itself be without cause which would contradict the principle of causality. . . we shall be able to determine the social types of suicide by classifying them not directly by their preliminarily described characteristics but by the causes which produce them. (Durkheim 1951: 146–47)

TYPOLOGY OF SUICIDE

Suicide is classified by Durkheim in terms of the causes. As an effect of group condition the suicidal tending is found to be as a result of either excessive individuation and lack of social integration or absolute integration with the collective and lack of individuation. Also, there is a third type which is caused by a general lack of order in the society or normlessness. Accordingly, the three types of suicide are:

i. Egoistic suicide
ii. Altruistic suicide, and
iii. Anomic suicide.

Again, while tabulating the three categories Durkheim noted a mixed category of suicide, that is, the ego-anomic type.

Analysing the religious, family and political society, Durkheim confirmed the first of the three causes of suicide. It is due to the lack of integration of an individual to the social life that an individual tends to fall back upon one's own resources to seek meaning in life. The ego asserts itself to the point that one is driven to the act of self-homicide. It is due to the lack of purpose as social ties become too loose to hold individuals together. The result is *egoistic* suicide.

The opposite of egoistic suicide is the *altruistic* suicide. Here the hold of the society is more than what is necessary. The social ties are in excess and individual life is vigorously governed by customs and habits as in the case of pre-modern archaic societies. Such a group condition is manifested in weak development of the ego. The stranglehold of the collective over the individual results in altruistic suicide. If egoistic suicide is a result of excessive individuation, altruistic suicide is caused by its opposite — the absolute lack of individuation.

The third type of suicide is anomic suicide. This is the most prevalent type of suicide in modern society caused by normlessness. It is not a case of lack or excess of societal ties; instead it is a case of lack of regulation of individual from the society. Since the nineteenth-century Durkheim observed a phenomenal rise of anomic suicide as a result of increasing irregularities of norms in the society.

EGOISTIC SUICIDE

In his sociological endeavour to seek casual explanation of suicide in the structure of society only, Durkheim first analysed how the different religious confessions affect suicide. His data showed that in purely catholic countries like Spain, Portugal and Italy the incidence of suicide was very less compared to the protestant countries like Prussia, Saxony and Denmark. Switzerland offered a more instructive observation as it was populated by both the French and the German. Durkheim could observe the variable influence of the confession on the two different races. The Catholics showed a suicide rate four or five times lower than that of the Protestants. This conclusively proved that irrespective of nationality, religious society has a direct bearing on suicidal tendency.

Additionally, the data showed that generally, the suicidal rate is the least with respect to the Jews, that is, even lower than the Protestants. Apparently, the Jews would have been more inclined to suicide given that their social living used to be more exclusive and intellectually driven. But their low rate of suicide then must be due to the religious society despite aggravating social circumstances.

It is not due to different religious maxims that govern the followers' suicidal behaviour, as both Catholicism and Protestantism abhor acts of self destruction. But, it is more due to the way the different confessions bind the followers together. The Jews exercise extreme control over their social lives and subject themselves to severe discipline to withstand the harsh and hostile social environment that they face due to their numerical minority. The Protestants differ from the Catholics as their confession encourages free enquiry to a far greater degree than Catholicism. The essential function of all religions is to promote ties and act as a prophylactic agent against suicidal tendency. If the Protestants show a higher suicide rate, it is because the very nature of the confession allows greater concessions to individualistic spirit; it frees individuals from the strict hold of the church. Hence, lesser the ties with the collectivity, greater will be the suicide rate. Given the nature of the confessions, both Catholicism and Judaism provide greater preservation against suicide. The lack of such binding ties actually results in egoistic suicide.

> The more intense religious life, the more men are needed to direct it. The greater the number of dogmas and precepts the interpretation of which is not

> left to individual conscience, the more authorities are required to tell their meanings; moreover, the more numerous these authorities, the more closely they surround and the better they restrain the individual. (Durkheim 1951: 151)

Studying the data from family society, Durkheim offered to quality the popular notion that the unmarried state is less stressful which accounts for the apparent less incidence of suicide amongst unmarried group compared to married people. The raw data of unmarried people needs to be corrected according to him as a large proportion of people below the marriageable age skew the data in favour of unmarried group. This does not explain the effect of family society or marriage upon suicidal tendency. Hence, only the populace above marriageable age is to be analysed. Durkheim realized that marriage has a coefficient of preservation against suicide as it has a salutary effect on individual lives irrespective of sex. But at the event of the death of the spouse, however, the widower faces a less favourable situation than a widow. Durkheim explained this by reasoning that a man enjoys more salutary effect in a married life compared to a woman, and as such the lack of which affects him more severely than a woman. Again, towards the later years of marriage the preservative effect of family society is more due to children than the effect of marriage.

Summarily, married people enjoy a better coefficient of preservation against suicide but it varies with the sexes, with men availing a better protection. The reason is not due to matrimonial selection but due to the influence of the domestic environment. The family society provides the necessary ties which neutralize the suicidal tendency. The immunity provided by family even increases with the density of the family, that is, with the increase in the number of its elements. Drawing conclusion from the statistical data of family society, Durkheim commented on egoistic suicide:

> But for a group to be said to have less common life than another means that it is less powerfully integrated; for the state of integration of a social aggregate can only reflect the intensity of the collective life circulating in it. It is more unified and powerful the more active and constant is the intercourse among its members. (Durkheim 1951: 202)

Referring to the political societies too, Durkheim contended that societal ties have a direct bearing on suicidal tendency. He substantiated this with the help of suicide statistics, that '. . . suicide, generally rare in young societies in process of evolution and concentration, increases as they disintegrate' (Durkheim 1951: 203). The statistical data refutes the popular contention that only during great political upheavals incidences of suicide rises. In fact, during such national political crises and wars it comes down heavily. Since, during such occasions of social disturbances collective sentiments are intensified, be it partisanship, patriotism or political faith. It results in stronger integration of the society. To confront the common danger people close ranks. Again it goes to show that the degree of integration is inversely related to suicidal tendency.

The egoistic type of suicide is then explained in term of the weakening of the collective force acting individuals. As Durkheim confirmed,

> Egoism is not merely a contributing factor in it; it is its generating cause. In this case the bond attaching man in life relaxes because that attaching him to society is itself slack. The incidents of private life.... which seem the direct inspiration of suicide and are considered its determining causes are in reality only incidental causes. The individual yields to the slightest shock of circumstance because the state of society has made him a ready prey to suicide. (Durkheim 1951: 215)

ALTRUISTIC SUICIDE

While discussing the egoist type of society, if Durkheim held that collective ties protect individuals from acts of self destruction, he was also aware that such integration needs to be appropriate and adequate only, an excess of which may even have aggravating effects on an individual's life. Altruistic suicide is a type which is marked by an absolute submission of the individual to the collective life. Here, the hold of the society and its collective life is so strong that the ego fails to have a life of its own, and is rather subsumed in the collective.

The popular notion that suicide was unknown among lower (pre-modern) societies, was refuted by Durkheim. He drew upon historical data to show that in such lower societies the communal life used to be too encapsulating for individuals. An excess of integration leads one to surrender individual lives and take recourse to self-homicide in the service of the greater collectivity.

The historical data showed that,

i. Men used to commit suicide at sick beds and on the threshold of old age
ii. Women used to plunge into the funeral pyre on their husband's death, and
iii. The followers used to take their own lives to save themselves from ignominy on the defeat and death of their chiefs.

Instances of all the above from pre-modern societies show that such acts were considered as a duty to the collective order. In contrast to the egoistic type, here, suicide is due to too rudimentary individuation. Society no longer holds its members in strict tutelage. Thus, in case of altruistic suicide '. . . ego is not its own property, where it is blended with something not itself, where the goal of conduct is exterior to itself, that is, in one of the groups in which it participates' (Durkheim 1951: 221).

Durkheim further classified altruistic suicide into three sub-types. They are:

i. Obligatory altruistic suicide
ii. Optional altruistic suicide, and
iii. Acute altruistic suicide.

Obligatory altruistic suicide is the one where the incumbents do so as they participate with the social group with a purpose but the goal is located in the collective and the act is undertaken as a duty. Here, the element of sacrifice is underscored and it is imposed by society for social ends. The best examples are drawn from such traditional practices where the destiny of one is entwined with that of the others.

Optional altruistic suicide is not so imposed by the society. Such acts lack any immediate or apparent motives. It is a case of voluntary sacrifice. Examples of such are drawn from China, Japan, North American Indians, India, etc. For example, in Polynesian lower societies, where on the slightest of offence to the society prompts an individual to take one's own life. It also happens when an individual kills himself purely for the joy of sacrifice without attaching much value to it. The act itself becomes source or object of gratification.

While it is true that in all cases of altruistic suicide, individuals seek to strip himself of his personal being in order to be submerged with the collective which he considers as his true essence. He has no life of his own but such impersonality reaches its peak in case of the acute altruistic suicide.

Collectively, although altruistic suicides are mostly to be found in lower societies which Durkheim called 'the theatre par excellence of altruistic suicide', it is also to be found in modern societies. Military society is such a case where one finds the hold of discipline and morality strips a member of his own ego. The regimented composite military life accounts for high rates of altruistic suicides in military population.

ANOMIC SUICIDE

Having discussed the relationship between collective ties of integration in a society and suicidal tendency, Durkheim finally examined the regulatory role played by society on an individual's life. Anomic suicide is a result of normlessness in a society. In fact, modern society in Durkheim's scheme would be witnessing mostly this third type of suicide — suicide as a result of lack of order in society.

Durkheim showed with the help of statistical data that economic crises have an aggravating effect on suicidal tendency. Whatever disturbs the normal collective states (prosperity as well as depression) causes such suicidal acts. A stable order is realized only when means are proportional to goals and needs. Aspiring for an unattainable goal is to condemn oneself to perpetual unhappiness. Passions and desires might be ever growing and physiological mechanism may fail to control them. One needs therefore an external force, that is, in the form of society to execute the regulatory mechanism. Under normal circumstances the society, given its moral authority, performs this task. But during periods of crises such control is slackened.

Citing data from economic history of many European countries, Durkhiem showed that such crises could be caused by either a depression, or a boon or opulence:

> Industrial or financial crises increase suicides, this is not because they cause poverty, since crises of prosperity have the same result; it is because they are crisis, that is disturbances of the collective order. Every disturbances of equilibrium, even though it achieves greater comfort and heightening of general vitality, is an impulse to voluntary death. (Durkheim 1951: 246)

According to Durkheim, anomic suicide is rampant in the sphere of trade and industry. Religion lacks a hold over economic life. Utilitarianism as well as anarchism holds sway over economic life and it gets de-regularized. A collective disorder claims its victims.

The manifold and changing relations between individual and collective actually provide the key for a sociological understanding of suicide. Durkheim explained it as a social fact by relating it to other sets of social fact. Apparently, the incidents of private life drive one to commit the act of self-homicide, but for Durkheim these are all incidental causes. Instead, it is the nature, degree and extent of the *collective conscience* of a society which orients an individual. Either one becomes a prey to the suicidal tendency or is being protected from such. Actually, individual causes of suicide are infinite and varied. Such individual causes cannot explain the social suicide rate. Individual causes would cancel each other out or such individual qualities may be of general nature. Individual proclivity can only be understood as a prolongation of a social or collective state. In Durkheimian sociology, the society is supreme and an individual is transcended by the collective way of thinking, acting and believing. At a collective level, then, suicide could be explained in terms of excess or lack of collective sentiments and norms and also, in terms of the regulatory function of the collective order.

SUMMARY

While it is true that Emile Durkheim is the pioneer in advancing a precise sociological method of study as well as defining the exact scope of the discipline, it was with a purpose. The growing de-regulation of social life and the decay of morality of modern society prompted him to search for such sociological laws not as an end in itself. The task was to predict and effect desirable change in the emergent society. The search for positive social laws was thought of as necessary instruments to produce a better social order. In a reformist mould Durkheim shaped his sociology while addressing the key areas of modern industrial sociology. He held society as supreme moral order while highlighting the collaborative exercise between individuals as well as with the society. As a sociomoral system, Dhurkheim looked at society. While the need for social order was highlighted, the notion of individual rights and the need for it was also noted in his theory.

Key Words

- *Comparative Method*
- *Conscience Collective*
- *Division of Labour*
- *Positivist Method*
- *Scientific Method*
- *Social Fact*
- *Solidarity*
- *Types of Suicide*

Glossary

Altruistic Suicide: Acts of self-homicide as a result of over-conformity with group or collective life.

Anomic Suicide: Acts of self-homicide as a result of lack of sufficient socio-moral rules that bind people together meaningfully.

Anomie: The lack of appropriate social organization as result of insufficient socio-moral rules that regulate inter-personal and group activity.

Conscience Collective: The totality of beliefs and sentiments common to the average members of a society which forms a determinate system with a life of its own.

Egoistic Suicide: Acts of self-homicide as a result of a lack of collective sentiments and an over assertion of one's ego.

Empiricism: The method of claiming knowledge based on systematic observation of reality as amenable to senses.

Function: Contribution of an individual or a group towards the maintenance of group life or the social whole as such.

Mechanical Solidarity: The solidarity out of similarity or likeness, which marks the forms of simple societies.

Organic Solidarity: The solidarity based on the complementarity of differentiated parts which marks a complex society.

Positivism: The epistemological perspective which claims that authentic knowledge is that which is based on sense, experience and positive verification. That, the scientific method is equally applicable to the physical as well as social world.

Social Facts: The emergent properties and realities of a collectivity that cannot be understood in terms of the motives, inclinations, or actions of individual actors.

Discussion Points

- Durkheim's method of study.
- Study of modernity.
- Importance of studying crime and punishment.
- Suicide as a social fact.

4

Max Weber (1864–1920)

If Karl Marx is considered the foremost social philosopher of the nineteenth-century, Max Weber is very specific to the discipline of sociology. Marx is important as a classical thinker for students of sociology, but Max Weber is the greater master of the discipline. Beyond positivism, Weber infused new life to the social science methodology. Intellectually he was the most comprehensive scholar of the nineteenth- and early twentieth-century world of sociology. Addressing substantive questions on issues of ideas and history of the world, Weber placed sociology on a firm disciplinary ground.

Weber's multifarious interests and personality possibly hold clue to his range of important formulations. Such formulations take care of the crucial issue of the subjective nature of the subject matter of sociology to problems of tripartite distinction between class, status and power. His interests moved from the role of ideas in economy to the issues of politics. Quite aptly, then Max Weber exhibits an interesting scholarly profile. Naturally such an involved academic thinker cannot be free from controversies. Some applaud him as the one who goes out of way to engage in lawsuits and disputes with the powerful to side with the less-powerful; a man of honour who never compromised on the question of moral ethics. On the other side, he had his detractors who held him as an inspiration for the Germany's stint with Nazism. As a nationalist conservatist, Weber is often understood to have provoked endless debates.

Often Weber's personal biography — the turmoil and the tension — is brought to the fore to depict him as a pessimist. For us, it would suffice to acknowledge that Weber had taken a dip into the antimonies and contradictions of human existence, so much so that he could see himself as a sociologist, as the one who would like to see how much one could stand for. He even admitted in a scholarly way that, the only course left open to an individual in a modern rational world is to learn how to live with the completing and incommensurable demands of reasoned analysis and ethical commitment.

A BIOGRAPHICAL SKETCH

Max Weber was born on 21 April 1864 in Erfurt, Saxony. His parents were from prosperous families. His father, also named Max, was a German lawyer and politician. The family lived in Berlin and his father was an important member of a middle-of-the-road party of the German Reichstag. Max Weber senior represented the National Liberal Party in the Imperial Parliament. While believing in constitutional democracy, senior Weber was authoritarian and sided with the 'iron rule' of the Chancellor Bismarck.

On the other hand, Weber's mother Helene was a devout Protestant. Raised in a pious family, she was governed by a strict ethical code. She used to moralize over every detail of daily life, while Max Weber senior, her husband used to control the household in an old patriarchal way. While her husband sided with the establishment-oriented politics, she favoured the new welfare-oriented movements that were shaping up the nineteenth-century liberal wings of the churches.

Such contradictory forces acted on Weber's formative years. As an adolescent, he was more in sympathy with his mother's ideals, than his father's attitude of pragmatism and compromise. It is evident that, Weber's mother and father held strongly different moral and political positions. Inevitably, the normative conflict between them became strongly engrained in Weber's personality. In his family home in Berlin, he already got acquainted with some leading intellectual German personalities.

Weber studied jurisprudence at the University of Heidelberg and Berlin. He also did his military service and became a reserve officer of the army. With the degree in law he had his career in the courts and at the same time continued his studies in the fields of history of law and economics. Torn between the choices of whether to follow the career of a lawyer/civil servant or to opt for an academic vocation, Weber finally joined academics — first at Freiburg and later at the University of Heidelberg.

It is being popularly held that, the turning point of Weber's personal life history was the death of his father in 1897. His father was a self-important man who expected automatic deference from his wife and children alike. Weber had a stormy argument with him. After a few weeks of being turned out of his son's home, he died. This incident left a deep imprint in Weber's psyche as he suffered an emotional collapse within a short period of time. Due to sickness he had to withdraw from the pubic activity as well as his professorship. For several years he had to undergo rest cures in various resorts. Intermittent nervous breakdowns forced him to even resign from his academic post at Heidelberg.

After almost six years of such uncertainty, Weber resumed his scholarly activity, although time to time he did suffer from nervous exhaustion. Interestingly, most of his fam ous works were authored after 1903. *The Protestant Ethics and the Spirit of Capitalism* was the first work of this period of Weber's life. In this new phase of intellectual life he worked on the major methodological essays for which he is considered as the path breaker in the discipline of sociology. He took an active role in the formation of the German Sociological Society in 1910. Along with leading German thinkers like Georg Simmel, Werner Sombart, Ferdinand Tonnies and Robert Michels, he started working towards the discipline of sociology in order to develop it as an autonomous one. His work on met odological problems and on the problem of general categories for sociological analysis took shape in his next major work *Economy and Society*. The major part of this work was published posthumously.

At the onset of World War I in 1914, Weber was called back and he became an administrator of military hospitals. Initially he was enthusiastic about Germany's chances in the War, but as the war dragged on, he got disillusioned. At the end of the war, Weber took interests in national policy. He was part of the German delegation to the Versailles Peace Conference. Subsequently, he joined the new German Democratic Party and adopted a centrist position. More or less, Weber moved towards the academic career as politics was getting him nowhere. He began teaching at the universities of Vienna and Munich. Striking a middle ground between the left-wing revolutionaries and right-wing conservatists, he lectured on general economic history and on socialism. Against the institutional set up of academia and the value-loaded orientation and preaching by the university professors Weber launched his famous lectures on 'scholarship as a vocation' and 'politics as a vocation'.

At a time when Max Weber was recovering his intellectual and academic powers, he fell victim of an epidemic influenza to die at the age of only 56 in the year 1920. He could hardly and actually act as a sociologist for two decades yet his contribution is enormous. Also, it is quite easy to outline the connection between his tormented inner life and the intriguing scholarly insights in all his works.

INTELLECTUAL BACKGROUND

The German intellectual life is highly impacted upon by great idealist thinkers, be it George Hegel, Immanuel Kant, Johan Gottlieb Fichte or Wilhelm Dilthey. All such idealist thinking revolved around the question of how to understand history. The bone of contention was whether the natural and the human sciences could have the same method of study. Immanuel Kant (1724–1804) advanced a divergence in epistemology with regard to natural and human sciences.

While it is true that the methods of the natural sciences provide us verifiable knowledge about the external phenomenal world, it would be inappropriate to apprehend the subjective world of human beings. The social world is much more than what we experience through our senses. We know the world through our thought processes. The social word around us is so much in a flux of unending events that it can never be known directly. It is in this way that the Kantian philosophy critiques the positivist trend in under standing society.

For Kant, moral philosophy explores the very basis of our social being. The 'moral law' is transcendental and trans-historical in character and is an integral aspect of any human society, so much so that moral philosophy is not amenable to any empirical observation. Weber imbibed from the Kantian philosophy how empirical analysis and moral judgments are incommensurable. Wilhelm Dilthey (1833–1911) and his Historicism too had his influence on Weber's intellectual upbringing. Dilthey was a leading theorist of the nineteenth-century 'historical school'. The 'historicists' observe that the social life of a nation could not be understood by ahistorical abstractions. Culture and history are society specific, and hence, every social aspect needs to be historicized accordingly. It is Dilthey's direct influence on Weber that prompts him to seek interpretative instead of positivistic explanations for human sciences. Again neo-Kantian philosopher Heinrich Rickert's insistence on ideographic understanding, i.e., a hermeneutic comprehension of the meaning and effect of specific cultural objects had its bearing on Weber too. Of all the influences on Weber, it is no doubt that Immanuel Kant was special, but the role of Friedrich Nietzsche's (1844–1900) insistence on 'human will' cannot be overlooked. It is so eloquent in Weber's ultimate view of society as the product of human wills.

We have noted at the beginning that the German Idealist tradition influenced Weber, but not all idealists alike. Most importantly Hegel's conception of history of the world as a logical unfolding of ideas was rejected by Weber. He strongly opposed the assumption of progress as the long-term pattern in history. Interestingly Hegel's philosophy influenced Marx to forward theories of progress and contradictions. On the other hand, Kant's philosophy allowed Weber to focus more on the form and mental categories with the help of which the context of the real world could be comprehended. As a result the world of sociology is enriched with a new methodological rigour.

It is all but expected that the Max Weber's sociological method had to be a product of his earliest intellectual development which was being shaped by deep historical consciousness. Also, his nineteenth-century predecessors impacted upon him in his theorization of the specificity of the present.

METHOD OF SOCIOLOGY

Max Weber's idealist and neo-Kantian predecessors made a clean distinction between the historical cultural sciences and the natural sciences. For the historical cultural sciences it is the realm of mind and spirit, whereas it is the realm of nature for the latter. The task of the historical cultural is to base themselves on interpretative analysis. On the other hand, the natural sciences base themselves on *nomothetic* knowledge. '*Nomos*', the Greek word for law or general principle, is the legitimate aim of natural sciences. As a result of such demarcation this tradition of thought prescribes different methods as appropriate to the study of the contrasting subject-matters.

Despite his idealist underpinnings, Weber still worked for a status of sociology as a scientific discipline. He affirmed that social science must operate on a systematic level using concepts and general categories. While accepting the overall tenets of the idealist thoughts, especially neo-Kantian, Weber admitted that the methodology of the natural sciences was inappropriate for sociology. Sociology for him was at the last instance a cultural science, as human beings act, behave and relate to each other with the help of a range of signs and symbols which are all imbued with meanings. Such meanings are imputed by human beings which make the entire exercise purposive and oriented. Without falling back into the promise of positivism, he still advocated an appropriate method for studying society which would not sacrifice the scientific status of the discipline of sociology.

It would be inappropriate to shape sociology in the same image of natural sciences in precision and scope, yet that does not mean that social scientists cannot arrive at generalization from history. Weber saved sociology from the approach that invoked a radical contrast between man and the rest of the universe. He attempts to reconcile the two extreme strands of thought in the scholarship of the nineteenth-century Europe: the positivism of the natural sciences and German idealism and historicism. While he used Kantian idealism and historicism to criticize positivism — that social science could be just reduced to collecting the facts and formulating them as general law — he never tried to defend the role of ideas against a simplistic imitation of physical science. He steered a middle ground. A science of society has to respect the endless flux of events in history, the complex nature of history without reducing it to either absolute laws or to the realm of esoteric idealism.

Generally, Weber considered social sciences, be it economics, history or sociology, as essentially 'idiographic' disciplines. The overriding aim is not to produce general laws, but to understand the meaning of particular events. Ultimately it is a question of objectivity, on which Weber was of the firm opinion that values did constitute the subject-matter of a sociologist but the method of study could not be value-laden. The appropriate method for the human sciences is '*verstehen*'-understanding. History is a creation of human beings, who are all embodiments of value / subjectivities. Thus, in order to explain it we must put ourselves into the position of those people who created it. Our understanding depends on such a unique way to see things through the eyes of the subject-matter. Weber therefore provided a '*verstehen*' sociology which employed the methodological tool of '*ideal types*' and the conception of 'social action'.

VERSTEHEN SOCIOLOGY

The fundamental question raised by Max Weber, which subsequently revolutionized methodology in social sciences, was: 'In what sense are there "objectively valid truths" in these disciplines concerned with social and cultural phenomena?' (1949: 51). An objective social science has to be unbiased and value-free. This is possible only when the researcher is alert in not mixing up his/her values and interests with the research enquiry. Such a stance is in tune with Weber's general understanding of the unfolding of socio-historical process as a matter of growing rationalization of social life. As diametrically different from the object of study of natural and physical sciences, social sciences deal with a subject that has consciousness. This understanding of social sciences was a marked departure from the positivist attempt of Emile Durkheim. Weberian insistence on value-freedom and value-relevance is fundamental to any appreciation of his method.

Value-Freedom (*Werturteilsfreiheit*)

Value-freedom, *werturteilsfreiheit* in German, was the cornerstone of Max Weber's methodology. The ideal of a scientific endeavour is value-freedom. Causal hypotheses and explanations are the testing ground of social sciences. Value-judgments are an outcome of one's moral, political and aesthetic choices. The obligation of social sciences is to keep the casual explanations free from value-based preferences of the researcher. At the same time social sciences have to acknowledge value-relevance, given every aspect of human society is impregnated with values. Social science method has to work towards the ideal of keeping the two separate. Sociological method has to be set aside from values because facts and values belong to two different realms.

Weber addressed the problem by calling for a clear perception of reality as the scientific vocation. He was categorical in his opposition to preaching by professionals. He outlined his argument against propagation of any ideals by scientists by emphasizing the professional duty of a practitioner of any scientific vocation. The task of scientists is to present reality unimpaired by their own evaluations. Such reality, even if uncomfortable, is to be addressed and explained in a non-partisan manner. It is not that social scientists refrain from studying values; instead it is a critical task of understanding values without attempting to tamper with them.

Understanding Explanation (*Vertehendes Erklaren*)

A critical, but an empirical, treatment of values is all that Max Weber's method of doing social science asks for. Weber acknowledged the work of his colleague Simmel with regard to his concept of *verstehen*. The actual German word *verstehendes* stands for 'understanding' or 'interpretation'. Following Simmel, Weber held that meanings emerge not from the patterns of the external objects. Also, meanings do not flow automatically from the subjective thought processes of the autonomous individual. Meaning is a matter of a social interactional process; such constitution of meaning is a precondition for the emergence of both objects and subjects in the first place.

A social scientist does not merely observe but also interprets at the same time. Without a mode of understanding, social action cannot be penetrated as values are also to be understood and not just observed. In human disciplines one cannot avoid evaluation from entering into the subject matter. By employing the method of *verstehen* (understanding), one can advance scientific research. Equipped with the tool of *verstehen*, a social scientist can make the subject's evaluation on his/her ways of action. Values cannot be observed as 'facts', neither are they determined by 'facts'. Human social world is impregnated with values, which are many and are quite likely at odds with each other. In this way, value is always 'free'; an actor chooses among contending values in the rational world experiencing modernity. It is because of the possession of such freely available values that human beings qualify as cultural beings whereby they can act, relate and communicate symbolically. This aspect sets apart the social world from its natural world. Thus, for Max Weber ultimately social science is quasi cultural science.

> The "points of view" which are oriented towards "values" from which we consider cultural objects and from which they became "objects" of historical research, change. Because, and as long as they do, new "facts" will always be becoming historically "important".... This way of being conditioned by "subjective values" is, however, entirely alien in any case to those natural sciences which take mechanics as a model, and it constitutes, indeed, the distinctive contrasts between the historical and the natural sciences.... The concept of the "culture" of a particular people and age, the concept of "Christianity", of "Faust", and also — there is a tendency to overlook this — the concept of "Germany", etc. are individualized *value-concepts* formed as the objects of *historical* research, i.e., by relation with value-ideas. (Shills and Finch 1949:159–60)

From the above quote it becomes clear that for Weber, social science is a sort of self knowledge. Man's relation to his own motives, values, beliefs and customs is not like his relation to the natural or physical world. This relation is an intimate one. Thus, in the study of human affairs man is both the subject and the object of inquiry; hence the difference in the approach and method of knowing between the natural and social science. Social sciences proceed by asking different questions, as it wishes to know 'something different' from that of the natural scientists. Hence, the major interest in the subject-matter of sociology is not that abstract and quantitative that characterizes our objective in the natural and physical world. The objects of the social sciences are constituted for us by our values. Weber brings in the concept of 'value-relevance' (*Wertbeziehung*) to make this above distinction. The object of inquiry is to secure clarity about the situations in which men select and act on their values, which Weber said 'to give himself an account of the ultimate meaning of his own conduct' (Weber 1949: 152).

Finally, we can say that being impacted upon by the neo-Kantians, Max Weber held that as we study men in society, we essentially attempt to 'understand' our subject-matter by identifying ourselves with the human actors and imaginatively experiencing their intensions and motives. Simply put, this is a method *of verstehen*.

SOCIAL ACTION

Social action is the unit of sociological enquiry for Max Weber. What is *social fact* for Emile Durkheim, is social action for Weber. It is the cornerstone of Weber's non-positivist method for studying society. A society is a result of human interaction, and every interaction is a web of action indulged in by human beings who impute meanings into their acts and behaviours. The study of society rests on interpreting the meanings of such interaction.

> [Sociology is] ... the science whose object is to interpret the meaning of *social action* and thereby give a causal explanation of the way in which the action proceeds and the effects which it produces. By "action" in this definition is meant the human behaviour when and to the extent that the agent or agents see it as *subjectively meaningful*.... The meaning to which we refer may be either (a) the meaning actually intended ether by an individual agent on a particular historical occasion or by a number of agents on an approximate average in a given set of cases, or (b) the meaning attributed to the agent or agents, as types, in a pure type constructed in the abstract. In neither case is the "meaning" to be thought of as somehow objectively "correct" or "true" by some metaphysical criterion. This is the difference between the empirical sciences of action, such as sociology and history, and any kind of *apriori* discipline, such as jurisprudence, logic ethics, or aesthetics where aim is to extract from their subjective-matter "correct" or "valid" meaning. (Weber 1922: 136)

For Weber, sociology is primarily an interpretive discipline. But the next level of the endeavour is to engage in interpretive theorization, that is, finally one has to set up causal relationships as causal analysis only sustains the discipline as a scientific one. This is to be accomplished by engaging in a process of understanding as action to which actors attach a subjective meaning is the scope of Weberian sociology.

Action is social by virtue of the subjective meaning attached to it by the acting individuals. It also takes into account of the behaviour of the others and is thereby oriented in its course. What constitutes a society is not some transcendental externally existing reality which people follow. It is created by people interacting. Weber is categorical in his assertion that the society will stop existing the moment people stop orienting towards it meaningfully. It is man as a feeling, thinking, willing, acting and responsible being who constitutes the subject-matter of sociology. Therefore, the issues of a proper method of study for sociology are inescapably rooted in evaluations which are of cultural significance. Objective validity of social action is possible only in terms of value-relevance, that is, in terms of all the meanings imputed to the actors by the investigator.

Action which has no said orientation cannot be interpreted. In fact, an action which leads to no social consequences does not qualify as a social action. Since it cannot be interpreted, no causal explanation could be made on that. Moreover, sociologists are neither concerned with events of mere interconnections, nor with reactive behaviours as such. The central point that Weber put forward was that, social institutions consists of nothing more than people interacting, and putting certain interpretations upon each other's behaviour. The expectations that the actors carry of each other is pertinent for a given moment. These expectations need not be necessarily what is considered to be normatively 'right' or realistically 'accurate'. The actors involved in a process of interaction are quite likely to have different subjective interpretations of the entire process. For Weber, each actor can follow his own self-interest and see the interaction from his own point of view.

In his *General Economic History* (lectures of 1919–20), Weber admitted that action may be either be overt or covert / subjective. It may be of a positive intervention in a situation or of deliberately withdrawing from such interventions or passively acquiescing in the situation. Meaning may be of two kinds:

i. Actual existing meaning in the give context, and

ii. Theoretically arrived at by an interpreter attributing it to the hypothetical actor.

Weber also pointed out that, although social action is marked by almost unconscious uniformity, there is nevertheless a rudimentary consciousness of meaning even in such conventional behaviour. All interpretations of meaning like all scientific observation, must attempt for clarity, verification and comprehension. Hence a general sociology needs to explain highly complex types of action which may involve the articulation of many discrete acts. To achieve this end, a typology of meaningful action in terms of hypothetical cultural values which shape and constitute the web of social interaction is called for.

From his methodological standpoint, Weber employed the concept of *ideal types* and of *Vertehen* to arrive at such a typology. That is to say that, to explain something causally it is required that a sociologist must put himself in the place of the actor in order to emphathically share his world view and thereby avail a vantage point to understand the subjectively meaningful reasons chosen by such actor to act as he did. Weber develops a typology of social action, the various ways in which social section could be oriented. These types are a set of *ideal types* of social action. They areas follows:

i. Instrumental rationality (*Zweek rationalitat*)

ii. Value rationality (*Wertrationalitat*)

iii. Emotional action, and

iv. Traditional action.

The last two types of social action are forms of human orientation towards the world which lack any conscience reflection. Emotional action operates almost at the level of reactive behaviour. It does not take into account the behaviours of the others, and thus, as a direct expression of feeling it cannot impact upon the social world. Weber cited the example of sexual desires as a case of such action. Similarly, the action of crying when one is hurt is another example of emotional action whereas, traditional action is an action indulged in by human actors as a matter of habit. In this case also we do not find any reflection or expectation on/of the behaviours of the others in an interactive process. Like emotional action, this too hardly affects the world around. Instead, it acts as an obstacle to the principle of rationality. These are actions devoid of world-views. Weber puts both these actions as close to meaningless; they thus constitute hardly any scope for a sociological method of enquiry.

The two dominant forms of social action, instrumental and value rationality actually constitute the major scope as *social action* to be interpreted and analysed by the proposed method of *verstehen*. These are human actions which are highly meaningful and driven by ideas, motivations and objectives.

Instrumental rationality is a case of means–ends calculative way of acting in the social world. It involves a rational action which is firmly based on a means–ends calculation. One chooses here the appropriate means to accomplish one's desired goal. It is a conscious reflection on an organized view of the world. Weber cited the example of economic action at its highest *ideal type* level as a case of instrumental rationality. It is the most dominant form of rational action in the modern world. Another example of this type of social action is that of bureaucracy. The ideal typical form of administrative organization, bureaucracy, is that form of organization which is dominated by instrumental rationality. In fact, Weberian sociology is all about how this particular type of rational action came to dominate the major aspects of modern society.

If the 'value' of instrumental rationality is to be realized in the goal or end that the means combine with, in case of value-rationality no such end is reflected upon. This type of action is in a sense an end in itself. It carries with it its own value. Value-rationality is a value on to itself, where an actor does not realize a 'value' in the end result but the action itself serves its own value. Citing the examples from the political and religious world, Weber showed that such actions do not calculate on what would be the most appropriate or efficient way to reach an objective/goal. One indulges in such action driven by an intense attachment to the values of such actions themselves.

Essentially in Max Weber's work we encounter two kinds of rationality:

i. Rational action in relation to goals, and
ii. Rational action in relation to values.

IDEAL TYPES

Ideal types are considered to be the central methodological tools at the hands of Max Weber. Weber always stood for a general sociology where the categories and explanation are universalistic in nature. Only by operating on a systematic level can we use concepts which are applicable to all societies. History is an immense flow of events and society is constituted by a web of complex types of action. A general sociology has the task of explaining causally the articulation of many such discrete acts. We understand that all large-scale social interactional processes are constituted of cultural values, which make them meaningful. A sociologist needs to typify such meaningful action. For example, when we talk about 'capitalism' or 'bureaucracy' we must be able to point out the most essential aspects of the types of action associated with the concepts of 'capitalism' or 'bureaucracy'. The crucial tool to arrive at such typification is the methodological innovation of the *ideal types*.

We have already noted the impact of the German intellectual tradition of idealism on Weber's methodological intervention in social sciences. We know nothing of the reality around us except for the ways in which we understand them and categorize them. Quite apparently the external reality is the 'thing in itself'. As Immanuel Kant has proposed, we always perceive the reality with the help of our mental subjective categories. It is only through such subjectively construed mental forms that we 'capture' the word. We always place mental forms upon everything we might possibly see or even think about in order to perceive it intelligently. This is a Kantian contribution to the theory of knowledge. We know our world only through our ideas, which we impose upon the observable reality. This is true for a common man as well as for a specialist. For the common man if it is simply the ideas, the thought categories of everyday living; for a social scientist it is the *ideal type*, a methodological tool and concept developed by him through a careful act of abstraction.

As we know, society and history exhibit a discrete and continuous flow of events. These events are spread across millions of people, across a vast expanse of time and space. The primary task of 'science' is to select and summarize, as without such manageable scope of study one cannot systematize one's subject-matter for any organized knowledge. Therefore, the social scientist always selects particular patterns to focus upon. One arrives at the pattern only with the help of one's own thought categories; obviously, such thought categories of a social scientist are of special types. Such analytical categories which a social scientist employs in taking out a pattern from the immense variety of events and 'order' the flux of actions are the *idea types* for Max Weber.

> An ideal type is formed by the one-sided accentuation of one or more points of view and by the synthesis of a great many, diffuse, more or less present and occasionally absent concrete individual phenomena, which are arranged according to those one-sidedly emphasized viewpoints into a unified analytical construct. In its conceptual purity, this mental construct cannot be found empirically anywhere in reality. (Weber 1949: 90)

Weber in his methodological essays made it very clear that such *ideal types* are never realistic, but they are just ideal typification of reality that facilitates a social scientist by making social reality tractable. They are always idealized in the sense that they are one-sided pictures, a sort of model of 'pure types' that the world may approximate. Such one-sided ideal typifications are indispensable for a social scientist to apprehend historical complexity. Also, as the world itself is a mixture of many kinds of things, *ideal types* have to be shaped so that they can be used in combinations. From the flux of discrete events and tendencies *ideal types* help to grasp historical reality somewhere between such different tendencies.

Weber cited the example of 'bureaucracy' as an ideal type of an administrative organization. Such an ideal type of organization entails administration according to the rules, where every personnel have a strict position. Such a position is just one such in a hierarchy of positions governed by well-laid rules and regulations. Moreover, this arrangement reflects a clear chain of command and so forth. Weber is pretty clear about the fact that in realty no organization would exactly fit into this model. Therefore, he pairs 'bureaucracy' with another ideal-type, 'patrimonialism' which is a form of organization, characterized by features just opposite to that of 'bureaucracy'. It is centred on personnel networks and cliques. The rights and responsibilities of every position are not governed by any rational rules or regulations. Weber then goes on to describe and explain the history of various states of organizations as fluctuating somewhere between 'patrimonialism' and 'bureaucracy'. Thereby, he could also trace the conditions and circumstances that place an organization towards one end of the continuum or the other. As we have noted before, in Weber's view, history is an endless flux of particulars which can never be comprehended in their entirety. We, thus, need to use the methodological device of ideal types to track it down between the fixed reference points, which are nothing but ideal types of such a phenomenon. Essentially through conceptual abstractions from reality, ideal types are developed and are employed in order to grasp the complexities of social world. 'Capitalism' is again an ideal type of an economic institution which is constituted of a very large number of interconnected elements, some of which are structural, while some others are normative. Weber makes sense of 'capitalism' by accentuating central features (as theorized by an analyst) and suppressing or eliminating those elements which otherwise would make historically unique and specific realities. This again shows that the *ideal type* of 'capitalism' is unlikely to be an accurate representation of the real thing.

Weber's use of this methodological device of ideal types follows from his general view of sociology as a social science which examines variations within and between institutional forms. It is not a search for any metaphysical entity that institutions share in common. Hence, when Weber studies religion he is not inspired by the Durkhemian mode of searching for the essence of religion, which then could be shown as a 'basis' for all other religions. Instead, Weber looked for the details of dogmas and rites, as different dogmas inspire and motivate their followers towards different types of social action. By shifting our focus to the variety of institutional forms, their types and sub-types, ideal type as a methodological tool facilitates us to bring some conceptual order to the chaos of reality. As claimed by Weber, ideal type has an important function in an empirical investigation. It helps us to compare the empirical reality with its idealized form, as well as all the variations that exist in the empirical world. In this way it establishes the similarities and the divergences, which in turn stimulates understanding in order to explain them causally.

An act of 'stylization' is actually indulged in by a theorist in the conceptual abstraction from reality. In the construction of ideal types we retain only what seems characteristic. We need to carefully recognize that, such construction of ideal types does not call for any generalization of the features common to every institution. It is done almost at the level of a utopian rationalization. Thus, it is not that an ideal type carries the essence of the phenomenon it represents; instead it represents a positive substitute for them. To talk of essence would be a case of a value-judgement. The particular is distinct from the general, as every particular is unique. Likewise, every reality is unique and thereby distinct from the idea of it. Ideas are the building blocks of concept building. Concepts are indispensable for a theorist to grasp the world, which is done by transcending the 'reality' by ideas. If we can rigorously define the terms we use in our conceptual abstraction, we can compare our ideas with the reality, which it represents. Through such comparisons we realize the inadequacy of the correspondence and could move forward for further abstractions which make our thinking more profound. Such comparison is made possible when we work with ideal types. Ultimately, ideal types serve as the unit of comparison in Weberian sociology.

RATIONALITY

To appreciate Max Weber's contribution to the study of modern society, we need to acknowledge that rationality forms the central theme in his thought. Weber's basic philosophy is based on rationality in the sense that he thinks man to be moving towards greater and greater state of rationality. Understanding, therefore, his concept of rationality has many meanings — all of which are coherent and consistent, and build up a whole comprehensive picture.

Roughly speaking, rationality implies a means–end relationship. A rational person correctly chooses the means to fulfill the ends. There are two aspects of this:

i. That the means that lead to the end is subjectively perceived by the social action, and

ii. That the means will lead to the end objectively.

That a social actor has a means–end relationship does not automatically imply rationality because, the fulfilment or achievement of that end may be determined by the value of the particular social actor and does not involve objectivity. For example, the superstitious student who has lucky trousers for examinations may feel that wearing those lucky trousers may have some linkage to doing well in the examinations. Wearing the lucky trouser may be 'rational' enough for him. But how do we know that the choice of such means actually leads to that desired end across the board? The choice could be held to be rational if and only if such choice of means always and everywhere leads to that desired end, irrespective of who exercise such choice.Thus, in any given circumstance, we should be able to clearly test whether such means produce the same end or not. Weber's concept of rationality, therefore, includes the idea of reliability and validity — the two plinths of objectivity.

In the Weberian scheme, man is a rational animal for s/he possesses reason. Reason is basically a subjective category. It means that before the actual action, wo/man is able to subjectively link up the means and ends. However, human perception operates through concepts. Concepts are mental categories which are subjectively conceived about reality. They are just the ideas about the nature of things. A wo/man's social action in the context of reality retains the same kind of orientation as her/his subjectivity is, or as her/his concepts are. Subjectivity stands in between a social action and the reality. This subjectivity leads to the formation of ideas about 'what should be' — which is essentially of a normative content.

Normative/subjective valuations are largely individualistic or at least confined to a group facing a particular social situation. Also, such valuations are formed, sustained and changed with the change in the social situation or the social circumstances, which are again particular to an individual or group. Hence subjectivity defies universality and cannot be called rational. What one perceives as reality may be perceived as falsity by any other individual or group facing a different situation. Thus, until and unless one fulfills the condition of universality, one cannot satisfy the condition of reliability and validity.

There is another way by which Weber tried to show how rationality is objective. This can be shown by a simple example. The tribal in order to bring rain may roll down a stone. It may sometimes be coincidental to raining but logically it is not. But why does the tribal in the first place roll down the stone? S/he does it because s/he has seen others doing it. Thus, in all probability s/he does roll down the stone with the same expectation. This implies:

i. S/he maintains merely a pattern, and
ii. S/he hardly validates a means–end relationship.

Weber was of the opinion that the maintenance of pattern is at the opposite pole of rationality. Rationality, instead, treats each end and each means specifically and matches the means with the ends.

Weber saw reason as rationality. This means that prior to any action, the social actor's mind should be able to

i. Conceive the end and the means required to achieve it clearly, and
ii. Conceive of a particular social situation where s/he is not using the particular means, and whether the same end can be achieved or not. If s/he is accomplishing that, s/he is transcending his/her conceptions about the availability of the means and therefore sublimates his/her subjectivity. By this way, s/he tries to objectively verify the means–end relationship.

Weber proposed that, while conceiving a particular means–end relationship the origin of propositions are subjective but verification has to be objective. This is the sole difference between the tribal's way of perceiving reality (as cited above) and the scientific weather bureau's way of forecasting.

What, then, is the difference between the tribal and the scientist? The tribal may know much more about the clouds and the stars than what the scientist does; then, why do we not call the tribal to be rational? Actually, rationality does not mean what is known absolutely, but the fact the reality is knowable at any point of time. This knowability is rationality and hence objectivity. Nothing is knowable absolutely until and unless it transcends time and space. Thus, universality as we have noted before, is a marker of rationality. But how do we universalize?

In order to universalize, we place all the categories similar to each other in one group or class, after which we can compare and classify. Rationality entails systematic classification. Again, the entire exercise of universalism is for a particular purpose. For example, we see and classify or identity (by classifying) a particular set of categories existing at a particular point of time. We see a set on a conglomeration. Now, we are to understand the existence of this set, so that

i. We can predict the occurrence at a future date
ii. Infer its occurrence in the past, and
iii. Explain why it exists.

Until and unless we can explain the occurrence in the above three ways, we cannot call our exercise to be knowable. A little reflection will show that such an explanation needs one basic answer — what causes the pattern. Causality is the only unifying thread lying through the associative social actions. If we can say 'what causes what', then we can clearly get an idea of the means–end relationship. Thus, causality is the plinth of rationality. Only when we arrange, the observed reality systematically, we can find causality which in turn leads to knowability. The essence of knowability is the law and less perfect is perhaps the theory — both are statements of causality, of 'if-then' relationship.

The running theme in Weber's work is the idea of the progressive rationalization of life as the governing principle of Western civilization. As we have discussed above, rationalization for Weber means doing away with sentiments, tradition and rule of thumb in all spheres of life. These are replaced with explicit, abstract, intellectually calculable rules and procedures. Thereby, the modern world is a disenchanted one. The process of rationalization makes the world utilitarian by demystifying it. We need to be careful to note that, Weber did not share the optimism of the eighteenth-century thought of Enlightenment. In his seminal work *The Protestant Ethics and the Spirit of Capitalism*, he was of the opinion that rationalization does not 'indicate an increase and general knowledge of the conditions under which one lives' (Weber 1905: 139) Interestingly, he pointed out that over a period of time the entire structure suited on rationality becomes a self-sustaining process. Man's rationality, and mastery of his environment based on formal set of rules, systematic technologies and rationally planned enterprises get dislocated from the rationality that created them. Instead, the very efficiency and reliability constrict the need for wider knowledge and rational capacities of the men they dominate. That is to say that, Weber did not finally approach rationalization as an inevitable process of change, in which the rational ethics blossoms fully to brighten up the social and cultural world. Instead, he emphasized its altering character as it evolves, the way it gets 'routinized' and creates an 'iron-cage' for man.

ROLE OF IDEAS IN HISTORY

Max Weber's thesis on the relation between the Protestant ethic and the spirit of capitalism is probably the most controversial theory in the history of sociological thought. As against crude materialist understanding, in his *The Protestant Ethic and the Spirit of Capitalism* (1904–05/58), he theorized the interdependence of ideational and material factors in history. Specifically, Weber traced the influence of religious ideas upon the conduct of men and challenged the Marxist thesis that being decides consciousness.

By taking recourse to statistical evidence, Weber could see that there was a close relationship between some of the Protestant sects and successful business activity, not only in Germany or Europe, but also in the United States. As a sociologist searching for the subjective sides of social living, Weber invoked his methodological tools of 'ideal types' and the concept of 'social action' to interpret the meaning of the life-style practiced by these protestant sects. He could establish that the Protestants' conception of duty and calling allowed them to adopt a life-style that was best suited to the gainful economic activity characterizing capitalism in its formative stage.

SPIRIT OF CAPITALISM

However, instead of understanding Weber's thesis as a critique of Marx's theory of capitalism, we need to note that for Weber the scope of inquiry was 'spirit of capitalism', whereas for Marx it was the logic of capitalism. Having defined the 'spirit of capitalism' as the object of his inquiry, Weber proceeded to cite the correspondence between the 'spirit' and the religious ideas of the Reformation.

By 'spirit of capitalism', Weber focused on a tendency that appeared to be typical of modern society and on an attribute of behaviour that appeared to be universal. These were a general opposition to personal subservience and an economic conduct possessing an ethical content of its own. It involved a work-ethic — the idea of it as a duty which carried its own intrinsic reward.

According to Weber, throughout history and in all civilizations men have pursued gain in a speculative manner. But in the modern period such pursuits were distinguished from all the traditional economic actions by the encouragement of rational calculation. Modern capitalism as a great complex of interrelated institutions reflected the ideas and habits that favour a rational pursuit of economic gains. In effect, a 'manner of life' was fostered. Developing an ideal type of such economic action as noticed in the formative years of capitalism, Weber tried to see whether it could be matched with another ideal type of religious action (social action). The consideration from the Protestant ethic prompted him to develop an ideal type of religious action. The search for correlation and congeniality between the two set of ideal types rested on Weber's methodological position of searching for meaningful action and orientation in terms of ideas and motivations.

THE PROTESTANT ETHIC

Appalled by the corruption of the Church in the Middle Ages, the Protestant Reformation of the sixteenth-century attacked the authority of the Church and the Pope. In certain Protestant groups like Calvinists, Pietists, Methodists and Baptists, the manner of life was characterized by a distinct asceticism — ambiguously called Puritanism. The central point was to do away with traditional Catholicism which taught that magical rituals stood between God and the true believer. Martin Luther and St Calvin both held that an individual's personal relationship with God could not be hindered with such mediating institutions or priests. However, having removed the institutions and rituals of orthodox Catholicism, they were thrown back on their inner resources. For, it was in one's own mind and not through the agency of another that one must understand God's decrees which are as impenetrable as they are irrevocable.

A new concept of salvation emerged, which was not through the sacraments but through the efficacy of one's faith which is to be attested by the success attendant upon one's industry. Along with asceticism contributed to a rational molding of every aspect of life, which was seen as related to the will of God. Although there were four main streams of ascetic Protestantism, the majority of Weber's analysis was based on Calvin's teachings. The most important calling of a Calvinist was to participate in worldly affairs. This was related to the major point of Calvin's doctrine of predestination. This implied that everything that everyone does is already fore-determined. Naturally this created a lot of anxiety and fear in the minds of the believers. If only a few, the so-called elect, could be chosen to be saved, no such 'good work' as prescribed by the church could save them. Such a negation of the church made the Calvinists stress upon the value of asceticism which involved hard-work, thrift and diligence. Thus, the ideal-typical Puritan adopted a methodical life-style of asceticism which had the greatest significance for his/her inner life. The strong motivation to discipline one's life resulted thereby. The doctrine of pre-destination ended up producing hard work and self-discipline. As such Calvin suggested that the ordinary world was the place in which everyone must work out one's own salvation. It provided the release from the anxiety resultant from the belief in pre-destination.

Such a rationalization of personal conduct as shaped by religious ideas — Calvinism in particular — was conducive to the particular kind of 'spirit' that capitalism required. Thus, the 'spirit of capitalism' also involved a calling attitude which exactly fitted into the calling of the Protestant Puritan. Thereby, the particular religious ideas became a powerful source of social motivation.

If early capitalism required of its actors independent entrepreneurship and honest business based on rational calculation bereft of personal pleasure, Calvinism also demanded of its believers a coherent and continuous life of discipline. It produced individuals who were able to find ultimate significance in the most worldly and mundane of activities. The correspondence was therefore evident. Thereby, Weber drew our attention to another side of the process which was not theorized hitherto in the light of more material causations of capitalist development. But Weber's theory is to be seen only as establishing the relationship in its formative years. As he himself was aware that once created, the institutions of capitalism would gain its own logic of existence and would deviate from the original manner of life and conduct.

> The Puritan wanted to work in a Calling; we are forced to do so.... In Baxter's view the care for external goods should only lie on the shoulders of the 'saint like a light cloak which can be thrown aside at any moment'. But fate decreed that the cloak should become an iron-cage. (Weber 1958: 81)

SUMMARY

Unlike Marx or Durkheim, Weber was not interested in the possibility of a general theory of evolution. Weber's sociology is a historical sociology. His methodological rigour actually contributed the most in enriching sociology, which subsequently resulted in many methodological shifts in later sociological theory.

For Weber, human being is essentially a cultural being and cultural-reality results from the value-orientations of social actors. The role of interpretive understanding pioneered by him made sociology a more reflexive science in later years. His wide range of subjects and analysis finally merged on his somewhat pessimistic view of human society. Nevertheless, Weber's theory on rationality and bureaucracy as well as his thesis on capitalism would remain a great classical treatment and resource for further research in sociology.

KEY WORDS

- *Cultural Science*
- *Historicism*
- *Social Action*
- *Rationality*
- *Spirit of Capitalism*
- *Idealism*
- *Verstehen*
- *Ideal Types*
- *Protestant Ethics*

GLOSSARY

Cultural Science: As against natural sciences, dealing with the way social reality is made meaningful through an exchange of shared values and beliefs, facilitated by a symbolic order of signs and symbols.

Historicism: The methodological perspective that consider societies and cultures as historically unique entities.

Nomothetic Disciplines: Those which are subjected to explanation of orderly empirical relationships by reference to general laws.

Ideographic Disciplines: Those which seek for qualitative explanation for elements of social reality considered as unique and different from other aspects of social reality.

Protestant Ethic: An ascetic mode of life-conduct that encourages hard work, thrift and righteous forms of godliness.

Rationality: An orientation that involves or consists of a set of social actions governed by reason or reasoning, calculation and pursuit of one's interests based on means–end calculation.

Spirit of Capitalism: An orientation to make gainful pursuit based on careful planning and investment and disciplined work.

Social Action: Subject matter of Weber's sociology, which takes into account the actions and responses of others while acting meaningfully.

Verstehen: The German word for 'interpretation', which Weber underscored as the benchmark of conducting sociological enquiry, taking into account the meanings imputed by social actors in their actions.

Value Freedom: The methodological stance that allows a sociologist to analyse human value commitments without making reference to their desirability and worthiness.

Discussion Points

- Subjective strains in Weber.
- *Verstehen* sociology of Weber.
- The importance of ideal types and the study of social action.
- Rationality and the emergence of capitalist spirit.

5

Vilfredo Pareto (1848–1923)

Vilfredo Federico Damaso Pareto, the distinguished Italian sociologist, was influential during in the American sociological circle in his time, especially the 1930s. As the leading proponent of functional sociology in the USA, Talcott Parsons took a lot of interest in his works. Pareto's sociology subsequently has lost the importance, while only his theory of elites and circulation of elites has retained its relevance in contemporary thinking on society. Primarily, his sociological theories were formulated in reaction to Marx's social theory. He not only refuted Marx, but along with that he also questioned the very foundation of the Enlightenment philosophy. He critiqued the rationality principle of the Enlightenment and contended that human society is as much a result of non-rational factors such as human instincts. Nevertheless, he insisted on the logico-experimental method, thereby holding the scientific nature of sociology aloft.

A BIOGRAPHICAL SKETCH

Vilfredo Pareto was born in Paris in 1848. His mother was French while his father was an Italian nobleman. Pareto's family had been active in Italian polities and had to live in exile for a while because of his father's support for an independent and united Italian republic. In the late 1850s, the family could return to Italy. He received a degree in mathematics and physics and enrolled himself in the School of Engineering in 1867. He even served a railroad company in Rome as a consulting engineer. However, he left the job shortly and returned to Florence and even contested for the Italian parliament in 1881. As a strong proponent of free market trade, he campaigned hard but lost the election.

The defeat made him more bitter about the Italian government and its protectionist economic policies. He retreated to his villa in Fiesole and inherited a substantial asset which allowed him to engage in study and research. As an ardent supporter of free-market capitalism Pareto joined the Adam Smith Society in Florence and wrote profusely on free-market economics. Subsequently, he was offered the chair of political economy at the University of Lausanne in Switzerland in 1893. As a political economist, he is best known for his analysis of equilibrium models of demand and supply. His principal focus was on the instrumental rationality of an economic system of production and exchange. Be it socialist or capitalist, he believed that any system of production and distribution basically favours one group against another.

Pareto's first major work was published at the turn of the twentieth century. This major contribution to sociological theory was published in 1916 as *Treatise on General Sociology*, which was not noticed until the turbulent years of World War I finally got over. The book carried some of Pareto's scathing criticisms of the democratic principles. As a result, the Italian dictator Benito Mussolini appreciated his arguments and even offered him a seat in the Italian senate, which he declined. This work is best known in the world of sociology in the translated English version as *The Mind and Society: A Treatise on General Sociology* (1963).

Pareto lived a troubled personal life too. Although he stressed the functional importance of religion and authority in his sociological writings, in his private life he led a careless life. With the growing years he became more and more isolated from his fellow intellectuals. As a lonely figure he dispensed with his earlier liberal social philosophy and sided more with authoritarian principles. He had less respect for social reformism which he thought would do more harm than good for the common man. Often for valid reasons, Pareto is thought of as the theorist who prepared the theoretical ground for Italian Fascism. He died in 1923, but prior to that he appealed to the Fascist regime to moderate the use of force and to acknowledge the citizenship rights of every individual. He did not live to see the ultimate consequence of the Fascist rule in Italy.

SOCIAL AND INTELLECTUAL INFLUENCE

Pareto lived, right from his birth, through a period of acute political crisis that characterized the Italian society of the nineteenth-century and beyond. Italy as a nation did not emerge as a sovereign state when he was born in 1848 as it was still a patch work of many states. The period was marked by strong nationalist movements which were also internally split. After 1861, Italy was ruled by the bourgeoisie who came from the commercial and the industrial cities of the north. Southern Italy was mainly populated by superstitious and backward landlords and peasants who strongly opposed the bourgeois reforms. To make matters worse, the governing classes were corrupt and all the elections were fixed and forged. In World War I, too, Italy heavily suffered and as a consequence faced acute economic crisis. The socialist force gained more support after the war and a rapid polarization between the rightist and the leftists took place.

After the 1920s, Benito Mussolini gradually emerged as the rightist leader. He broke away from his earlier socialist policies to form the Italian Fascist Party. The party initially lost the election and became more pro-capitalist and hostile to the socialists. With a strong emphasis on enforcing discipline it gradually demolished all oppositions to seize power.

In such a social scenario, Pareto justified the coming to power of the Fascists. According to him, the failure of the Italian government in the post-war years to serve its people was the main reason for Mussolini to come to power. He considered Mussolini as the most competent politician to seize the opportunity. Essentially, he lauded the Fascists' skill and their lofty ideals. Pareto did not live long to see the final consequence of the fascist rule. The erratic and brutal rule of Mussolini, the displacement of private enterprise by state-run capitalism and all such subsequent development in Italy were not foreseen by Pareto.

Although Pareto was a firm believer in classical free-market economy he could see that the social and political philosophies of the American federalists could not come good for Italy. Initially, given the weak development of parliamentary democracy in Italy and its debilitating status as a nation-state, influenced Pareto to side with the ideals of bourgeois republicanism. The failure to secure an independent and united Italian republic by the idealist humanitarian nationalist leader Guiseppe Mazzini made Pareto sceptical. Politically, he was disenchanted with the possibilities of the French Republican philosophies and the German nationalist ideals for bearing a root in the Italian soil. Moved more and more towards an authoritarian philosophy.

The thoughts of the Italian political theorist Niccolo Machiavelli (1469–1527) appears to have impacted upon Pareto in a significant way. The political manual for how to rule, *The Prince* was Machiavelli's principal work, written in 1513 for the ruler of Florence. He made a political statement on the art of government. It stated that a successful rule is basically a technical art, which should be free from any moral sentiments. The technique is to consider the subject as perpetually governed by superstitions, non-rational petty ambition, while the ruler is equipped with rational expertise. The rulers should be cunning and intelligent to use fraud and deception to allow the subject to remain non-rational and superstitions; this way political authority could be established and made fault-free. The art of governance is the technique of rising above the confused beliefs of common people. The ruler needs to pay least attention to whether s/he is considered as honest. There is one moral obligation in the art of ruling. As the objective of any government is fixed and taken for granted, political theory is not a moral question but is full of technical expertise. Such an astute political cunningness in Machiavelli's theory appealed to Pareto.

Machiavelli's image of *The Prince* as one who would actually be successful in building a strong Italy never succeeded historically. Italy, since the days of Machiavelli, could never catch up with Britain, France or Germany in terms of political power. The Reformation had skipped Italy, while the Enlightenment ideals could hardly inspire the intellectual life of Italy. Pareto's inklings for Machiavellian thought were due to his disdain for the Enlightenment promises. He never believed that intellectuals could guide their lives and society with reflective self-enlightenment. The social milieu around him compelled Pareto to ponder that there is an intractable non-rational core to human nature — the inner-force of any society, so to say. Given the absolute disarray of the Italian society around him, with the church being still strong and widespread ignorance looming large, Pareto looked up for a strong ruler of discipline and authority.

Among the classical thinkers, Pareto admired Herbert Spencer, but considered him, as well as Auguste Comte, as insufficiently positivist. In Karl Marx he admired the idea of continuous struggle for domination among competing groups. Pareto infused such a concept of history in his classical elite theory but differed strongly with the Marxist proposition of the possibility of a classless society. Two of his contemporaries, Georges Sorel and Gaetano Mosca impressed him. Although Sorel, who was an anti-nationalist, agreed with Marx about the final and pivotal role of the proletariat, he argued that the working class could be organized only by some non-rational myths so essential to wage a revolutionary struggle. Pareto shared the view that human behaviour is governed largely by non-rational impulse. With Mosca, Pareto shared the view that it is only through manipulation that at any time in history, rulers are able to dominate a subordinate majority. Quite interestingly, although the very concept of 'circulation of elites' was used by Mosca first, Pareto used it extensively in his works without ever acknowledging the debt. Pareto, to a large extent was a product of his time which was marked by failures of rational principles of life. From a thinker of political economy Pareto drifted towards sociology, as he thought it was that subject area where he could trace the non-rational impulse of human behaviour.

SOCIETY IN EQUILIBRIUM

Pareto's conception of society carries an interesting feature, while he considers society in terms of an equilibrium state but the 'inner forces' of society is thought to be an amalgamation of imprecise sentimental factors. It is a sort of a Janus-faced image that he promoted for a society. The equilibrium state is a rational act while the forces which maintain such a state are thought to be largely irrational. This possibly was a result of Pareto's twin identity of a political economist and a sociologist rolled into one. Initially, he theorized the rationality of free market enterprise to account for the equilibrium state of society. Society as a system in equilibrium consists of interdependent parts and any change in any part affects the other parts and the whole as well.

As an economist Pareto held that the goals of economic activity are beyond dispute. They are rationally arrived at on the principle of 'utility maximization'. In general people adopt the policy of maximization of utility to achieve the desired economic goal. Hence, economics study logical, rational action — action which uses the most effective means to achieve objectively known goals. Therefore, concrete logical rational action uses the 'logico-experimental method'. Here, individuals test the truth content of any objective goal in terms of means–ends assertions and tries to build logical deductive links between those assertions. Such actions mark only the economic realm of society. Economic man uses observation and rational calculation to achieve the goal of maximizing his utility. The goal of such action is indisputable and not to be evaluated. It is a goal in itself. Only when the goal of action is set, a concrete logical action takes place which involves utilizing the means effectively to achieve that goal. Logically, it is not possible to evaluate such goal, except as means to other goals.

An economic model of equilibrium that Pareto proposed does not take into account human behaviour that one finds in the other spheres of society, such as cultural, legal, religious, political or art-related. Pareto switched to sociology to examine such aspects of society which he thought are governed by non-rational actions. For a society as a whole system cannot adapt to external natural environment without taking such non-rational actions into account. As ironically, it is these non-logical, thereby, non-rational sentiments that acts to maintain the system in a state of equilibrium. Economics can only deal with the types of logical action, but sociology can take care of the totality of all the logical and non-logical forces that govern human behaviour. These non-logical actions play a crucial part in maintaining social systems. The forces within society are non-logical which are accounted for by Pareto. Economics can study the static equilibrium of a society, whereas sociology can explain the dynamic aspect of equilibrium. Since sociology analyses the uniformities in patterns of non-logical action, it explains change as well, as the non-logical actions made up of sentiments and subjectivities are always in a state of flux.

The importance of the inner forces of society in maintaining the system in equilibrium was underscored by Pareto. Whenever a society is threatened by external forces, the inner forces come into play to push the system towards the point of equilibrium. Anything that disturbs the inner equilibrium, the sentiments of revulsion against that restores the system back. According to Pareto, there are two major kinds of non-logical action. *Impulses* result from a commitment to goals and values whose utility cannot be evaluated or disputed — they are good in themselves. And, the second type is such actions which employ means that are not effectively connected to the stated ends of action.

Extending this distinction between logical and non-logical action Pareto opined that there is nothing logical about human wishes and sentiments. Hence, if a ruler desires to make his subjects happy, that is also a non-logical thinking because logically one cannot derive the effectiveness of such desires or actions either. Only economists could apply the logical mode of thinking to develop anticipatory models of logical economic action-because in that sphere individuals employ rationality to maximize self-interests.

NON-LOGICAL ACTION

Pareto discussed more of non-logical action than logical action, as presumably logical actions are rare. He could cite only a few such actions in his treatise to exemplify non-logical action. These are formulation of scientific theory, economic action and the practice of trial in judiciary. Even then, he said that the sentiments of the judges, which are also shared with members of the group, to a perceptible extent determine the judicial decisions. The reference to an objective and logical legal provisions and acts is a mere post-facto reference. The contention of Pareto is that, judicial decisions, too, are arrived at through actions which are a product of sentiments, whereby, non-logical action predominates social life in general. As he explains in his treatise, 'court decisions depend largely on the interests and sentiments operative in a society at a given moment, and also upon individual whims and chance events, and but slightly, and sometimes not at all, upon codes or written law' (Pareto 1963: 466).

While making a distinction between logical and non-logical action, Pareto held that the behaviour of an individual in case of logical action may be observed and there is also a substantive rational theory, as well as its application in such action. On the contrary, in case of non-logical action, a behaviour is a mere expression of a sentiment. The psychic state of an individual is actually the foundation of such actions, although an individual tries to pass off such non-logical action as a logical one. More precisely the manifestations of sentiments are an expression of biopsychic/somatic basic states. The concepts of *residues* and d*erivations* in Pareto's sociology try to account for these biopsychic states, that is, biologically inherited psychic states drive individuals to act in a non-logical manner. There are *sentiments* which cannot be logically explained and they may change over time only very slowly. Essentially they are fixed, and the effects of sentiments are actually the *residues* in social action. These fixed and constant *residues* constitute the psychological substratum of social action. Pareto, however, did not offer any definition of such residues. 'Residues correspond to certain instincts in human beings and for that reason they are usually wanting in definiteness, in exact delimitation' (Pareto 1963: 213). Only rational or logical matters can be observed and described definitely; the rest, whatever is left undescribed, is residual. Such is Pareto's contention about residues without giving it any precise definition. Residues are fundamental for the maintenance of equilibrium of a society.

Although the residues cannot be precisely defined, they can be classified into six classes:

i. **Residues for Instinct for Combination:** They are to be found in inventors, speculators and most importantly in politicians. Here, the instinct is to combine things and synthesize information. This instinct of associating things or events with striking happenings, or phenomena result in terrorizing or inspiring awe and even which are associated with good fortune

ii. **Residues of Persistence of Aggregates:** These are to be found in churchmen, family men and 'good subordinates'. This instinct is the cause behind persistence of social groups and allows the designated group to gain inertia necessary to remain together

iii. **Residues for the Need of Expressing Sentiments:** These instincts are to be found in festivals, religious rituals, ceremonies. They allow expressions of sentiments by means of external acts

iv. **Residues Related to Sociality:** These instincts are realized in ancient college and medieval guides as well as in modern trade unions. They give rise to the persistence of fashion, feelings of pity and cruelty, and acts of self-sacrifice. These residues explain the uniformities and imitations which are noticeable in disciplined social life

v. **Residues of Individual Integrity:** These instincts are instrumental for maintaining the equilibrium of a society. As a complement of residues connected with sociality, these residues promote along with individual integrity, the development of personality. Pareto places these instructs as the only ones for which individuals specify a logical derivation which involves pure economic activity, and

vi. **The Sex Residue:** These instincts are responsible for shaping the legitimacy, adultery, celibacy and many other sentiments which are associated with the phenomenon of sexual activity.

Of all the six classes of residues, Pareto focused more on the first two classes, i.e., the residues for combinations and the residues of persistence of aggregates. The focus ensued from the fact that these two residues cover the major aspects of social life and they essentially govern human behaviour in Pareto's sociological scheme.

For Pareto, individual beings while engaging in non-logical actions tend to give an impression that they are performing the most preferred action to achieve the goal. As surface manifestations, derivations are explanations provided by incumbents indulged in non-logical action which constitute the underlying forces in social life. They are like justifications that individuals offer for the sentiments they manifest. Such derivations allow individuals to move toward the preferred goal states that basically arise out of the residues only. Pareto's treatment of derivations is then more detailed than his analysis of the residues. He had listed four classes of such derivations. They are as follows:

i. **Assertion:** It constitutes a dogmatic or axiomatic assertion of fact. This derivation is mostly associated with the residue of instinct for combination. The assertion of fact is an indirect way of expressing certain sentiments which are non-logical in character.

ii. **Authority:** It constitutes a single or multiple individuals in one sphere, but engulfs other people who are gullible enough to consider themselves as experts in other spheres. This derivation is associated mainly with the residues of persistence of aggregates. Pareto exemplified this on the claims of successful political leaders, whose authority actually stems from traditional or customary sentiments but are externally manifested as something arrived at 'logically'.

iii. **Accords with sentiments or principles:** These derivations are manifested as serving and maintaining common sentiments and principles. They are used with different kinds of residues. The best instance for such derivations is one where a person justifies his/her individual desires by arguing that s/he wants it for the interest of the common people; that is, essentially when personal sentiments are passed of as sentiments of the generality of mankind, it is a case of derivations of accords with sentiments or principles.

iv. **Verbal proofs:** These are derivations which indulge in using indefinite terms and vocabularies of doubtful or equivocal meaning. Pareto gave the examples of logical sophistries, ambiguous syllogism, a pun and all such verbal usages which rest on vagueness. Basically, such derivations are operated through sheer force of rhetoric.

However, given Pareto's examples to explicate different kinds of verbal explanations of conduct, it becomes obvious that there is no close connection between the classes of residues and of derivations, each cross-cutting the other. More specifically, although he attempted to treat the classes of residues and derivations as definitive, his illustrations of derivations as the expression of specified underlying residues are not always clear-cut.

Apparently Pareto's understanding of social equilibrium is a result of his early stints in engineering. He understood equilibrium in terms of social utility which demands a correct balance between logical and non-logical action, that is, a balance between the economic interests as manifested in logical actions of utility maximization and the rest of the society marked by non-logical action. The demarcation that he created between logical and new logical aspects of society catches human beings in a dilemma. The fixed nature of psychological substratum that he assigned to social life condemns human beings to the control of forces which they are unable to take charge of. Thus, in his sociology, Pareto sees the state of the modern individual as one lacking liberating agency.

ELITE THEORY: CIRCULATION OF ELITES

The view of society proposed by Pareto rests primarily on his focus on residues and their classification as providing the psychological substratum of human nature. A society achieves its social equilibrium on the dead weight of the residues. Derivations can change across society and time. However, throughout history the residues are constant and in preferred goal states. Different periods of history make social change appear as undulating.

Every society is marked by individuals with different abilities and interests, and of course with different classes or groups of such individuals. Since all human societies are heterogeneous, there are competitions among groups who are differentially competent as governed by their residues. Heterogeneity of society makes for change in the content of the derivations. The undulating movement of history is all the social change that one can expect which is observable in the conflict and struggle between different groups or classes.

Pareto's elite theory and his conceptualization of 'circulation of elites' constitute his major contribution to sociology. Elites are individuals of highest performance in their respective fields. There are two main strata in any human society: the elite and the non-elite. Additionally, there are two principal classes of elites: the governing elite and the non-governing elite. Governing elite consists of individuals who directly or indirectly play an important role in the manipulation of political power. On the other hand, the non-governing elite consist of capable men not in power positions. The governing elite comprises of people who actually rule but are always in a precarious position. The elite rule is characterized by a state of slow and continuous transformation. Pareto explains such social change through the concept of 'circulation of elites'.

The differential distribution of residues among the members of elites decides the character of the group. Pareto mainly concentrated on the residues of *instinct for combination* and *persistence of aggregates* to designate the two types of elite and their relative positions of strength. A correct combination of instinct for combination and persistence of aggregates allows a governing elite to stay in power. After a period of rule a ruling elite tends to show decadence as the members tend to lose the sense of cohesiveness they possessed at an earlier time. As the rule of the elite group prolongs, superior elements accumulate in the governed (non-governing elite) classes. When the residues of instinct for combinations are on the wane among the members of the governing elite, leaders from the lower order with the appropriate attributes of cunning and imagination will constitute an aspiring non-governing elite group. They move in to challenge and displace the older entrenched elite group. Basically a circulation of elites takes place, as always the majority of the populace in any society is always ruled by a minority elite group. Historically, the elites of the two types rotate in positions of political power. Pareto suggested that for ensuring social equilibrium a ruling elite should be dominated by the residues for instinct of combinations, and the non-governing elites be constituted mainly by individuals who have a greater share of the residues of persistence of aggregates.

For Pareto, it is desirable that the ruling elite possesses more of intelligence and cunning than be constituted of individuals who promote only group solidarity. Actually, he imagined two groups of contending elites as one dominated by instincts of cunning and the other by instincts of force. Those dominated by the instincts for combinations (cunning, intelligence etc.) are metaphorically seen as the 'lions', while the ones dominated by the residues of persistence of aggregates are seen as the 'foxes'. Hence, the circulation of elites is a political process of change of one by another, between the 'foxes' and the 'lions' and is cyclical by nature and definition. The theory of social change which actually is expressed by the concept of circulation of elites posits an uneasy oscillation of individuals around the overlapping, and sometimes antithetical, extremes of human sentiments. But history reveals no significant change in terms of the way through which social equilibrium is maintained. Social equilibrium in Pareto's model of society is not static but one which constantly regains its position in a process of dynamic change. Such change is only a matter of a change in the content of non-rational belief.

> Revolutions come about through accumulations in the higher strata of society — either because of a slowing-down in class circulation, or from other causes — of decadent elements no longer possessing the residues suitable for keeping them in power, and shrinking from the use of force; while meantime in the lower strata of society elements of superior quality are coming to the fore, possessing residues suitable for exercising the functions of government and wiling enough to use force. (Pareto 1963: 1431).

SUMMARY

Primarily Pareto depicted society as a system in equilibrium. Such equilibrium is a result of some inner forces of the society which cannot be logically observed or explained because of the very fact that they themselves are non logical actions constituted of sentiments. Individual members of the society are exposed to these forces which determine the point of equilibrium in the society. The domain of logical action is that of economics only, beyond which all the other spheres of society are based on sentiment. As such, he did not contend that sociology could entail monism. He rejects explanations of social life to single factors or causes. He treated residues and derivations as the most important forces in the social system. However no such precise model of equilibrium did he present depicting the actual operation and balance of the inner forces of sentiment and residues.

KEY WORDS

- *Derivations*
- *Elites*
- *Equilibrium*
- *Logico-experimental Method*
- *Non-logical Action*
- *Residues*

GLOSSARY

Derivations: Non-logical explanations that allow people to behave what they want to believe, and which differ and signify different societies and group orientations.

Induction: The method of arriving at scientific truth through observation of, and generalization from, collected empirical data.

Logical Action: An instance of instrumental action which ensures that effective means are employed to secure stated goals.

Non-logical Action: Action that is not instrumental, but impulsive or irrational. It involves the adoption of ineffective means to secure stated goals.

Residues: Sentiments conceptualized in psychic terms.

Sentiments: The premise of non-logical actions, the fixed orientations of people.

Utility Maximization: The logic of instrumental action which is premised on the most effective means of securing the goals set.

DISCUSSION POINTS

- Social background of Pareto's theory.
- Logical and non-logical actions.
- Theory of Circulation of Elites.

6

Functional School of Thought

From the 1940s the functional perspective in sociology emerged as the most dominant theoretical school in the discipline and it continued to rule for two decades. It was mainly the American sociology where functionalism prospered. It is considered as the most disputed sociological perspective in the history of sociology. Quite appropriately, Don Martindale commented that the most primary theoretical and methodological debates in post-war social science have centred on functionalism and alternatives to it. It is true that beyond the 1960s the functional school lost its appeal and vigour, but it continued to impress sociological thinking as an alternative qualified version of the orthodox paradigm came to existence. Organismic analogy is the basic premise of functionalism which conceptualized the society as a whole constituted of functional parts (Martindale 1965).

The perspective of functionalism attempts to explain society in terms of the system needs, while at the same time it stresses on the role of structure of a society in shaping human behaviour. Thus, quite often it has been interchangeably used with the term structural functionalism. Synoptically the functional perspective is captured by Wallace and Wolf:

> According to this view social systems tend to perform certain tasks that are necessary for their survival, and sociological analysis, therefore, involves a search for the social structures that perform these tasks or meet the needs of the social system. (Wallace and Wolf 1999: 17)

Analogy with living organism forms the basic guiding idea of functional theories. It rests on the idea that like any living organism, society as a stable system is constituted of different parts which are interrelated. They function meaningfully in an interrelated way for the maintenance of the whole, i.e., the society. Inherent in this theory is the idea of interdependence of functionally specific parts and the requirement of the whole as being met by such functions performed by the constituting parts. Obviously such a perspective has to emphasize on the idea of system stability or equilibrium. Any change in any of the parts leads to a disturbance of that state of equilibrium. An equilibrium state only ensures a smooth functioning of the society. As a macro sociological theory functionalism, therefore, constitutes a consensual view of society. The focus of such a view is on the social institutions and patterns, the smooth functioning of which is held as basic requirement for ensuring social order and stability.

The other aspect of functionalism which follows directly from its insistence on social equilibrium is that a common set of value permeates through the whole body of the society. Equilibrium is a result of value consensus perspective. Society as a system can function properly only when all it members share and agree on basic values, thought to be good for the society. The normative structure of a society is then a shared one, and thus any damage to that is thought to be destabilizing the entire system as such. Containing change is theorized by functionalists as something of primary importance for the sake of survival of the system. A homeostatic model of society advanced by functionalism, therefore, ignores the issues of conflict and structural change of a social system. On the question of social change it only admits a low scale change from within, which does not actually alter the existing structure.

In modern sociological thought the contribution of Talcolt Parsons and Robert King Merton is widely acknowledged. However, the sociological thinking of Auguste Comte, Herbert Spencer and Emile Durkheim actually served as the backdrop for the modern development of the functional school. Also, Max Weber's influence on Talcolt Parsons needs to be noted to appreciate Parsons's grand theory of structural functionalism.

INTELLECTUAL INFLUENCES ON FUNCTIONALISM

Many of the ideas of modern functionalist thinkers are rooted in Auguste Comte's attempt to lay the foundation of a science of society by effecting a distinction between social processes that hold society together and the mechanisms of change. Basically invoking an organismic understanding for human society, Comte found it useful to make a distinction between social processes and mechanisms of change like the way it is being done in biology between anatomy and physiology. For Comte, the social processes which lead stability to society are *social statics*, and mechanisms of change are *social dynamics*. While social dynamics tell us about the laws of social change or progress, social statics tell us about the constitutive units like the individual, family and other such aspects of society. Science of society actually starts by examining these social statics and subsequently arrives at the laws of change, which are always ordered.

HERBERT SPENCER

We can notice a very rudimentary organismic analogy in Comte's early positivistic attempts. Actually it was Herbert Spencer (1820–1903), the British social thinker, who organized the organic analogy more coherently to be applied for an understanding of human society. Spencer considered society as a super-organic body and that there are certain basic similarities between society and living body. As a *Social Darwinist*, he held that social institutions, like plants and animals, grow in an evolutionary scheme and progressively become complex. They are also interdependent on each other to constitute the whole. Spencer adapted the Darwinian theory of natural selection to suggest that individual human beings who are capable would prosper and proliferate when unhindered by external interventions. Only, the 'unfit' would perish. They adapt to the environment by fulfilling certain universal requisites of the society.

As such an evolutionary scheme was proposed by Spencer where the concept of differentiation was very important. As a society grows in size, like organic bodies, it involves both multiplications of individuals as well as compounding of the groups. The increase in size brings in more complex social structure as a result of growing differentiation. It is not that only the social structures get differentiated, but also the functions of the interrelated parts get increasingly differentiated. In turn, this progressive differentiation entails greater interdependence amongst differentiated parts. Like any living organism, society too evolves from a simple undifferentiated state to compound and more compound states through progressive differentiation. The concept of *differentiation* was all too important for later day functionalists to adopt into their schemes.

In his *Principles of Sociology* (1898), Spencer made clear his ideas of difference between modern and pre-modern societies. Specialized roles and institutions are the characteristic features of modern society. As a society progresses, along with its size it involves a proliferation of specialized roles. In a complex differentiated structure only individuals with a competence over any specific role and institutions with specialized function could only survive. And such survival is made possible through increased interdependence. We see that the functional school too used the same framework to account for the stable functioning of a society. From an undifferentiated state of incoherence a coherent and differentiated state of a society emerges where the functional requirements act as the principal organizing axis of any society.

EMILE DURKHEIM

Apart from the influences of Comte and Spencer, significant contributions from social anthropologists B. Malinowski and Radcliffe-Brown also helped the development of functionalism is sociology. But among sociologists it was the French sociologist Emile Durkheim who first used the functional approach in his analysis of society.

In his major works, Durkheim was strongly influenced by Spencer's biological analogy of society. He tried to explain the contribution of the parts of the organism towards the need of the whole. Apart from using biologically inspired terms, the major assumptions of Durkheim reflected those of the organicists. Those are:

i. Society viewed as an entity in itself, and as distinguished from and irreducible to its parts
ii. Parts of society as fulfilling basic needs or requisites of the whole
iii. Basic needs of a society have to be fulfilled if 'abnormal' states are to be avoided, and
iv. Societies have equilibrium states around which normal function occurs. (Turner 1974)

All of the preceding assumptions permeate through Durkheim's works. Inspired by Comte's positivist as well as functionalist premises, he developed a view of society as a sum total of constitutive individuals groups, organizations and institutions. Such a notion of society figures prominently in all subsequent theories of functionalists. The functionalists later on tried to explain society in terms of the ways it realizes the functions required to maintain itself in an equilibrium state. Durkheim's adoption of the functional perspective is best available from his work, *The Dualism of Human Nature and Its Social Conditions* (1914).

> A great number of our mental states, including some of the most important ones, are of social origin. In this case then, it is the whole that, in a large measure, produces the part; consequently, it is impossible to attempt to explain the whole without explaining the part without explaining, at least, the part as a result of the whole. (Durkheim 1973: 149)

The work of Durkheim which most significantly inspired Talcott Parsons, the greatest theorist of the school, was *The Elementary Forms of the Religious Life* (1912). He selected the simplest practices of religion among the most primitive people to show the 'pan-religionism' of most pre-modern societies. The theory was to examine the functions that religion plays in organizing the collective sentiments and activities of the people. From the secondary sources, Durkheim selected a primitive Australian tribe *Arunta* and analysed the practice of *totemism* amongst them. Taking totemism as the simplest form of religion amongst the *Arunta* he theorized at a general plane that group life is the efficient cause of all religions and also, that the sacred–profane division is universal and functional for the social life as a whole. Parsons took the clue from Durkheim's study of the *sacred*. It influenced Parsons's structural theory of functions. It was Durkheim who prompted Parsons to see the worth of a structural functioning system as a complex of need and working for the stable continuance of the whole. Similarly, Durkheim's contention in his *The Division of Labour in Society* (1893) that crime and deviance as functional at a normal rate, and that it provides an occasion for a dramatic display of social solidarity goes a long way to impact functional theorizing on society.

THE ANTHROPOLOGICAL TRADITION

Bronislaw Malinowski, one of the proponents of functionalism in anthropological studies, along with Radcliffe-Brown had an overwhelming influence in functional sociology. Also the French structural anthropologist Claude Levi-Strauss's analysis of structural system in terms of binary opposition invoked the idea of examining all social phenomena as systems of communication. Implanting the principles of structural linguistics Strauss's analysis went on to show how the different arrangement of its parts (interplay of the signifier and the signified) creates meanings.

However, the major input of functionalism in sociology came from B. Malinowski. The term *functionalism* was actually coined by him. While studying the Australian aboriginal tribes of the Western Pacific islands he concluded that it was possible to link up functionally the various types of cultural response such as economic, legal, scientific, magical and religious to human physiological needs (Timasheff 1967); that is, biological determinism was employed by Malinowski to understand culture, and the proposition that followed from such a theory helped functionalists to develop the notion of *functional requisites* with a focus on institution as the functional isolate.

Another major exponent of functional anthropology was Radcliffe-Brown who tried to correct the teleological implications associated with organismic analogy associated with orthodox functional understanding. Thus, instead of *system needs* he preferred the term *necessary condition of existence* and advanced a more structural theory. He rejected the practice of relating items to individual needs. For him, structure is the network of actually existing relationship and function is the recurrent activity that contributes to the maintenance of the whole.

The propositions of Radcliffe-Brown that impacted upon functional theory are that, in the beginning society needs to be studied by its morphology, which includes in its definition, comparison and classification. The process within the structure takes place as a result of function; that, for a society to survive there must be a minimal consistency of relationship and solidarity between parts of a social system; and finally, that, each society or type of society exhibits certain basic structural features and various practices are related to these so as to contribute to their survival. On the whole, Radcliffe-Brown treated social structure and its requirements as something irreducible. Later day functionalists gained insights from all these anthropological exercise to take note of the various consistent patterns of behaviour and to relate them to the logic of the existence of the whole society.

TALCOTT PARSONS

Talcott Parsons is considered as the undisputed leader of functionalism who dominated the world of sociology, especially the American sociology since the publication of his *The Structure of Social Action* in 1937. Over the years he shifted his focus from *action theory* to the *system analysis*, but remained as a grand theorist of the functional school. He influenced a whole range of scholars, especially in the departments of Sociology of the American universities, the epicentre of which was the Harvard.

Born in Colorado Springs in 1902, Talcott Parsons hailed from a religious and intellectual background. In his undergraduate school he studied biology and social sciences at Amherst College. The idea of interdependence of an organism's parts which he learnt from biology shaped his subsequent idea of a social system. Subsequently he moved to the London School of Economics where Malinowski's ideas impressed him too. He left from Heidelberg, Germany immediately after that and although Max Weber was no more alive but his ideas continued to reverberate through Heidelberg. Parsons was immediately attracted to Weber's *action theory*. This was evident in his doctoral work from Heidelberg. He returned to Harvard and secured a post in 1927 and eventually became the first sociology faculty at Harvard. As a visiting professor he taught at various universities like Pennsylvania, Rutgers, California (Berkeley), but retired only from Harvard as emeritus professor. He died in 1979.

As one of the most prominent theorists of his time Parsons inspired a whole range of his students. Many of whom later emerged as leading sociologists of their own right. The most prominent of them was Robert King Merton, who reflected upon Parsons's theory and advanced it further. Parsons is considered as a grand theorist who with a single theoretical model tried to explain all social behaviour across time and space. Essentially his model was a structural–functional one. Although quite an abstract model, it is considered as the most powerful theoretical model to have emerged in the twentieth-century sociology.

SOCIAL ACTION THEORY

The Structure of Social Action (1937) was Parsons's first major work which had a strong imprint of Max Weber's methodology of understanding human society. Weber's insistence on understanding the normative order of a society in terms of value-orientations of interacting individuals appealed to Parsons. He accepted Weber's methodology to study society as made up of interacting individuals and he reiterated that such interactions are affected by the social environment. He also stressed upon the fact that, interactions are a part of the greater action system which ought to be integrated into a grand conceptual scheme.

Parson's action theory rests on the distinction between *action* and *behaviour*. Acknowledging the subjective nature of human interactions, he held that it is not behaviour, which is just a reactive response, occasioned by a stimulus. Action on the contrary indicates an active intervention of the action as one who is in cognizance of his/her situation and act weighing all the alternative lines of action.

For Parsons, the basic unit of sociological study is the unit *act*, which implies an action. An actor orients his/her action towards an end but s/he has alternative choices as far as means towards the end is concerned. However, in situations where there are no such choices, there is at least a 'normative orientation' to govern an action (Parsons 1949). Through such actions we get the structures and processes which are always meaningfully intended and implemented in actual concrete situations. While adopting the most appropriate means an actor always pursues a goal negotiating the social environment of such action. Thus, an actor is always bound by a social system.

SYSTEM ANALYSIS

It was later that Parsons shifted more towards a theory of social system and tried to explain how the structure and processes of social systems govern an unit act or the social action. In *The Social System* (1951), Parsons elaborated upon his theory of social action to bring in the notion of the complex of status and role to theoretically construct the idea of social system.

Social system is a theoretical construct which emerges from the process of interaction between plurality of actors in a situation which has at least a physical or an environmental aspect. Actors interact because they are motivated in terms of optimization of gratification. Their relation to each other as well as to their situation is defined and mediated in terms of culturally structured and shared symbols. Further, Parsons elaborated the scheme of structuring a complete system of social action by suggesting that the social system is just one of the three aspects of that:

> [A] social system is only one of three aspects of the structuring of a completely concrete system of social action. The other two are the personality systems of the individual actors and the cultural system which is built into their action. Each of the three must be considered to be an independent focus of the organization of the elements of the action system in the sense that no one of them is theoretically reducible to terms of one or a combination of the other two. Each is indispensable to the other two in the sense that without personalities and culture there would be no social system and so on around the roster of logical possibilities. (Parsons 1951: 5–6)

A system of social action then rests on an interrelationship between the social, cultural and personality system and which is marked by reciprocal support mechanism. A requisite minimum amount of support is being mutually shared so that a system and all of the subsystems strike a point of equilibrium.

Interestingly, Parsons did not put interaction as the basic unit for study in *The Social System*. It is the status–role complex which forms the basic unit. This complex is neither an aspect of actors nor an aspect of interaction but rather it is a structural component of the social system. Status refers to the structural position within a social system and role is what an actor does in that position. Thus, actors are considered a bundle of statuses and roles which are of functional significance for the social system.

A general theory of action Parsons could develop moving away from a voluntaristic theory of action by acknowledging that goal-seeking actors avail choices in terms of selecting their means, but within the constraints of norms, values, ideas as well as situational constraints. A plurality of interactive relationship with one or more members of the society, which a single actor indulges in, cannot be understood without a functional analysis of the interrelatedness affected by the interaction of a plurality of all such actors.

The interrelatedness of the social, cultural and political system is explained by Parsons by meticulously conceptualizing the social system as a result of interactions between oriented actors. Accordingly, actors are oriented to situations in terms of motives and values. Motive means the need and readiness to mobilize energy. While valuation means conceptions about what is appropriate. Interaction pattern is sustained as a result of sharing of the normative order by the oriented actors. Subsequent institutionalization of such patterned interactions is to be conceptualized as a social system. In this grand scheme, Parsons introduces the conceptualization of the cultural system and the personality system. Effectively to realize the social system made up of unit actions one also needs to see motives as a result of the personality system and values as a result of the cultural system. These sub-systems are analytically independent from one another but are interpenetrating and inter-connected. Parsons' functional explanation rests on such a general theory of action which is a composite of the three inter-penetrating systems of social, cultural and personal.

FUNCTIONAL REQUISITES

The notion of *functional requisites* was used by Parsons to understand the systemic features of the social, cultural and personality systems. Integration between and among systems (sub-systems, synonymously) is a basic survival requisite. For the purpose of integration each of the systems must fulfill two basic functional requisites. They are:

i. A sufficient proportion of the actors in each of the systems must adequately be motivated to carry out the expected role as required by the particular system, and
ii. Cultural patterns which fail to provide the minimum normative order to govern the actors or put unrealistic demand on people need to be avoided by a system. This is required to avoid deviance and conflict.

The cultural system is of primary importance as it does not only mediate interaction among actors, it also integrates the personality and the social system. Through the norms and values culture is embodied in the social system and the same is internalized by the actors in the personality system. Culture is therefore an internalized aspect of the personality system. As a patterned ordered system of symbols the cultural system is the major binding force of the various elements of the social world. The symbols are the objects of orientation to actors. Culture is largely symbolic whereby it is readily transmitted from one system to another. And finally, in the social system it provides institutionalized patterns (Ritzer 1996).

Further, 'need-disposition' is thought to be the basic component of the personality system. According to *need-disposition,* actors either accept or reject objects presented in the environment or, they may even seek new ones if those made available are failing to satisfy need-disposition. Such need-dispositions need not be all that innate but are shaped by social setting as well (Parsons 1951).

Parsons' usage of the term 'functional prerequisites' reflects his overriding concern with the maintenance of order within the social system. But by talking about the integration of value patterns and need-dispositions, he brings up the issue of the relationship between actors and social structures. Thus, the processes of socialization and internalization figure prominently in Parsonian sociology. As he said, 'The combination of value-orientation patterns which is acquired [by the actor in socialization] *must in a very important degree be a function of the fundamental role structure and dominant valves of the social system*' (Parsons 1951: 227).

Along with the process of socialization Parsons also advanced the idea of social control as another mechanism of ensuring social order. Only a gentle measure of social control is indicated by him as a supplement to socialization which would allow the social system to maintain its equilibrium. But at the last instance, Parsons was more focused on the system as a whole. It is his structural–functional scheme that explained how the structure of the system acts on and maintains the constitutive actors.

PATTERN VARIABLES

Parsons is regarded as a grand theorist because of his vigorous detailing and meticulous examination of every aspect of social system and its constitution. To account for the variable properties of social systems he developed a set of concepts called pattern-variables. With the help of this set Parsons tried to capture and categorize the modes of orientation in the personality system, the value patterns in the cultural system and the normative requirements in the social system. The five set of pattern variables are placed in a way so as to account for comparisons of values in different cultures at a very general plane. 'The variables are pharased as polar dichotomies, that, depending on the system under analysis, allow a rough categorization of decisions by actors, the value orientations of culture, or the normative demands on status–role' (Turner 2003: 42). The five set of variable properties coined as pattern variables are as follows:

i. **Affectivity and affective neutrality:** This concerns the presence of emotional content in an interactive situation.
ii. **Diffuseness and specificity:** This concerns the spread of the demands and obligations in an interactive situation.
iii. **Universalism and particularism:** This variable denotes whether evaluation and judgment of others in an interactive situation is standardized on the basis of a general norm, or such evaluation is person specific and discreet.
iv. **Achievement and ascription:** This variable deals with the issue of whether an actor is assessed on the basis of performance or on the basis of in born/ascribed statuses.

v. **Collectivity and self-orientation:** This variable deals with the issue of whether an action is motivated by group interest or directed towards self-interest only.

The five variables are called pattern-variables as any action can be placed within the matrix of the five dichotomies and examined universally as belonging to or approximating which type of social action. Deciding upon these universal dichotomies one can then classify a social action, on a larger scale; a social system as such as belonging to pre-modern or modern state of human social living.

FUNCTIONAL IMPERATIVES

As a dynamic theorist, Talcott Parsons kept on qualifying upon his own theories continuously and advancing fresh insights onto the study of society. He, along with Robert Bales and Edward Shils in 1953, co-authored *Working Papers in the Theory of Action*. In this work he proposed the concept of *functional imperatives* and further elaborated the same concept in *Economy and Society* (1956, co-authored with Neil Smelser). Parsons became categorical with four sub-systems of a social system, such as the economic (behavioural organization), political, fiduciary and societal community.

The four functional imperatives are adaptation, goal attainment, integration and latency. It is popularly known as the AGIL scheme of Parsons in sociological literature. Moving beyond his earlier proposition of functional prerequisites, Parsons talks about four sub-systems in a society as performing four distinct functions for the maintenance of the whole system. In fact they are the imperatives for each of the sub-systems without which the stability of the social system would be precarious.

The functional imperatives are:

i. **Adaptation:** This refers to the problem of securing from the environment sufficient resources and distributing them throughout the system. It demands adapting to the environment and its changing conditions. This function is to be performed by the *economic* sub-system.

ii. **Goal attainment:** This refers to establishing priorities among system goals and mobilizing system resources for attaining such goals. This function is accomplished by the *political s*ub-system.

iii. **Integration:** This refers to the crucial aspect of coordinating and regulating the interactions between actors and subsystems within the greater social system. The *societal community* with law as the principal element performs this task as an imperative.

iv. **Latency:** This refers to the functions of tension maintenance and pattern management. This is to be accomplished by the fiduciary system, with schools, family and religion as the principal institutions. Accordingly actors are sufficiently motivated by appropriate socialization to ensure the perusal of a common set of goals and values.

Initially, Parsons was less enthusiastic in his action theory about the behavioural organism, where he mainly focused on the other three — social, cultural and personality system. He simply noted the behavioural system as a source of energy for the rest of the society (Ritzer 1996). But after he had developed the functional imperative scheme of AGIL, he effected the four functional imperatives to operate through the four sub-systems, where along with the social, cultural and personality system, the behavioural organization is also highlighted. Thus, when applied to the four sub-systems, the AGIL scheme attains specific and distinct operational areas. The behavioural organization carries out the role of adaptation in order to survive in the environment. The personality system performs the role of goal-attainment by motivating individuals towards desired goals. The function of integration is accomplished by the social system, while the cultural system ensures that appropriate norms, values and expectations of the society are internalized by the individuals — the function of latency.

In sum, Parsons's functional theory is premised on the fundamental concepts of organic evolution. The concepts which run through his model are that of variation, selection, adaptation, differentiation and finally, integration. He is popularly known as a system analyst. A grand systemic study of society — society conceptualized as a system being constituted by sub-systems, and mutual interdependence between the sub-system with each performing a particular function, is the core of Parsons's model of society. The aspect of coordination and sharing of a common normative order is given primary importance, which rests on as well as relies on the capacity to garner sufficient resources from the environment. An equilibrium model of society is thereby presented in the most detailed way, while it is theoretically quite abstract but provides insights for empirical studies as well.

ROBERT KING MERTON (1910–2003)

As a functionalist, R. K. Merton's credit goes as one who could critique T. Parsons and the orthodox versions of functionalism but still could advance on improved version of functionalism. Instead of opting for an overarching grand theory, he looked out for more empirically grounded theories of functionalism. He suggested that a continued run of the functionalist theory rested on making theory closer to empirical research. Merton was instrumental in enriching functionalism with new ideas and concepts to make it recover the lost prestige, which was due to the system–equilibrium model of the orthodox version.

Robert King Merton came from a humble background of Jewish origin. Born in 1910 to immigrant Jewish parents, he spent his early years in a South Philadelphia slum. From an early age he was attracted towards cultural and intellectual activities. He studied in the Temple University with a scholarship and was introduced to sociology by none other than the translator of Emile Durkheim, George E. Simpson. Interestingly, Merton confessed in his autobiographical work that he chose his intellectual interest from Durkheim's theoretical treatment of varied subjects and the empirical bent of his sociology (Merton 1994). After receiving a fellowship Merton joined Harvard, where he came in touch with both Pitrim Sorokin and Talcott Parsons. Sorokin oriented him with the wide areas of the European social thought, but Merton was impressed with Parsons's great works. He obtained his doctorate from the Harvard in 1936.

In his own admission Merton said that apart from Durkheim it was George Simmel's sociology which inspired him. From the great masters he adopted the spirit of developing sociological theories of social structure and cultural change which would help him to understand the process through which social institutions characterize human society. As against subject specialization he followed the path of studying a variety of sociological subjects. The empiricist Paul F. Lazarsfeld, Merton's colleague inspired him too to see the bearing of empirical research on theoretical constructs (Merton 1994). His basic thrust was to make functionalism a dynamic one with an empirical bent, which was in contrast with Parson's abstract theories.

CRITIQUE OF ORTHODOX FUNCTIONALISM

The non-empirical propositions based on abstract, theoretical systems, according to Merton, had led to assumptions that all systems have needs and requisites that must be met and that certain structures are indispensable in meeting these ends. That was the tradition of functional theorizing mainly influenced by the anthropological tradition as well as by Talcott Parsons' theory of social system. In order to modify and qualify the functionalist heritage Merton pointed out that the orthodox version rested on three postulates which need to be reassessed (Merton 1949).

The three postulates are as follows:

i. **Functional unity of society:** It holds that all standardized social activities or cultural items are functional for the entire society and cultural systems. Merton said that this may hold good for primitive societies which were small in size and least complex but cannot be held to be true for all societies. Such high level of integration can only be an empirical variable. Such an image of society as perfectly integrated and homogenous actually works on a naïve assumption that all elements in a society are 'good' for the whole and work towards harmony of the society. By introducing the term 'dysfunction' Merton instead postulated that, some parts/elements of a society may not have such a positive function for the whole as such. The concept of dysfunction, Merton said, 'which implies the concept of strain, stress and tension on the structural level, provides an analytical approach to the study of dynamics and change' (Merton 1949: 53).

ii. **Universal functionalism:** It holds that all standardized social and cultural forms and structures only fulfill positive functions. In fact this follows from the first postulate, i.e., there are no dispensable elements in a social arrangement. This is almost an anthropological fundamentalism, which justifies every element of a culture just in terms of its existence. Merton opined that such a situation may contradict empirical reality. It is premature and a prior assumption that each and every item or part is functional for the whole, as there may be items which are having non-functional consequences for the society and as such irrelevant.

iii. **Indispensability:** It holds an extreme position that all standardized social and cultural items are indispensable and necessary conditions for the social whole; that the equilibrium stable state of a society cannot be attained without each of these elements. Such an image of society tantamount to suggest that except the given there cannot be any alternatives. Merton critiqued this postulate to indicate that there could be functional alternatives, which he termed as *functional equivalents* in a society. These modifications are a must to admit that there are variations in a society and such variability of its institutions could only enthuse detailed empirical study of a society. In fact this variability is the promise of an enriched study of a society and that of the subject matter as well.

THEORIES OF THE MIDDLE RANGE

Neither abstract theorization nor crude empiricism could serve the purpose of sociological study. Merton treaded a middle path, suggesting 'theories of the middle range'. He asserted that, functional theory must work with a limited set of assumptions. From such limited assumptions only specific hypotheses need to be developed and subsequently put to empirical testing. This could be accomplished by acknowledging the bearing of theory on research and vice-versa.

> Middle-range theory is principally used in sociology to guide empirical inquiry. It is intermediate to general theories of social systems which are too remote from particular classes of social behaviour, organization and change to account for what is observed and to those detailed orderly descriptions of particulars that are not generalized at all. Middle range theory involves abstractions, of course, but they are close enough to observed data to be incorporated in propositions that permit empirical testing. Middle-range theories deal with delimited aspects of social phenomena, as is indicated by their labels. One speaks of a theory of reference groups, of social mobility, or role-conflict and of the formation of social norms just as one speaks of a theory of prices, a germ theory of disease, or a kinetic theory of gases. (Merton 1949: 39)

Illustrating with the theory of role-set Merton showed that broad theoretical orientation of great classicists, be it Marx, Sorokin or Parsons, cannot adequately account for such. For him systems of sociological thought, although, are projected as logically close-knit and mutually exclusive sets of doctrine but comprehensive sociological theories are actually sufficiently loose-knit and internally diversified. Only middle-range theories with a measure of empirical confirmation are better suited as comprehensive theories.

In order to drive his point home, Merton makes a distinction between *role-set* and 'multiple roles'. Traditionally, 'multiple roles' referred to the various social statuses, could be even in different institutional spheres, in which individuals find themselves. It could not recognize the complex of roles which could be associated with a single social status. But role-set as a component of a social structure leads one to infer that individuals with adequate social regularity perform the components of countless role-sets through multiple social structures. To begin with, role-set theory implies that a single social status gives rise to a single associated role, but it implies an array of roles. Without being restrained by extreme conflicts in their role-sets, individuals perform the functional task of managing such situations. This qualified understanding of role-set occasions new studies of discovering and identifying the social mechanisms which facilitate such an array of roles to be performed. According to Merton, only empirical studies could account for the social processes which have designated consequences for designated parts of social structure. In a nutshell, sociological theories of the middle range explain elements of social structure. This is in contrast to the grand theories which are successful in providing only concrete historical descriptions of particular social systems.

AN ALTERNATIVE PARADIGM FOR FUNCTIONAL ANALYSIS

In order to correct the static orthodox version of functionalism Merton attempted to codify functional analysis in sociology all through. He promoted a new paradigm of relevant concepts and problems as an alternative approach. The different aspects of this alternative and qualified paradigm are as follows:

i. The object of analysis for a functionalist theorist must represent a standardized item, such as social roles, institutional patterns, social processes, social norms, group organization etc., i.e., only patterned and recurrent items of a society need to be imputed with the notion of function
ii. The conception of the motives or purposes of individuals involved in a social system, i.e., the subjective dispositions of the individuals must gain the attention of a functional analyst, at some point or the other, of the research, and
iii. The obvious confusion between subjective dispositions and objective consequences must be eradicated with a proper understanding of the term *function*. For Merton, function is not the same thing as purpose or motivation; rather functions are defined as, 'those observed consequences which make for the adaptation or adjustment of a given system' (Merton 1949: 105).

 To resolve this confusion between the subjective dispositions and objective consequences of an item Merton introduced the concepts of *manifest* and *latent* functions. In simple terms, manifest functions are those that are intended, whereas latent functions refer to the ones which are unintended. This distinction addresses the problem of distinguishing between the cases in which the subjective aim-in-view coincides with the objective consequence, and the cases in which they diverge. Such an analytical distinction is related to Merton's contention of unanticipated consequences. One may do things which are aimed at some goal but end up achieving something else. For a sociologist studying the intended consequences are far easy, but the challenge is more in identifying those which are unintended and where mostly the actors are unaware of it.

Latent function is one type of unanticipated function which is functional for the society. But there are other two types of unanticipated functions — one that is dysfunctional, i.e., damaging for the social structure, and the other being one which is irrelevant or non-functional for the designated system.

iv. Given the understandings of variability of function it is required for functional analysis to consider a range of units for which an item has designated consequences. This is so, as same items may be functional for some individuals and sub-groups and dysfunctional for others.

v. Often *ex post facto* functional requirements are understood by functionalists. To avoid such tautological analysis one must establish types of functional requirements (universal or specific) and procedures for validating the assumptions of these requirements.

vi. One must attend to concrete and detailed accounts of the mechanisms which operate to perform a designated function, i.e., functions are fulfilled through social and not psychological mechanisms. Thus, such mechanisms like rituals, division of social labour or role-segmentation etc., need to be studied.

vii. Variability of social structures is to be recognized. As such the functional indispensability is to be dismissed in favour of functional alternatives or substitutes.

viii. However, the range of variation of social structure is not without bound. Items fulfill designated functions variously but within the structural context. The integration of the parts or the interdependence of the elements of a social structure limits the variation. Therefore, the effective possibility of change is bound by the structure.

ix. The very concept of dysfunction points to the areas of stress, strain and tension on the structural level. The orthodox functional focus on the static unchanging character needs to be abandoned in favour of an analytical approach which appreciates the examination of dynamics and change in a society.

x. A functional analysis must be ready with a rigorous statement of the sociological procedures of analysis which should be amenable to the logic of experimentation. One needs to validate functional analysis, which can be done through systematic reviews of the possibilities and limitations of comparative study.

xi. From the sociology of knowledge perspective, functional analysis must be aware and sensitive to the issue of ideological implications of a study. Intrinsically functional analysis is value-free; nevertheless, particular analyses or hypotheses may have an identifiable, ideological role, where such a possibility needs to be accounted for, if one is interested to accomplish the alternative paradigm for functional analysis.

The paradigm offers a provisional guide, a codified manual for engaging in functional analysis. It raises functionalism to a new height of acceptance, at least a new lease of life for functionalism. Merton anticipated the stiff criticism that Parsonian functionalism would invite, and thus, he developed an improved version of that. Possibly, the greatest contribution of Merton goes in his attempt to make functionalism dynamic by stripping it from abstract rationalistic approach to a more empirical-based perspective. Thus, the close association between theory and research gets a thorough methodological treatment from Merton's use of functionalism. Prior to Merton structural functionalists were interested in analysing functions of one social structure or institution for another. But he made the analysis more empirically grounded by focusing on groups, organizations, societies and cultures.

SUMMARY

Since its coming during the 1940s, functionalism has been the centre of major sociological attention. It emerged as the most dominant sociological theory, especially in the United States, in the 1950s and 1960s. Subsequently, it declined mainly due to its obsession with stability and value consensus model of society. Talcott Parsons led the way to develop a view of society which rested on the principle of a shared normative order. Merton's intervention definitely extended the life of functionalism, with the introduction of some valid new concepts. However the perspective remained focused on system equilibrium. Society and systems do comprise interdependent parts, but the issues of structural change and conflict remained unattended in this perspective.

KEY WORDS

- *Action Theory*
- *Dynamic Functionalism*
- *Functionalism*
- *Funtional Imperatives*
- *Pattern Variables*
- *Social System*
- *Value Consensus*

GLOSSARY

Action Theory: Recognizing motives as part of human actions, it tries to explain ends, purposes and ideals when looking at actions.

Functionalism: A broad perspective in Sociology which holds society as constituted of interrelated parts, and each part contributing to the maintenance of the whole.

Latent Function: That which is neither recognized nor intended. A latent function of a behaviour is not explicitly stated, recognized or intended by the people involved.

Manifest Function: In functional sociology, any function of an actor, institution or other social phenomenon that is planned and intentional.

Middle Range Theory: Theory which attempts to integrate theory and empirical research.

Pattern Variables: Five dichotomies to show the contrasting values to which individuals orient themselves in social interaction. One side of the dichotomies reflects the value patterns dominant in traditional society, the other reflects the dominant values of modern society.

Social System: Undestanding society as an interrelated structure constituted of social action, and which is marked of from ecological, biological, psychical and technical systems.

Discussion Points

- Theoretical influences on Functional Theory.
- Parsons's System Analysis.
- Critique of Orthodox Functionalism.
- Merton's Middle-range Theory.

7

Conflict Theory

The emergence of conflict theory in sociology, in a way, was in reaction to structural functionalism. The dominance of the functional theories during the 1950s and 1960s created an image of society which is stable and integrated. Any challenge to an existing order was viewed as an aberration or deviance. Value consensus was considered as the cornerstone of society, and hence, conflict used to be discarded as originating outside the social system. As against such a conservative bias in functional theories, many sociologists alternatively focused on the concept of power and distribution of power in social structure. Conflict theories emerged as a counter to the consensual view of society proposed by the functional theorists. The systemic exercise of power, the structural causation of conflict and inequality were the areas of new focus in sociological theories. Conflict theories basically emerged with these areas as the core concern. The growing unrest in socio-political world and a disenchantment with conservative position made conflict theory popular in the 1970s. But the groundwork was done much earlier. In fact, the roots of a conflict view of society can be traced back to the works of classical thinkers like Karl Marx, Max Weber and Georg Simmel.

KARL MARX

Marxian theory of society could be acknowledged as the timeless theory that would fuel any kind of conflict or critical approach to society. The cornerstone of Marx's theory was his attempt to make theory an accomplice in changing the world. As his famous phrase goes, *philosophers have hitherto interpreted the world, the task however is to change it*. Obviously, the concept of change is integral to Marx's analysis of society. And, for all conflict theorists of later years change is the key notion.

Using the materialist method of analysing the various stages of society, Marx primarily showed how contradictions are inherent in human social structure; that, such contradictions are systemic and are a result of the way a mode of production is organized in a society. He further showed the dialectical nature of the contradiction. To diagnose the root cause of the contradiction one needs to disentangle the production system and the relation of production in any society as such production is the primary life giving and sustaining force in all human societies.

Methodologically, Marx was thorough with his application of the dialectical-materialist method. He showed that history is not an automatic creation of great kings or any supernatural power or any mystical forces, but a result of creative human labour. Again, men make history not just as they please, but under certain constraints and situations given to them. Yet, human beings have the great creativity to effect change by altering the course of history. He showed how actually the human history has changed from a stage of primitive communism to ancient society, then to feudal society and finally to the capitalist one. The role of division of labour and the appropriation of the means of production played a major part in this course of history. The division of society along class lines and the emergence of private property are all attributed to the fundamental mode of production of any society. Class struggle is conceptualized as the motive force of any society. The class analysis of society recognizes that the interests of one class at any given time coincide with the development of the productive forces and their impulse towards new social structures. Ruling classes defend the established and the traditional because these correspond to their interests. Finally, the notion of two fundamentally opposing classes representing distinctively opposite interests is advanced. It ends with the conviction that the proletariat is the last of the classes and that its liberation demands the abolition of all classes for a classless society (Marx 1932[1848]).

Another dimension of Marx's theory that impressed the conflict theorists is that of the conditions of advanced division of labour which alienate human beings from their species — nature. Labour for Marx is a collective creative activity but as long as its differentiation leads to the enrichment of the few and poverty for the majority, it is dehumanizing. In its historical development labour then becomes the negation of its own principle. The condition reaches its peak under capitalist mode of production, where the actual social nature of production stands in direct conflict with the private nature of appropriation. This denies the producers any control over the movement of their products and subjects them to the autonomous power of the products. This confusion and transposition of human being's nature is historically conditioned and therefore, can for that reason be overcome (Marx 1844/1964). Such a dialectical and historical approach of Marx promises an understanding of the unified structure of reality in terms of an intricate relationship between the material and ideal/cultural factors. The centrality accorded to class conflict in this model survived time to provide the elementary premise of all conflict theories.

MAX WEBER

Max Weber expanded the understanding of social class by expanding its scope to include the entire life opportunities that individuals enjoy in a given society, i.e., social status or prestige as well as political influence is important constituents of a social class. Unlike Marx, Weber's sociology allows an understanding that irrespective of whether one is possessing economic power or not, one can still be empowered by social status and prestige. The very concept of power is central in Max Weber's sociological thought. Every human interaction is marked by power relationship and human society is a web of power relationship.

Every human interaction is a relationship of command and obedience and power is conceptualized as the capability of one to exercise such command over the other. Weber developed his notion of authority as a legitimate use of power. Weberian sociology provides an image of society where authority is a universal element of social structure. By implication it suggests that a society is made possible because of such functional role of authority. In his analytical discussion on the types of authority and sources of legitimacy, Weber exemplified how the interests of the ruling group work toward the maintenance of the existing order. This is so because the interests of the dominant group are the values that justify the exercise of the specific rule giving it the necessary legitimacy. As long as the dominated subordinates conform to the same values, the legitimacy of the rule is assured and in situations of defiance conflict is inevitable. The source of change is located at this question of conforming or defying an existing legitimate order. 'According to the kind of legitimacy which is claimed, the type of obedience, the kind of administrative staff developed to guarantee it, all the mode of exercising authority, will all differ fundamentally' (Weber 1978: 213).

Conflict theories gained crucial inputs from Weber's treatment of power as an essential ingredient of social relationships. Further, the wider social base of power as theorized by Weber influenced conflict theorists to move beyond the Marxian frame of analysis of conflict — that, any social order is built upon an exercise of power which is coercive, actual or otherwise, remained a running thread in all the works of conflict theorists.

GEORGE SIMMEL

Apart from the classical theories of Marx and Weber, Georg Simmel's sociological writings had a tremendous impact upon conflict theories. Simmel (1958–18) shared the same historical time and space with his fellow German classical thinker Max Weber as well as Emile Durkheim. Yet despite his seminal contribution to dialectical thinking on society he received less attention in the world of sociology. Although his works were in league with the other three great thinkers Marx, Durkheim and Weber, Simmel was eclipsed by the three. Possibly it was due to the fact that Simmel did not hold any regular academic position in sociology, neither did he write as much academically as the others. His incisive writings were mostly directed at a wider audience (Ritzer, 1983: 141–62). However, he had a remarkable influence on early American sociologists as a micro-sociologist.

Simmel's theory created an image of society which is three-tiered, where the higher levels emerge from the lower levels. These three levels of society provide three distinct areas of study for sociology. At the basic level he suggested the operation of 'pure' sociology, or formal sociology. At this level the psychological components of social life are to be accounted for through microscopic assumptions. Next emerges the scope for 'general' sociology which is the area for the study of the social and cultural products of human history. 'Philosophical' sociology which deals with the epistemological and metaphysical aspects of society constitutes the highest level.

With his focus on microscopic assumptions about human interactions, Simmel put much attention on the 'lowest level', i.e., the formal level, where he studied the societal forms of subordination, super ordination exchange and sociability. The task of sociology primarily is to explicate the forms of interaction of individuals, as society is made up of such interactions. Interaction is a matter of reciprocal human relationships. Simmel was interested in both sociation and forms. This becomes clear from his method to abstract the societal forms out of the diverse interaction of individuals. The diverse situations are marked by competition and subordination. He wrote:

> It proceeds like grammar, which isolates the pure forms of language from their contents through which these forms, nevertheless, come to life. In a comparable manner, social groups which are the most diverse imaginable in purpose and general significance, may nevertheless show identical forms of behavior toward one another on the part of their individual members. We find superiority and subordination, competition, division of labor, formation of parties, representation, inner solidarity coupled with exclusiveness toward the outside, and innumerable similar features in the state, in a religious community, in a band of conspirators, in an economic association, in an art school, in the family. However diverse the interests are that give rise to these sociations, the forms in which the interests are realized may yet be identical. (Wolff 1959: 22)

By indicating that the three basic levels of social reality are interrelated Simmel advanced a dialectical approach. This dialectical thinking is multi-causal and multi-directional in the sense that he asserted that there are no strict divisions between social phenomena. Like Marx, Simmel, too, viewed society as held together by conflicting groups, but his view of the future is not so positive like Marx. Rather the image of society he foresaw was quite close to that of Max Weber — that is, one moves towards an 'iron cage', a shackling condition.

The sociation, critical for the continuance of social life is the reciprocal relationship between the superior and the subordinate. However, domination is not always unilateral. Mostly submission is also passive but an active group condition. These insights from Simmel greatly impacted upon conflict theorization of the later decades. Also, as Simmel moved from the lower level of social reality to the higher level, he showed in his analysis that the emergent large-scale structures tend to become separate from the constituent individuals and can even dominate them. This is the source of conflict and contradiction between the individual and all larger society. In fact, a deep conflict may arise between individual culture and the cultural level of social reality, i.e., the 'objective culture' according to Simmel.

By inter-relating the cultural and individual levels Simmel used his micro-sociology to offer a conflict view of society. While his view gained attention in the American sociological world for some time, his lasting contribution was mainly in the subsequent development of conflict theories of society. The two German-born sociologists, Lewis Coser and Ralf Dahrendorf were the leading conflict theorists of the 1950s, while C. Wright Mills was the most prolific American sociologist to dominate world sociology.

LEWIS COSER (1913–2003)

At a time when functional theories held sway in American university departments of sociology, Lewis Coser emerged as one who looked at the unity of society entirely from a different angle. When conflict was seen as a destabilizing aspect of any social order, Coser introduced the idea of functional role of conflict in ensuring social order. Interestingly, he theorized on the role of conflict in society to solidify a loosely structured social group. Against totalizing tendencies of institutions he opted for a less integrated model of society.

Born in Berlin, Germany, in 1913, Lewis Coser had a typical life emerged in the American sociology as a name to reckon with. Hailing from a Jewish family he earned the wrath of the Nazi regime due to his socialist leanings. He had to leave for Paris after his schooling and had to struggle hard to pursue academics during the years of depression. He could enroll himself at the prestigious Sorbonne University with a scholarship.

At the Sorbonne, Coser had interesting shifts from studying literature to the study of social theory. Initially it was only the sociology of Emile Durkheim with whom he was acquainted with. The other exposure was to the classic works of Karl Marx. But he shunned Marxist orthodoxy and in his own words was an 'unorthodox Marxist with strong admixtures of Durkheimian thought' (Coser 1993: 3).

Coser finally was destined for America as he could leave France and found ground as an antifascist refugee. He got himself enrolled at Columbia University to study sociology in 1948. At Columbia he met Robert Merton who from then onwards remained as Coser's greatest influence. In 1954, he received his doctorate degree from Columbia.

Coser taught at various departments. Even before his doctorate, he taught at the University of Chicago. He then taught at Brandeis University before moving to the State University of New York at Stony Brook. After his retirement, he continued at the Stony Brook as an emeritus professor. He was also an adjunct professor of sociology at Boston College. Always in favour of an open society, Coser treaded a non-conventional path in academics. He, along with Irving Hose, co-founded the magazine Dissent in 1954.

The objective of the magazine was to arouse and inspire intellectuals against the McCarthyist intolerance. He contributed to a wide range of journals with academic as well as not-so-academic writings and consistently promoted the idea of freedom from any totalizing regimes or power structures.

SOCIAL AND INTELLECTUAL INFLUENCES

It is quite obvious from his life history that Coser learnt the effect of conflict first hand. Born in Germany, he experienced the tyranny of the Nazi regime. Being a Jew he had to escape his homeland. Thus, the turbulent years of his growing up and the intolerance of the powerful had their imprints on Coser's subsequent academic interest.

Initially, Durkheim's functional view of society as a system of variously interrelated parts attracted Coser while he was in Sorbonne, Paris. It was here that, he learnt from Durkheim's great works that imbalances, tensions and conflict are integral to any social system, and that the different constituent parts of a society function under different conditions. Similarly, George Simmel's detailing of conflict at different levels of social reality and the notion of cross-cutting allegiances was used by Coser to seek the possibility that even antagonisms can also bind society together. At the same time Coser took interest in Marx's social theory but not in an orthodox way. He tried to combine all these great classicists' works and develop a theory of conflict in terms of its intensity, duration and functions.

Coser was also impacted upon by his contemporaries like Talcott Parsons and Robert Merton. In fact Merton was his supervisor only at the Columbia University. Merton shared a very intimate relationship with him and was the man who inspired him to complete the great work *Masters of Sociological Thought* (1977), which stands as a brilliant review of social theory. Although Coser was strongly against Talcott Parson's model of equilibrium for all society, he held him in high regard. Finally, Coser credited his wife Rose Laub Coser for clarifying and formulating many of his own thoughts. In fact, Rose Laub herself was a graduate student of sociology at the Columbia University and she introduced Coser to Robert Merton.

FUNCTIONAL-CONFLICT THEORY

The Functions of Social Contract (1956) is Coser's seminal work on functional-conflict theory. Simmel's treatment of contradictions as crucial dimension of social reality was adopted by Coser in his work. In this fundamental work on functional-conflict theory, Coser advanced 16 distinct propositions to substantiate his theory that conflict promotes cohesion. The Durkheimian understanding of the role of crime in stimulating a dramatic display of social solidarity appears to have been in the back of Coser's mind in such a formulation. Basically, he reformulated the idea of conflict which was present in the classical sociological theories by defining conflict as 'a struggle over values and claims to scarce status, power and resources in which the aims of the opponents are to neutralize, injure or eliminate their rivals' (Coser 1956: 8). In his scheme conflict is multidimensional, as it could be between individuals, between individuals and collectivities, and also between groups of individuals. The nature of relationship between the incumbents decides the exercise of power of one over the other to influence the behaviour in accordance with one's wishes.

Coser was close to Marx's theory of 'being decides consciousness' and attempted to explain how structural factors interact with people's underlying emotions. The role of values and emotions in generating conflict was crucial for Coser to analyse conflict in order to understand the nature, source and degree of conflict.

> The revolutionary and activist Marxism first developed by Marx and Engels in the late 1840s found an echo among 20th century intellectuals.... Social existence determined social consciousness. The receptivity to variant Marxist doctrine was largely conditioned by the values and attitudes of men and women whose concrete social and historical existence was mirrored in their World view, whether as producers or as consumers of ideas. (Coser 1972: 200)

Moving beyond Marx, Coser indicated a wide range of factors which decide the nature of conflict, from those located at the emotional level of the family to the social structural factors. He was close to Simmel to reason that it is due to close contact between individuals that opportunities for hostility increases, as love and hate are the twin impulses in human nature. The closer the proximity the greater is the chance of conflict. He further suggested that, the root cause of all conflict is scarce resources — material as well as non-material. Conflict emerges as and when a deprived group starts questioning the legitimacy of an existing pattern of such distribution. More than absolute deprivation it is the relative deprivation between groups that triggers open conflict.

With the help of sixteen postulates in his *The Functions of Social Conflict*, Coser deliberated upon the exact nature of functions as performed by conflict. Conflict essentially binds people at the group level which is occasioned by a group's awareness of its differences with others. Conflict with others strengthens group consciousness and realization of its exclusivity — which result in stronger bondage within a group. The intensity of conflict is directly proportional to the intensity of group solidarity. Thus, in close social relationships, there is a greater possibility of hostility. However, close and intimate relationships have a tendency to contain and suppress conflict. Despite such suppression if conflict still breaks out then it attains a disruptive character. This is also aggravated by an accumulation of hostility. At the last instance, it is the inter-group conflict that fosters among individual group members to close their ranks. Loyalty and dedication to the group identity is enhanced as a result. Thus, in contrary to orthodox functional theory of dismissing conflict as damaging, Coser indicated that at different levels of social reality, the in-group and out-group feelings are actually strengthened by actual or threat of hostility.

BEYOND ORGANISMIC ANALOGY

Coser's contention of understanding conflict in social structure as functional for the continuance of the whole also carries with it the prospects of social change. He accomplished this by theorizing beyond the organismic analogy that governs orthodox functional theories of society. Society, unlike living organism does not die, neither does it has a starting point. Rather it continues to exist through continuous changes of its form.

Coser made a distinction between *change within a system* and *change of a system*. He put more emphasis on change of a system because change within is just a process of adjustment internal to an existing social structure. It is gradual and slow. It is mainly confined to individual efforts and as such it offers no institutional change. Whereas, change of the system is radical as it involves a break from an existing system in favour of new institutions. With a change in norms and expectations the system designated undergoes an actual change. The sources of such a change of the system may be external to the system as well as internal to the same. Such a process of change is intrinsic to any social structure and is indefinite. Thus, sociology needs to be alert to this aspect of social reality instead of remaining confined to the areas of regularity and patterns of social behaviour. Such patterns may be the visible dominant fact of society but a conflict approach must analyse why such a pattern of behaviour is dominant. Inevitably such alertness would direct one to the aspects of social reality which are being dominated upon. The subject of conflict and change are crucial areas of investigation, which need not only stand for disruption or disorder, but allows still better cohesion and are functional for a society,

C. WRIGHT MILLS (1916–62)

At a time when American sociology was under the grip and awe of the towering presence of Talcott Parsons, C. Wright Mills made a radical intervention in the academic and intellectual world in general. He went about to demystify the liberal democratic image of the US polity as such and critiqued the status-quoist sociology of Parsons. The system analysis school premised on vigorous functionalist concepts was questioned by Mills severely. Although he was not an orthodox Marxist he kept alive the Marxist tradition in American sociology almost single-handedly.

Born in 1916 in Waco, Texas, C. Wright Mills came from a conventional middle-class family. He obtained his graduation degree from the University of Texas by 1939. He left Texas to pursue his doctoral degree from the University of Wisconsin and even before his doctorate degree he taught for a while at the University of Maryland. After his doctorate he joined the Columbia University in 1945 continuing there until his death in 1962.

Mills was a radical for his days and contributed regularly for many left-wing publications. The world of sociology is indebted to Mills primarily because of his two works, *The Power Elite* (1956) and *The Sociological Imagination* (1959). His other works are *New Men of Power* (1948), *White Collar* (1951), *The Causes of World War Three* (1958) and *The Marxists* (1962). Although Mills had a critical look at the world around him and in fact, within the academic circles also he used to be fiercely combative challenging even his professors time to time. Although in his later years he was impressed with Marx's writings he never adopted a rigid position and did not hesitate even to take on the Soviet on the question of freedom and censorship even when he was honoured by the Soviet as a major critic of American democracy. He died early and led a tumultuous life of just 45 years. It was through him that radical sociology made an inroad into world sociology.

SOCIAL AND INTELLECTUAL INFLUENCE

Mills had a short but colourful career as a sociologist. Primarily he exhibited a combative character in challenging every dominant views and norms of American society. Many commentators on Mills have noted his out of the way attitude towards even his teachers and colleagues. As such he was greatly annoyed by the facade of liberalism that marked the American academic world. Possibly his rebel self was a reaction to the conservative climate of his time. He carried the tag of a Texas Cowboy throughout his career.

In reality Mills was a product of a time in American intellectual and social life which was marked by almost enforced conformity. Many academicians as well as intellectuals opted for a safer position and avoided criticism which would have earned the wrath of the government. Thus, Mills was occupying a very marginal position and opposed the policy of keeping silent severely. At the risk of being branded as subvert or a communist he did not soften his stand.

It is not that Mills was trained in Marxist social theories from the beginning. Only at a later stage, around 1950s he read a few of Marx's writings which were available in English. As such his works were not guided by any sophisticated Marxian theory. Overall, he was committed to the historical method, which one can claim as the influence of Marx on him. Primarily Mills' sociology grew out of a severe criticism of the then trend of sociology in the United States as well as that of the American society. The positivist thinking in sociology he strongly opposed and he took on Talcott Parsons grand functional analysis of society. The system analysis he thought was a de facto justification of the existing social order. On one hand he criticized the abstract theories and on the other he opposed the crude empiricism of his colleague Paul Lazarsfeld of Columbia. Lazarsfeld was a leading empirical researcher, but Mills felt that such indiscriminate data collection cannot really explain society and its historical structures with a sound theory. In a way, Mills's understanding of social reality was close to Weber's analysis, which made a broader examination of the issue of inequality and power.

POWER

The concept of power is of critical importance in C. Wright Mills's sociology. In his very first major work, *The New Men of Power* (1948), he offered an understanding of the working class which was quite contrary to classical Marxist proposition. By focusing on the concept of political power he showed that in actuality the working class is denied of such power. They can only address to their day-to-day issues but cannot emerge as a revolutionary class. He blamed it mostly on the role of the trade union leaders who he thought were unable to work towards the best interests of the workers. Instead they were co-opted by the business class, who actually wield the power.

Subsequent to this quite pessimistic view of the possibility of militant working class movement, Mills engaged himself more with closer scrutiny of the concept of power. He examined all the different aspects of power — right from the nature of power to the myths and irrationality of power. An encompassing understanding of power was thus mooted by him:

> Power has to do with whatever decisions men make about the arrangements under which they live, and about the events which make up the history of their homes. Events that are beyond human decisions do happen; social arrangements do change without the benefit of explicit decision. But in so far as such decisions are made, the problem of who is involved in making them is the basic problem of power. (Mills 1958: 29)

The liberal polity of the United States was always under scrutiny, as Mills thought that the legitimacy generated is essentially a manipulated one. The liberal democracy gives only an impression of consent-oriented but in actuality the powerful groups attain such consent through acts of manipulation. He moved beyond Weber's notion of authority as power backed by legitimacy to indicate the operation of two other types of power. One is done through *manipulation*, while the other is the extreme form of *coercion*. Given the institutionalization of power in the American polity, as understood by Mills, there is hardly any possibility for the general masses to have an access over power and take part in any effective decision-making process.

The central theme of Mills' most powerful book, *The Power Elite* (1956), was that the polity of the United States is basically governed by a unique integration and cooperation between the industrial, political and military structures. These three institutional structures are almost rolled into one in terms of interests. Those who occupy the highest positions in these three structures form a clique; they are interchangeable and it is this group who actually form the power elite. Thus, it is a combined group of military elite, business elite and political elite. It is a sort of tripartite elite. He heavily substantiated this analysis by drawing upon events from the concurrent American socio-political history.

> The power elite composed of men whose positions enable them to transcend the ordinary environments of ordinary men and women; they are in positions to make decisions having major consequences. Whether they do or do not make such decisions is less important than the fact that they do occupy such pivotal positions: their failure to act, their failure to make decisions, is itself an act

> that is often of greater consequence than the decisions they do make. For they are in command of the major hierarchies and organization of modern society. ... They occupy the strategic command posts of the social structure, in which are now centered the effective means of the power and the wealth and the celebrity which they enjoy. (Mills 1956: 3–4)

The unity of the members of the power elite group is accounted for by Mills as having similar socio-economic background. They share similar tastes, lifestyles and goals as they come from similar back grounds; their commonality facilitates smooth and easy intermixing and interchangeability of the elite posts between the three powerful groups. Those who are placed immediately below the power elites are the advisers, opinion makers or the spokespersons. They assist the power elites in maintaining the status quo. The status quo is in the best interests of the powerful. The result is the dispossession of power from the common citizens. The potential for conflict is rooted at this asymmetry of power.

Mills did not contend that the rise of a new middle class would in reality be a challenge to the power elites. The new middle class comprised mostly of service personnel, civil servants, technicians, managers and low level supervisors. They are the white collar workers who essentially cater to the power elites as they enjoy some advantageous positions in the society. Also, the top occupants of the white collar jobs are none other than the old captains of industries. Principally, with the increase in professional specialization the white collar sections enlarge in size but such specialization actually make individuals more concerned with personal needs than collective. As such, Mills saw no collective revolt against the powerful capitalist rule in the American polity.

INTELLECTUAL CRAFTSMANSHIP

Finally, Mills proposed a radical view of conducting sociological studies. In his *The Sociological Imagination (*1959), he imagined a sociologist as an intellectual craftsman. In order to develop a critical view of society methodologically one needs to free oneself from the conservative hold of positivism as the method of sociological study. Principally, Mills directed his attack on Parson's abstract theoretical schemes which used concepts far removed from ground reality. Such system analysis only justified a conservative society. Mills dismissed such status-quoist sociology. Again, he was equally skeptical about the other extreme which was represented by Paul Lazarsfeld. The disparate collection of data based on techniques of questionnaire and interview could not account for sound theories of society which can take account of its historically evolved structures. A sociologist needs to be aware of the historical social context in which one is conducting a study and its interface with one's own personal biography. Such a reflective mode of research is the promise of conflict theory. Conflict theories of society can only be advanced with sociological imagination.

> The sociological imagination enables its possessor to understand the larger historical scene in terms of its meanings for the inner life and the external career of a variety of individuals. It enables him to take into account how individuals, in the welter of their daily experience, often become falsely conscious of their social positions. Within that welter, the framework of modern society is sought and within that framework the psychologies of a variety of men and women are formulated. By such means the personal uneasiness of individuals is focused upon explicit troubles and the indifference of publics is transformed into involvement with public. (Mills, 1959: 5)

RALPH DAHRENDORF

As a conflict theorist, Ralph Dahrendort is unique to propose that a society has both the aspects of consensus as well as conflict. He is also clear in his understanding that no single sociological theory can encompass both these aspects and processes of a society. Thus, there is a requirement for types of sociological theories. This is premised on his thinking that there cannot be conflict unless some degree of consensus has already emerged in a society.

Prior to the emergence of the Nazi rule in Germany, Dahrendort was born in Hamburg in 1929. He had to pass through the strife-torn period in Germany as his father was a Social Democratic politician. His father lost his job and was even arrested once the Nazis came to power is 1933. Daherendorf was himself hounded by the Nazis because of his political activism being directed against the Nazi rule. He was arrested too and sent to concentration camp. However, he escaped in 1945 with the intervention of the Russian force.

Dahrendorf has two doctorate degrees to his credit. He earned his doctorate in philosophy in the year 1952 from Hamburg. Later on he earned his doctorate in sociology from the London School of Economics. He served the position of director of the London School of Economics from 1974 to 1984. Widely respected for his thorough sociological arguments, he held academic positions not only in Europe, but also in the United States.

Initially, Dahrendorf was influenced by structural functionalism and admitted to the fact that a social system is held together by voluntary cooperation or a shared normative order, or both. Subsequently, Marx and Simmel's writings prompted him to recognize the other face of society, i.e., society being held together as a result of 'enforced constraint'. While adopting the conflict perspective he believed that tension is constant in society because the order of society is a result of coercion. Given the social milieu of his early life and the dramatic socio-political changes in Germany — the rise and the fall of the Nazis — he was enthusiastic about the prospects of change in society. This is infused in his sociological theory of conflict which entertains the possibility of radical change of society at any given point of time. However, he was not the theorist to consider the economic structures of society as the sole determinant of conflict. In this sense he was not a naïve Marxist to opt for any reductionist theory.

AGAINST THE EQUILIBRIUM MODEL

Dahrendorf strongly felt that the dominant theoretical approaches in sociology during the 1960s tried to analyse the social structure in terms of elements characteristic of immobile societies. The result is a utopian image of society. He equated the equilibrium model of society with the moral and metaphysical view that would be found in Plato's Republic. According to the Republic, justice means that everybody does what is proper for him to do. On the other hand, the equilibrium model holds that every member of the society plays his role towards a common goal. Both the views converge to project the image of an ideal and perfect society. Such a perfect society according to Dahrendorf is a utopia as neither it explains familial reality nor has grown out of such reality (Dahrendorf 1968).

Daharendorf held structural functional theory utopian not because some of the assumptions it makes are unrealistic but because it is exclusively concerned with spelling out the conditions of the functioning of a utopian social system. It is clearly in contradiction with empirical evidence that, society is held together as a result of value consensus. It is hard to see how a social system based on universal consensus could explain structurally generated conflicts.

Instead, Dahrendorf opined that all units of social organization are continuously changing unless some force intervenes to arrest this change. Thus, while adopting a conflict perspective one must identify the factors that interfere with the normal process of change, rather than to look for variables involved in bringing about change. The desire to solve the riddles of experience is the starting point of conflict theory, whereas structural functionalism introduces unrealistic concepts, not to explain a real problem but to defend a social system that never existed. Conflict theory asks for a critical involvement with reality.

Dahrendorf considered that change is ubiquitous in time and space and there is no use of making a distinction between 'change within' and 'change of'. As a great creative force there are variations in forms of conflict which always need not be violent or uncontrolled. Only temporarily conflict can be suppressed, regulated or channelized but cannot be abolished at all. The most important notion of conflict is that of constraint-that, society and social organizations are held together not by consensus but by constraint, i.e., by coercion of some by others. If we say 'value' system of a society, then it is the value of the ruling class and not of the common mass. Hence, any notion of shared value system is the enforced value system of the ruling class.

IMPERATIVELY COORDINATED ASSOCIATIONS AND CONFLICT

Dahrendorf argued that in all human societies there are positions that enable their bearers to exercise power. These positions are endowed with sovereignty and obedience is enforced. The most important single aspect of power is the control of sanctions. Be it direct or applied, and even a mere anticipation of the effect of sanction may suffice to guarantee compliance with the law. This also implies that, there is always resistance to the exercise of power. Legitimacy is a precarious issue here, as those who are in power manage to stay in power because of their strength and society being held together by the exercise of their strength. As he puts it, 'some positions are entrusted with a right to exercise control over other positions in order to ensure effective coercion; it means, in other words, that there is a differential distribution of power and authority' (Dahrendorf 1959: 165). Thus, the differential distribution of power and authority is the basis of conflict. Conflict analysis then needs to identify the variously equipped authority roles. Only then can one examine further the differential distribution of power and authority. Dahrendorf adhered largely to the Weberian notion of authority to recognize that in organizations and institutions power held by people is backed by legitimate authority.Thus, class conflict occurs more as a result of dispute over the distribution of authority in a given authority structure.

To explain the authority structure in any society, Dahrendorf used the concept of *imperatively coordinated associations*. Authority is only restricted to the position that one holds, as it is position specific. One who loses the position loses the authority automatically. Similarly, one who is in a position of authority in one structure can be in a subordinate position in some other structure. Every society is marked by a distinguishable organization of roles endowed with different authority. The imperatively controlled associations are associations of people controlled by a hierarchy or authority positions. Further these associations are coordinated as organized aggregates of roles and authority, which within each association is dichotomous — that of domination and subjection. Those in positions of domination seek to maintain the status quo while those in positions of subjection seek to change it. Conflict is thereby an inevitable structural feature of any society (Dahendorf 1959).

At the root of any social change is social conflict. Referring to Lewis Coser, Dahrendorf held that the conservative function of conflict is only one side of social reality. Conflict also leads to fundamental change and development of society. He disagreed with Marx on the question of class conflict as he did not accept the two-class polarization indicated by Marx. He felt that the proletariat class cannot ultimately form the conflict group. But at the same time he thought that to ignore Marx would be irresponsible because it was Marx who first made a systematic analysis of the structural causation of conflict. Dahrendorf promoted an alternate class theory:

> The systematic explanation of that particular form of structure-changing conflict which is carried on by aggregates or groups growing out of the authority structure of social organizations. The general theory of class precedes the empirical analysis of given societies in terms of class in that it states the underlying regularities of class conflict in a form that in principle allows application to all societies. But the following formulation of the theory of class does not claim universal applicability, for such applicability is always subject to the test of empirical research; it is confined, instead, to that type of society which we have described as industrial society. (Dahrendort 1959: 152)

With the coming of the industrial society Dahrendorf indicated the formation of a new type of conflict. With industrial society there is a clear correlation between the distribution of authority and social stratification. Here, the authority is more specific and one can no longer talk about an aggregate roles endowed with authority are in conflict with another set of roles dispossessed of such authority. Instead, authority is restricted to people as incumbents in given, limited roles. Although an industrial enterprise is also an imperatively coordinated association but the interests of the workers is generally in conflict with the interest of the management.

SUMMARY

At a time when structural functionalism was holding a complete sway in sociological thinking, conflict theory made a significant intervention in sociology to challenge the conservative mould of theorization of society. Structural functionalism had its contribution to sociology by emphasizing on the interrelatedness of society and focusing on large-scale structural studies. But conflict theories of the 1950s and 1960s made a case for altering the focus of study not by rejecting the study of large scale structures, but by questioning the very premise of the functional view. Value consensus is an unrealistic view of society; instead, it is a question of power and interests of the powerful which decides value for a society. Order of society is a desired goal but at the same time one needs to probe the aspects of asymmetry of power and inequality inherent in any social structure. It is essential to understand any order as an enforced one and recognizing conflict as inevitable feature of society. Conflict theory of different varieties basically offers a dynamic view of society — that, a society is constantly under tension to undergo change. The differential distribution of power in society is a primary cause of conflict. The different causes of conflict and the different nature of social change are theorized by different thinkers. Greatly influenced by classical thinkers like Marx, Weber and Simmel, the contributors of conflict theory tried to come up with significant propositions which enriched sociology. As such, conflict theory was a great turn-around for sociology to take account of new and newer challenges of a fast changing social world.

KEY WORDS

- *Conflict*
- *Constraint*
- *Functional Conflict*
- *Imperatively-coordinated Associations*
- *Power*
- *Power Elite*
- *Sociation*

GLOSSARY

Class Struggle: An active expression of conflict of interests between contending social classes.

Conflict Theory: As against a consensual view of society, it draws attention to power differential in any society. It does so by emphasizing the social, political or material inequality of a *social group*.

Functional Conflict: As against disintegrative consequences of conflict, it suggests greater group cohesion and interaction under hostile situations, which in turn promotes higher level of integration.

Legitimacy: The popular acceptance of exercise of power, whereby it becomes an authority.

Power Elite: A closely knit alliance of military, government and corporate officials perceived as the centre of wealth and political power in the US.

Discussion Points

- Theoretical influences on Conflict Theory.
- Functional Conflict Theory.
- The importance of power in Conflict Theory.
- Dahrendorf's Model of Conflict.

8

Symbolic Interactionism

As a perspective in Sociological Theory, symbolic interactionism rests on a premise that society forms the context in which the self develops. Essentially, this perspective devotes itself to an understanding of how the individual self interacts with the society and in turn gets affected. It attempts to theorize on how society's own existence is dependent on acting individuals to create social groups and structures. The relationship between individuals and society and the medium of communication that facilitates such relationship are the important subject matter for symbolic interactionist school of thought. The primary concern of symbolic interactionism is with the impact of meanings and symbols on human action and interaction. It is the meanings and symbols that allow human individual social action to get entangled into social interaction. Social interaction is the clue for any human society to exist. It is in the process of social interaction that individuals symbolically communicate meanings to other individuals, who too are engaged in the same process. A mutual interpretation allows interaction to take place — that is the distinctive characteristic of a society.

During the 1920s and 1930s, sociology in the United States was re-orienting itself away from the hitherto abstract theory and research based on secondary data. The move was towards the study of the empirical world and to develop appropriate theoretical frame work for that. The watershed for this trajectory of sociology was the co-authored work of W. I. Thomas and Florian Znaniecki's The Polish Peasant in Europe and America published in 1918. Although it a macro-sociological study of social disorganization among Polish migrants, it indicated the possibility of utilizing a variety of data sources and signalled the coming of microscopic, social psychological orientation in sociology. The epicentre for this new turn in sociology was the sociology department of University of Chicago. The Chicago School was instrumental in taking sociology beyond the macroscopic perspectives of the classical thinkers like Karl Marx, Max Weber and Emile Durkheim. Robert Park was the key sociologist to shape the new orientation by focusing on an individual's meaningful social action and interaction.

Although, we read the main tenets of symbolic interactionist school in George Herbert Mead's writings, it was actually Herbert Blumer (1900–87) who coined the term 'symbolic interactionism' in 1937 out of his analysis and reading of G. H. Mead and others. Mainly out of the work of Mead and Charles Hortan Cooley, Blumer phrased the term and continued to energize the theoretical framework for quite some time to keep it alive. Although the chief symbolic interactionist is G. H. Mead and a subsequent extension of the same is to be found in the *Dramaturgical* analysis of Erving Goffman, it is pertinent to acknowledge the contribution of C. H. Cooley in the shaping up of Mead's ideas.

CHARLES HORTON COOLEY (1864–1929)

Charles Cooley's sociology is popularly associated with the Chicago school but he actually belonged to the University of Michigan. This is because he offered interesting insights into the social–psychological aspects of social life, which was to be the cornerstone of the Chicago school's approach later on.

Cooley's interest in self and consciousness was primarily a result of his association with William James. James, a psychologist at the Harvard University theorized for a fresh examination of the individual–society ties. Looking beyond biological determinism and instinct theory to account for human behavior, James emphasized upon habit. He argued that new habits are acquired by individuals and through that they modify these behaviours (Martindale 1988).

Linked to the idea of acquiring new habits was James' analytical distinction between 'Me' and 'I'. In fact, this distinction served as the backbone of the subsequent full-fledged development of symbolic interactionism as a sociological perspective. 'Me' for James is the self that is known. An individual is simultaneously a knower and a known. 'Me' as the empirical self is the congregate of all that an individual possesses — all his/her actions geared towards self-generation. But, 'I' as the pure ego signifies that self who is a knower. It is a result of self-reflection. This component of self as a known entity allows individuals to view themselves as objects. This in turn allows them to modify their behaviours time to time as per the demands of the social environment. This elemental notion of self-society interaction was to serve Cooley in his development of the further insights into the social–psychological aspects of social life.

LOOKING-GLASS SELF

Charles Cooley premised his theory on the dynamics of self-society, as always in a process of 'Learning'. Individuals are not exclusively free-willing entities; instead they learn to act as society wants them to. It is the bearing of society, thereby, all other individuals with whom an individual constitutes his/her social environment and shapes up one's consciousness. It is to say that our consciousness is a result of a continuing process of social interaction. The process of socialization is thereby indicated as the most important component of an individual's psyche.

Cooley introduced the concept of the *looking-glass self* to explicate how an individual develops his/her self out of his/her interaction with others. By looking-glass self, Cooley meant that an individual's self-conception arises from a perception and interpretation of the reactions of others and an emotional feeling about such reactions of others. Hence, no self could be an isolated self as an individual's self development goes through a dynamic process of interaction with others. 'There is no sense of 'I' . . . without its correlative sense of you, or he, or they' (Cooley 1964: 182). Thereby, Cooley touched upon an important aspect of socialization — a predominant subject for sociology.

Related to the concept of looking-glass self, Cooley also emphasized on the concept of primary groups. It is the primary group where in a child first learns to take others into the development of the self. As we all know, primary groups are face-to-face groups, where a child is being initiated to take part with the larger society. These are the most intimate and immediate groups, e.g., the family and the other close members of an individual's life. By the very membership of such groups, a child first starts developing his/her looking-glass self. It is the primary site where a child, essentially ego-centered, starts taking others into his/her conscious self. It is through such consideration of others that one becomes a meaningful member of the society. This explains how individual selves are all results of social situations. Quite obviously then, one finds in Cooley an echo of Max Weber, but with a more rigorous focus on social–psychological aspects of individual behaviour. Almost like Weber, Cooley made a case for an application of the method of sympathetic introspection, that is, to place oneself as an analyst into the place of the subjects that one wishes to study. This is a suggested method for a sociologist to arrive at the meanings and motives and which could only be accomplished by analyzing what the subject as actors might do in various circumstances. Cooley's ideas served as the building blocks for subsequent development of symbolic internationism at the at the hands of G. H. Mead and Herbert Blumer.

GEORGE HERBERT MEAD: A BRIEF BIOGRAPHY AND INFLUENCES

Essentially a philosopher, George Herbert Mead was associated with the Chicago school and it is his theoretical treatment on the development of self that went on to be considered as that of symbolic interactionism subsequently. Born in South Hadley, Massachusetts in 1863, Mead hailed from a family with a comfortable standard of living. Quite unlike the great classical thinkers of sociology, who were all radicals in their own ways, Mead was a clear conformist. In fact, he represented the face of the typical late nineteenth-century and early twentieth-century American values of democracy and social reform.

In 1883, Mead received his Bachelor's degree from Oberlin College. The overall pedagogical influence of his College days was that of conservatism. Mead went on to opt for scientific optimism and social reform as against religious faith. Before getting himself enrolled at Harvard in 1887, Mead had to take up a few jobs (as a secondary-school teacher, railroad surveyor) due to financial constraints. Simultaneously, he was getting drawn more towards contemporary writings on empirical science which helped him to move towards a field where he could serve humanity.

At Harvard, Mead was drawn towards psychology as well as philosophy. After spending a couple of years at Harvard, he left for Germany to attend the Universities of Leipzig and Berlin. In 1891, he returned to the US and joined the University of Michigan. At Michigan he came in touch with the Charles H. Cooley, whose ideas on individual–society relationship and the importance of socialization impacted upon him. Also, around the same time Mead struck an intellectual chord with the humanist philosopher John Dewey (1859–1952). Drawing upon social psychology, Mead continued to advance Dewey's social reformist concerns. In 1894, he moved to the University of Chicago at the behest of Dewey and there taught regularly for the rest of his life.

G. H. Mead was typical product of his time — the turn-of-the-century American ideals of social progress. Opposed to abstract speculation he relied on practical action based on the American values of voluntarism and self-discipline. In fact, the emergent democratic values were lauded as necessary conditions for the progress of scientific knowledge. Such a social framework provided Mead the intellectual environment to theorize on social interaction coupled with self-discipline. He tried to understand how individuals choose their own actions while embedded in social interaction. Such social interaction is premised on cooperation. It was all a product of an era that called for an academic pursuit of knowledge as governed by a strong scientific justification for social reform. In fact the ambience of the Chicago school promoted this focus on the individual, social reform and thereby, social interaction. The influence of the progressive–era optimism on Mead is well documented by historian Robert M. Crunden in *Ministers of Reform: The Progressive Achievement in American Civilization 1889–1920* (1985).

Mead's theory on the emergence of individual self as contingent upon adaptation to social reality can be traced to the influence of George Hegel and Charles Darwin. Primarily, these two thinkers had a decisive impact upon Mead's understanding of social reality. Without conforming to the Hegelian perspective of the quasi-mystical presence of an 'Absolute Spirit', Mead saw society as an emergent reality; that a society emerges out of a dialectical relationship of self and other in a process of social interaction. Such interactions are exclusively facilitated by the sharing of symbols; hence, it is a process of symbolic communication and mutual role taking. The Hegelian influence is complete as

Mead theorized that individuals attain selfhood only within the context of a social situation. It includes the crucial process of identification with the other groups/members of that social setting.

As far as Darwin is concerned, Mead adopted the idea that life is an ongoing process of adapting to the external. Such adaptations are marked by random variations as well as selection with respect to changing environmental conditions. Thereby, Mead could insert the element of flexibility to individual life and selfhood. Again, adhering to the pragmatic philosophies of William James and John Dewey, he emphasized on the goal orientation of individual action. He distanced himself from psychological behaviorists and was against the idea of human behaviour as a result of a stimulus-response sequence. Instead, Mead focused on the emergent goal-oriented human action which is a result of pragmatic self-reflection. Thus, instead of psychological behaviourism he opted for social behaviorism. This social–behaviouristic approach in Mead led the foundation for the perspective of symbolic interactionism. The intricate relationship between the mind, self and society is the framework of such a perspective.

THE SOCIAL

G. H. Meads's *Mind, Self and Society* (1934) was posthumously published and was the effort of his students, who compiled his lecture notes on the courses he taught at the university. The running theme of all his notes was that traditional social psychology cannot explain social life by focusing on individual psychology. Instead the priority was given on the social:

> We are not, in social psychology, building up the behavior of the social group in terms of the behavior of separate individuals composing it; rather, we are starting out with a given social whole of complex group activity, into which we analyze (as elements) the behavior of each of the separate individuals composing it . . . We attempt, that is, to explain the conduct of the social group, rather than to account for the organized conduct of the social group in terms of the conduct of the separate individuals belonging to it. For social psychology, the whole (society) is prior to the part (the individual), not the part to the whole; and the part is explained in terms of the whole, not the whole in terms of the part or parts. (Mead 1934: 7)

Thus, society comes first for the development of the individual self . What distinguishes a human society and humans from the rest is that it is constituted of 'selves', i.e., individual human beings are both subject and object of their own acts. The idea of society advanced by Mead is that which is premised on the existence of interacting individual beings. They interact on the basis of role-taking and sharing common symbols for communication. However, the dialectical relationship between the self and society accords primacy to the society. To have a self, one needs to be a member of a community and be shaped by the attitudes shared by the community. Without the pre-existence of an ongoing social group an individual cannot develop a self. A self-conscious individual is a logical improbability, as it is the society which initiates the process of the development of one's self. Thus, mind is not just a matter of consciousness. Instead, it is a product of its embeddedness in social experience and social processes.

Mind, self and society are considered to be the exclusive compilation of Mead's thought. The text itself carries a great deal of deliberation on the question of importance of socialization in the development of an individual's self. Apparently, Mead did spend more lectures on the question of *mind* and *self*. But at the backdrop of this development of *mind* and *self*, lies a societal context. Therefore, society remains a fundamental concept in his works. Society exists prior to the particular individual, so that acting individuals can cooperate, share and even adapt to the random variations in social situation.

THE MIND

According to G. H. Mead, mind is not just a matter of consciousness. It is rather a matter of social experience. In other words, the ability to communicate meanings to others and at the same time to reflect upon it governs the emergence of the mind. An individual does respond to one's environment but not just as a stimulus–response mode. One responds with the active involvement of the mind. But mind here is not a thing in itself. It arises and develops as a process. It is not just a result of uncontrolled responses to the social environment. The responses are pragmatic and goal-directed.

The pragmatic and goal-oriented responses of individual beings allows an individual the ability to choose, select and delay their responses. Such choices among ranges of actions in turn allow an individual being to be better adapted to one's environment, unlike lower animals.

Development of one's actions is a function of one's reflections on social experiences. Such reflections are of course, in turn, functions of one's consciousness. Consciousness which is exclusively subjective does not come into the play in the development of mind. What is important is that part, which represents reflexive intelligence. Hence, meaning and perception of an individual being are not fixed in external nature. It is the relationship between the individual beings and their social situations that shapes perceptions and meanings. We can say thus that the whole process of experience and perception of such, reflecting on such meanings taking oneself as an object is *mind* as Mead understands.

This idea of the *mind* is the result of the way Mead understood consciousness:

> Consciousness is functional not substantive; and in either of the main senses of the term it must be located in the objective world rather than in the brain — it belongs to, or is a characteristic of, the environment in which we find ourselves. What is located, what does take place, in the brain, however, is the physiological process whereby we lose and regain consciousness. (Mead 1934/1962: 112)

Mead rescued meaning from being a psychical entity. Interestingly, he understood meaning as existing prior to the awareness or consciousness of such meaning, as meaning is embedded already within the social act. But it can be shared only when it is coded in symbols. Consciousness is a result of such an occasion, when meanings associated with symbols allows reflexive intelligence. Mind and meaning as a product of a to-and-fro relationship with the social environment is synoptically thus put by Mead:

> . . . the adjustment to one another of the acts of different human individuals within the human social process; an adjustment which takes place through communication; by gestures on the lower planes of human evolution, and by significant symbols (gestures which possess meanings and are hence more than mere substitute stimuli) on the higher planes of human evolution. The central factor in such adjustment is "meaning". Meaning arises and lies within the field of the relation between the gesture of a given human organism and the subsequent behavior of this organism as indicated to another human organism by the gesture. If that gesture does so indicate to another organism the subsequent (or resultant) behavior of the given organism, then it has meaning. (Mead 1934/62: 75–76)

The basic mechanism in the social act and in the social process is the *gesture*. Unlike lower animals, human beings take recourse to significant symbols. Whereas lower animals indulge in non-significant symbols — that is, based on non-reflexive reactive behaviours; human beings use significant symbols. Gestures are significant symbols when they are capable of arousing in the individual (who is the subject of such gestures) the same kind of response, not necessarily identical, as they arouse onto whom the gestures are directed at. It is only with the help of such significant symbols that human beings communicate truly. Not much of physical gestures constitute significant symbols, as the subject is hardly able to experience physical gestures on their own. It is the vocal utterances that elicit adequate reflection, although not all vocalizations qualify as significant symbols. Language is that set of vocal gestures which is composed of significant symbols — the building blocks for the foundation of any meaningful communication. In turn, language is the great builder of self, mind and society.

It is this possession and use of language that sets human beings apart from the rest of the natural world. It allows them to control and regulate their responses and reactions to the environment. In a way, language is that mechanism of control that facilitates adjustment and intelligent reflection between an individual and the environment. Sharing a language is sharing the same significant symbols. Such a sharing of the common symbols allows people to put themselves in the role of the others and to understand the other through his/her eyes. Thereby, Mead theorized reflexivity as the starting point of any development of the self.

THE SELF

The *self* is possibly the most critical concept in Mead's theory. By studying the activities and socialization of children Mead developed the concept of self as involving a process through which actors reflect on themselves as objects. This gives the self a unique characteristic of being both a subject and an object rolled into one.

> The self has a character which is different from that of the physiological organism proper. The self is something which has a development; it is not initially there, at birth, but arises in the process of social experience and activity, that it develops in the given individual as a result of his/her relations to that process as a whole and to other individuals within that process. The intelligence of the lower forms of animal life, like a great deal of human intelligence, does not involve a self. (Mead 1934/62: 135)

Mead had suggested that just by the possession of a living body one does not acquire a self; that the body is not a self but becomes one when a mind has developed. To be more precise, self and mind are dialectically related. If the development of a mind is a precondition for the development of a self; the self and its reflexivity has a bearing on the development of a mind too. Although the self is a mental process yet it is contingent upon social experiences. Mead stated,

> Human society as we know could not exist without minds and selves, since all its most characteristic features presuppose the possession of minds and selves by the individual members; but its individual members would not possess minds and selves if these had not arisen within or emerged out of human social process in its lower stages of development. (Mead 1934/62: 127)

Reflexivity is that mechanism which facilitates the development of the self, the idea and purpose of which is to examine and judge oneself through the eyes of the others with whom one is locked in social interaction. Mead called it 'the turning back of the experience of the individual upon himself'. It is like getting out of one's own shoes in order to evaluate oneself. Thereby, the self as a subject becomes an object to itself. The experiential world is extremely crucial for the development of the self but an individual cannot experience oneself directly. It is being accomplished only, when an individual indirectly puts oneself in the position of others and reflecting upon from that 'outside' standpoint.

DEVELOPMENT OF THE SELF: 'I' AND 'ME'

Self is not a fixed mechanism as it is simultaneously the subject and the object of its own behaviour. Essentially, in Meads' terms, it is a process that involves judging, planning and finally reflecting upon one's line of action. Therefore, the development of the self as a process is conceptualized by Mead as a two-phase affair. Studying the early socialization process of children, he pointed out that a baby is always born without a sense of themselves as objects — as a new born only responds automatically to external stimuli. It is only through the subsequent phases of interaction with others that the newborn develops a sense of the self. The 'I' and the 'Me' are the two phases of the self as a process. In a way, the self is a result of an interplay between the 'I' and the 'Me'.

Social life is not marked by a series of events — a continuous flow of stimulus-response situations. Instead, such a flow of events is intermittently interrupted as a process of noting and is followed by judging and reflecting whereby, every action becomes a coordinated action. The self arises at such points of reflective action, i.e., a self which is a socialized self always negotiates with an un-socialized self. If 'Me' is the socialized self, 'I' is that un-socialized self.

The 'I' is that impulsive aspect of the self which represents the creative or imaginative phase of the self. Importantly, the 'I' is also conscious of the breaks and interruptions of the flow of events and offers a resolution through a new line of action. As the subject of one's actions, the 'I' reflects and knows the ongoing circumstances and situations, but the 'I' is not known or reflected on. Hence, it operates at the realm of the spontaneous and, therefore, un-socialized.

In contrast, the 'Me' is the known or reflected-on aspect of the self. It is formed as the object of others' actions and views as well as one's own reflections on oneself. Any society has its norms and expectations; the 'Me' aspect of the self acknowledges that and adjusts or adapts to it. The impulsive elements of the self are molded accordingly by the 'Me' phase of the self. So, the 'Me' is a sort of a judgmental aspect of the self, which takes into account the attitudes of other members of society in the full-fledged development of the self. This makes the development of a self as a stable and a consistent aspect social life. The interplay between the reflecting 'I' and the judgmental 'Me' gives rise to a society where the process of mutual adjustment and adaptation are the salient features.

As active agents of society, human beings do not merely respond to their environment in a passive way. Between different lines of action they select, choose, reflect and judge taking account of other similarly placed individual beings. In this 'interruption' of events and actions (instead of automatic responses) the individual brings in his/her past learning and knowledge of different roles at such similar situations and expectations of the 'other' in question. Also, an individual is not bound to present the same self in all such similar situations, or to all other individuals. Thereby, Mead explored the conditions of flexibility and pluralism in the constitution of the self in modern society.

The different patterns of interaction at different stages of their lives govern the development of the self of human beings. Mead focused on the two stages in childhood development to account for the genesis of the self.

The *play stage* and the *game stage* are the two distinct stages through which an individual attains a full-fledged sense of the self. Rather, the emergence of the social self is contingent upon the passage of an individual from the play stage to the game stage. A new-born baby does not have the capacity to use significant symbols to share an interactive world. It is in the play stage that such a capacity is developed. At its best, the new-born only imitates the people around him/her. But while playing the roles of others, in this play stage the child slowly starts learning the roles of others, it is a case of simple role-playing.

In this first stage, that is, the play stage a child begins to learn the attitude of his/her parents, siblings etc, who are close to him/her. Thus, s/he takes on the attitude of particular others to herself/himself. The learning process continues through various forms of play. However, it is important to note that prior to the coming of the play stage proper, there is a third stage. It is an elementary stage of imitation. It is an elementary stage of learning, whereby, a child first starts to imitate and learn the gestures of particular others. This is immediately followed by a development of the child's capacity to learn the use of language and the meanings of symbols. A child starts playing out the roles of particular others with the help of certain symbols. This is the starting point of a child's growing up as both subject and object. The formation of the self is a result of this elementary development in a child's life. At this point it is the child's imagination that enables him/her to 'act out' the roles of others.

The final stage is the game stage. In the full sense of the term the self develops at the game stage. The difference of the game stage with the play stage is that, unlike the play stage where a child acts out the roles of particular others, here s/he is enabled to take the role of everyone else. Drawing an analogy with the game of basketball, Mead explained:

> But in a game where a number of individuals are involves, then the child taking one role must be ready to take the role of everyone else. If he gets in a ball nine he must have the responses of each position involved in his own position. He must know what everyone else is going to do in order to carry out his own play. He has to take all of these roles. They do not all have to be present in consciousness at the same time, but at some moments he has to have three or four individuals present in his own attitude, such as the one as the one who is going to throw the ball, the one who is going to catch it, and so on. These responses must be, in some degree, present in his own make-up. In the game, then, there is a set of responses of such others so organized that the attitude of one calls out the appropriate attitudes of the other. (Mead 1934/1962: 151)

It is a case of knowing the rules of the game that allows every individual to participate in the game. It is a transition from just role playing of a series of discrete individuals to a participation in a standardized order. This ensures the development of a self in the full sense, whereby, the self emerges as a part and parcel of the entire community. The personality of an individual cannot develop in the play stage, but it can blossom to the fullest only in the game stage as a child learns to function in organized groups. Different interacting individuals have different roles, and the child picks up appropriate roles through evaluation and reflexivity.

Instead of the discrete particular others, a child acknowledges a *generalized other* only in the game stage. Over and above the discreteness of different individuals, *generalized other* as a concept stands for the attitudes of the whole community. It is a sort of a standardized behaviour of the community within which an individual interacts. The development of an individual self is then a matter of responding to a generalized other symbolically. Instead of a simple process of taking up the roles of discrete individuals, by taking the role of the generalized other an individual ensures an evaluation of oneself from the point of view of the community as such. The root of socialization lies exactly at this process.

SOCIAL EXPERIENCE AND THE ACT

It is clear that for Mead, society is a result of individuals who are capable of interactions. Such interactions result from role taking and meaningful shared communications. His central text *Mind, Self, and Society* delineated individual social experiences in relation to society. Human society is therefore a society of 'selves', whereas, the self involves the process which involves actors reflecting on themselves as objects. A stimulus–response situation is fore-grounded in Mead's theory. By theorizing on the self as both the object and the subject of its behaviour, Mead understood the self as a process that comes into existence when an individual 'acts' — which is not just an instant and automatic response to a stimulus. In possession of symbols human beings do not act instantly in an unthinking manner. They think and decide on their own as to the appropriate way of acting in given situations. Again, they react on the basis of their perceptions, understanding and estimations of the situations in which they are placed.

In his *The Philosophy of the Act* (1938), Mead analysed the act in terms of four interrelated stages, *Impulse* being the first stage. The impulse is the immediate sensuous stimulation. Still, an individual's reaction to this impulse is not completely free from contemplation or decision making. Impulse also involves both the actor and the environment by the fact that unlike lower animals, humans satisfy this impulse taking into consideration the environmental situations. For example, both non–human and human does respond to the impulse of hunger. But a human being will consider the various choices of action — to eat immediately or to postpone it for a while, to search for food which would be appropriate etc. Thus, the impulse stage is an urge to react to an environment, which is followed by the second stage of *perception*. 'Perception is a relation between a highly developed physiological organism and an object, or an environment in which selection emphasizes certain elements. This relation involves duration and a process. The process is that of action through media which affect the sense organs of the biologic individual' (Mead 1938: 8).

In the second stage the actor searches for, and reacts to, with the help of their senses as well as mental images in order to satisfy the impulses. Confronted with a plurality of stimulus individuals exhibit their ability to select purposefully. By the very fact that something is being perceived, it becomes an object to an individual. Thus, the object and its perception are dialectically related too.

After the object is being perceived, the individual needs to take action with regard to it. At this stage human beings contemplate on all possible lines of action. This stage is called *manipulation*. It represents the conscious action that only higher animals like human beings can take recourse to. Hence, the response of human beings to the environment is not an immediate one. To satisfy the impulse, human beings indulge in manipulations which could either be conforming to the environment in terms of alternatives or making the environment conform to their purpose.

The final stage is that of consummation. In this fourth stage an individual actually takes the action in order to satisfy the original impulse. Any act finally is being consummated through an inter-relatedness between all these four stages.

> The full completion of the act which the distance stimulus initiates is found in some such consummation as that of eating. It is not the consummation of the act, however, which is the perceptual thing that the distance stimulus sets going. One eats things. In other words, there is an experience of contact with the object which constitutes its perceptual reality and which comes in between the beginning of the act and its consummation. To this experience is referred both the visual experience and consummatory act. They both become characters or adjectives of the thing. ... We approach the distant stimulus with the manipulatory processes already excited. We are ready to grasp the hammer before we reach it, and the attitude of manipulatory response directs this approach. (Mead 1938: 23–24)

If Mead considered the act as the basic unit of his theory, social act is that act whose impulse attracts/involves responses from all those who are in the environment. The very possession of symbols and a common sharing of gestures through such symbols allow all individuals to engage in social acts. In Mead, we find that socialization is emphasized to develop the sense of self, but the process of interaction remains vital for such socialization to take place at the first instance. Human being as a thinking being is highlighted in this perspective of symbolic interactionism.

HERBERT BLUMER (1900–87)

The credit of presenting symbolic interactionism as a coherent body of sociological thought goes to Herbert Blumer. In fact, Blumer coined the term 'symbolic interactionism'. Unlike his teacher Mead, Blumer was a sociologist. He taught sociology at the University of Chicago from 1927 to 1952. He held the centre stage in the Chicago school of symbolic interactionism. As he moved out of Chicago to the University of California at Berkeley, after 1952, the Chicago school started losing its old glory.

Blumer, although coming from a sociological background, was attracted towards Mead's courses on social psychology in Chicago. Subsequently, he organized Mead's scattered thinking into a body of sociological thought — which he termed as 'symbolic interactionist'. Blumer represented the fact of the Chicago style of symbolic interactionism. He tried to resolve the issue of reductionist behaviorism in nascent symbolic interactionism as well as the grand sociologism promoted by the emergent structural–functional school during his time. Instead, he focused on the crucial process by which actors impute meanings onto the forces acting upon them as well as on their own behaviours. It goes to Blumer's credit to carry forward Mead's theory and incorporate it in the building of sociological theory.

SYMBOLIC INTERACTIONISM AS A PERSPECTIVE

As a sociological perspective, Herbert Blumer tried to free symbolic interactionism from the trap of reductionist behaviorism as well as grand sociologism. He was against all kinds of psychological reductionism which ignores the actual process by which meanings are generated and given to every act by the actors themselves. In terms of external stimuli human behaviours cannot be fully understood. It is neither the mental impulse that, propels individual actors, nor any large-scale external forces that can adequately account for human behavior.

As a sociological perspective, Blumer posited symbolic interactionism as one that emphasizes the thinking capacity of human beings that allows them not only to indulge in interactions but also to modify and alter meanings in order to weave and sustain social interactions. Such thought processes are impregnated with symbols, which are in turn learnt simultaneously and variously in the very social interactions only. Human groups and society is a result of this unique capacity for thought amongst human beings. Thus, Blumer could develop a theory which gives human agency not just as an outcome of mental impulse and neither as a pawn to larger social structural forces.

Blumer successfully summarized the three premises on which symbolic interactionism rests on. He, as noted before, compiled the writings of Mead to come up with a systematized theory of symbolic interactionism.

> Symbolic interactionism rests in the last analysis on three simple premises. The first premise is that human beings act forward things on the basis of the meanings that the things have for them. ... The second premise is that the meaning of such things is derived from, or arises out of, the social interaction that one has with one's fellows. The third premise is that these meanings are handled in, and modified through, an interpictative process used by the person in dealing with the things he encounters. (Blumer 1969: 2)

The three premises are interrelated and the central thrust of which is the act of interpretation. The interpretation of each other's actions is the building block of symbolic interactionism. This interaction is a matter of intelligible communication facilitated by the possession of a common language. The act of interpretation is emphasized by Blumer in order to theorize upon human behaviour more than just a case of stimulus-response situation. One interprets not just as an alternative response on the basis of learned meanings, but through a process of self-interaction — forming the meanings, reviewing and if necessary altering the meanings etc. The methodological implication of such a theorization of human society is profound. Individuals, collectively and variously, are all engaged in such acts of interpretation give rise to social acts. Such social acts are nothing but a complex network of acts which signals interdependency, and that, such interdependency marks all aspects of society and is a dynamic one.

The methodological implication of Blumer's theorization on symbolic interactionism is that explorative empirical researches are made crucially significant for sociological theory building. Additionally, small-scale studies are highlighted. Blumer was more in favour of a 'naturalistic' study of human behaviour. The everyday context, the day-to-day interaction of individual beings engaged in social interaction is that natural sphere which promises a more authentic study of human group life. Such a 'naturalistic' approach of Blumer rests on an explorative research design which allows a study to move freely and explore the unfamiliar. This inductive insistence of Blumer was to develop analytical schemes out of empirical studies. Thereby, a micro approach could generate a theory of society in terms of its structure as well. Such analytical schemes are equipped to explain the relations between man and society. The role of such micro studies is thereby seen as intrinsic to any scientific theory society. 'Theory, inquiry and empirical fact are interwoven in a texture of operation with theory guiding inquiry, inquiry seeking and isolating facts, and facts affecting theory. The fruitfulness of their interplay is the means by which an empirical science develops' (Blumer 1954: 3).

It is to the credit of Blumer that symbolic interactionism could develop with a strong methodological grounding. As against abstract concepts and grand theories, Blumer advanced empirical observation as the mode of clarification and even revision of concepts.

ERVING GOFFMAN (1922–82)

A Brief Biographical Sketch

Like Blumer, Erving Goffman also belonged to the Chicago school of symbolic interactionism. Goffman is best known for his work *Presentation of Self in Everyday Life* (1959). He was born in Canada, 1922. He finished his graduation in 1945 from the University of Toronto. Subsequently, he shifted to the University of Chicago and obtained his doctorate degree in 1953. Incidentally, Blumer was Goffman's teacher at Chicago.

For his doctoral thesis Goffman took up intensive field-study of a small island community. It was the Shetland Island, where he studied 300 families. These families were all placed in close proximity to each other, which allowed Goffman to study their ways, manners and techniques of day-to-day interactions (Adams and Sydie 2001). He researched on the various ways that those islanders interacted not only with each other but also with the outsiders. The result was his thesis on how people present themselves before the world and the ways they negotiate differentially to make effective communication.

In 1957, Goffman joined Blumer at Berkeley. He remained there till 1969 and finally took up professorship at the University of Pennsylvania. The way people perform and alter their performances within a social set-up could best be realized by a researcher by skillfully concealing the role of a researcher — Goffman adopted such a tool of research to enrich the tradition of symbolic interactionism. Apart from the inputs from social anthropology, Emile Durkheim's functional analysis of rituals shaped Goffman's sociology. The ceremonial practices and the role of rituals were seen as the crucial links between the individual and society. However, collectively speaking, the face-to-face interaction remained the central tenet in Goffman's sociology. The influences of the Chicago school of empirical study along with the useful insights drawn from the field of social anthropology influenced him to expand the scope of symbolic interactionism. To give rise to a sociology of everyday life, Goffman introduced the field of dramaturgy. It was mainly out of a series of studies and analyses of conversation that Goffman presented a theory of dramaturgy to account for human behaviour.

Goffman is considered to have presented the most comprehensive account of the self in symbolic interactionism. The fundamental idea that the self is not just a possession of any individual but a product of one's interaction with the society was further elaborated upon by Goffman. The influence George Herbert Mead was obvious in his conception of the self. Goffman suggested a dramaturgical approach by invoking the sense of social life as almost analogous to dramatic performances that take place on a stage. Also, he was the key sociologist to give shape to the sociology of everyday life. His ideas were instrumental for the subsequent development of ethno-methodological school of thought in sociology. The distinctiveness of Goffman lies in the fact that he could successfully blend the descriptive studies of symbolic interactionism with the empirical tradition of social anthropology.

Stable Self-image

An image of the self is all that individuals in this world are ceaselessly presenting in their daily lives. Drawing upon Mead's theory of the tension between the spontaneous self and its social constraints, Goffman theorized on how people resolve to come up with a stable self-image.

All individuals present a self which fulfills the expectations that are placed on them. That is to suggest that while presenting their selves to the society, individuals do not waver. Social living consisting of social interaction is a matter of performances for Goffman. Thus, he advanced an analogy with stage performance and social living. Hence, the approach is that of dramaturgy. A successful performer is one who presents a stable and firm self-image by resolving all the disturbances and constraints that accompany such performative processes. The self 'is a dramatic effect arising … from a scene that is presented' (Goffman 1959: 253). What is stable is what is accepted as normal.

The principal text of Goffman's dramaturgical approach is his *Presentation of Self in Everyday Life* (1959). In the very preface of this book he made clear the perspective of his dramaturgical approach.

> . . . that of the theatrical performance; the principles derived are dramaturgical ones. I shall consider the way in which the individual in ordinary work situations presents himself and his activity to others, the ways in which he guides and controls the impression they form of him, and the kinds of things he may and may not do while sustaining his performance before them. (Goffman 1959: XI)

Simply put, a theatrical analogy was put forward by Goffman to suggest that all human interactions are essentially dramatic performances. Self is a result of a dramatic interaction between the actor and the audience. Therefore, every individual strives to work on an identity and present it to others that satisfy the expectation of them as well as provide them with information about what to expect from him/her. A negotiated sense of self is what Goffman attempted to deliberate upon. A stable self is a result of a successful performance on the stage, which involves presenting not only an idealized picture of one's self but also the capacity to weather possible disruptions in the process. At the last instance actors attempt to make the characters believable.

Technique of Dramaturgy

By comparing life to a theatrical performance, Goffman argued for a method in sociology which could focus on day-to-day interactive actions of individual beings. Such interactions were thought to be constituted of actors who perform for an audience and accomplish the task of acquiring a self through such performance.

> In developing the conceptual framework employed by him report, some language of the stage was used. I spoke of performers and audiences, of routines and parts; of performances coming off or falling flat; of cues, stage settings and back stages; of dramaturgical needs dramaturgical skills, and dramaturgical strategies. Now it should be admitted that this attempt to press a mere analogy so far was in part rhetoric and a maneuver. The claim that all the World's a stage is sufficiently commonplace for readers to be familiar with its limitations and tolerant of its presentation, knowing that at any time they will easily be able to demonstrate to themselves that it is not to be taken too seriously. An action staged in a theatre is a relatively contrived illusion and an admitted one; unlike ordinary life. (Goffman 1959: 254)

Drawing upon an analogy with the theatre stage, Goffman had a structural view of the actor–audience setting. He made a distinction between the front stage and the backstage — similar to an actual theatre setting. According to Goffman, the front stage is 'that part of the individual's performance which regularly functions in a general and fixed fashion to define the situation for those who observe the performance. Front, then, is the expressive equipment of a standard kind intentionally or unwillingly employed by the individual during his performance' (Goffman1959: 22).

The front stage is that stage which is apparent and obvious. Here individuals perform as per the expectation of the audience. For those who are observing the performance, the situation is portrayed and defined by the performer as 'true'. In fact to make the performance look authentic, such intentional performances make use of appropriate props with respect to be roles they play. The front stage in further differentiated by Goffman into two parts: the setting and the personal front. The setting refers to the physical site without which the performer cannot perform ordinarily. For example, a taxi driver requires a cab to play his exact role, as a surgeon requires a sterile operation theatre to execute. Whereas the personal front refers to those props which directly mark the performer with the exact role that one is executing. These consist of the items that the observing audience would ordinarily expect from the performers to carry with them into the setting (Ritzer 1996). For example, a surgeon is required to dress in his/her appropriate medical gown as well as carry specific instruments with him/her to execute the role of being a surgeon.

There is a further subdivision of the personal front into *appearance* and *manner*. For a normal performance, the appearance and the manner need to synchronize. Appearance speaks of the performer's social status, whereas manner signifies to the audience the kind of role that the performer is expected to play in the given situation. Overall, according to Goffman, the front stage is already given, and hence it cannot be created by the action but can only be selected by them. A successful performance entails the ability of an actor to present an idealized picture of himself/herself. For that, s/he tends to show that s/he is intimate with the audience. Mystification is the technique employed by an actor, often, to mitigate any discordant issues that might disrupt the process of interaction. Such creating of 'distance' is useful to invoke credibility of the identity so projected. In actuality, on such an allegorical stage performance, Goffman suggested a team of performers. A smooth blending and coordination of individual acts actually takes place on such front stage.

Beyond the front stage, there is the back stage in Goffman's analysis of symbolic interactionism. As the term suggests, it is the stage hidden from the view of the audience. It is the actual preparatory place where the real actors could let their guards down and indulge in informal actions. It is the crucial site for the performers to engage in various manipulative techniques. Goffman advocated this as an act of *impression management*. This art of impression management protects one in presentation of the self. It helps to guard against unexpected disruptions or inopportune intrusions which might arise during any front stage performance. To cope up with unforeseen circumstances, impression management is the key so that the front stage is kept at a distance from the back stage. The true feelings which are expressed in the back stage are carefully protected thereby, so that an idealized interaction is facilitated.

Goffman, subsequent to *Presentation of Self in Everyday Life*, also talked about the concept of *role distance*. In *Encounters* (1961), he wrote:

> It is important to note that in performing a role the individual must see to it that the impressions of him that are conveyed in the situation are compatible with the role-appropriate personal qualities effectively imputed to him: these

> personal qualities, effectively imputed and effectively claimed, combine with a position's title, when there is one, to provide a basis of self-image for the incumbent and a basis for the image of his role that others will have of him. (Goffman 1961: 87)

The concept of role-distance is invoked by Goffman to account for the degree to which individuals distance themselves from the role-performance. One indulges in such separation in order to protect one's self-image as idealized. In the absence of effective role-distance, an individual runs the risk of getting stigmatized. As it is clear from the term 'stigma', here an individual earns a negative self-identity. It signifies a gap between 'what it is' and 'what it ought to be', that is, while advancing the dramaturgical approach in symbolic interactionism, Goffman acknowledged the possible gap between the virtual and the actual social identity. Often in interactive situations persons failing to conform to the 'norm', that is, the expected identity/role-playing are stigmatized. Such dishonour or disgrace is a source of tension, which is again theorized by Goffman as to be contained through dramaturgical techniques. In his *Stigma: Notes on the Management of Spoiled Identity* (1963), Goffman analysed stigma as a type of deviance from the normal. Finally, in his *Frame Analysis: An Essay on the Organization of Experience* (1974), Goffman showed his inclination to move away from his earlier orthodox everyday study of interactions. Rather, he suggested an approach beyond the confines of everyday symbolic interactions, to acknowledge the functioning of the small-scale structures of social life. In a way, he took into consideration the societal frames that impinge upon individuals and enable them to perceive and render their actions meaningful. That an individual's experience and perception are ordered by certain social frames and not just left to as any absolute matter of choice. Possibly, Goffman realized the limitation of considering everything as enacted on a theatrical-stage. Rather, the pre-existence of structured meanings too affect individual life and, thereby, social life significantly.

SUMMARY

As against the more classical macrosociological tradition of sociological theories, symbolic interactionism emphasized on the micro relations of social life. The basic idea of this perspective is that social reality is a constructed one; that it is a result of human interaction, interaction as facilitated by the use of symbols. Meaningful words and gestures constitute the world of symbols for human society. Methodologically it promotes a naturalistic approach. Interacting individuals in that natural environment constitute the scope of study for researchers. It is in this way that symbolic interactionists also resist any tendency to bring in preconceived notions about such 'free flowing' interactions. As such, the entire theoretical approach advocates an inductive qualitative method of studying micro social situations. A flexible method, thereby, allows a rich collection of data on human behaviour. The core idea of symbolic interactionism could be traced to George Cooley's initial ideas, which were subsequently developed by G. H. Mead. Herbert

Blumer organized the ideas and presented an organized body of symbolic interactionist theory. Finally, Erving Goffman's thesis on presentation of the self rounded up the issue of how a social reality is incumbent upon the participants' negotiation with their natural environment. The interface of sociology with psychology is underscored in this school of thought.

KEY WORDS

- *Dramaturgy*
- *Interactionism*
- *Looking-glass Self*
- *Primary Groups*
- *Reflexive Intelligence*
- *Self*
- *Social Behaviourism*

GLOSSARY

Dramaturgy: The sociological perspective arising out of the symbolic interactionist school which holds that self is a sense which is a dramatic effect emerging from the immediate scene being presented.

Game Stage: The stage of self-development that follows the play stage. It involves the process of learning to take up the role of the generalized other, which facilitates group activity.

Generalized Other: The overall attitude and activity of a group when considered irrespective of the particular.

I: The imaginative, instinctive and creative aspect of the self.

Looking-glass Self: A sociological concept which explains a formation of self-image via reflection in a situation of interaction.

Me: The known, reflected upon aspect of the self.

Play Stage: The initial phase of self-development which involves the process of learning to take the role.

Role-taking: The ability of imagining oneself into the position of another to whom an action or behaviour is directed, in order to assess how would the other respond or feel.

Self: Constituted of the two alternating phases of 'I' and 'Me', a process which is a result of taking the role of the other through imagination, planning and selecting action.

Social Act: An act which suggests that individual behaviour is a stimulus for the response of another.

Symbolic Interactionism: As a sociological perspective, it takes into account the process of social interaction in the formation of meanings for individuals.

Discussion Points

- The looking-glass self.
- The dynamics of 'I' and 'Me' in Mead.
- The drammaturgical analysis of Goffman.

9

Social Exchange Theory

Social exchange theory was founded by George Homans. Man as a rational being lies at the foundation of such a theory. The individual as a rational being is seen as rationally calculating loss or gains, pleasures and pains in order to maximize profits. Thereby the exchange theory implies that an individual being is universally motivated by self-interest. Accordingly, as per the provisions of the social environment individual beings maximize their profits in social interaction. By exchanging gains and loss, or rewards and punishment, human beings interact with each other.

INTELLECTUAL ROOTS

It is being held popularly that social exchange theory was largely guided by the early twentieth-century rational choice theory as developed in neo-classical economics. While the influence of rational choice theory, as well as that of utilitarianism and game theory is generally obvious, the basic idea of society as a result of mutual reciprocal behaviour is drawn from cultural anthropology.

Cultural anthropology primarily aimed at establishing that beyond particularism and uniqueness, all human societies are bound by a thread of common goals and aspirations. Cultural anthropologists in their orthodox pursuit studied the balance and order of primitive societies in terms of a 'give and take' social behaviour. In other words, reciprocity was theorized as the most essential aspect of social life. The leading anthropologist Bronislaw Malinowski's study of the Trobrianders of the Melanesian Islands, or the comparative account of many primitive society studies by Marcel Mauss emphasized the social role of gift exchange. The theory of function of gift exchange as creating bondage on the basis of reciprocity impacted upon George Homan's thinking of a social exchange.

Apart from this elemental influence, psychological behaviourism also played a role in the development of exchange theory in sociology. The principal idea of behaviourism is that, the environment in which a behaviour takes place is impacted upon by the behaviour and affects the subject in turn as a consequence. It is a cyclical understanding of the affect and effect of the environment, be it social or physical, on human behaviour.

As an individual behaves in a society, it affects the society either positively or negatively. A behavioural sociologist would study whether the impact is rewarding or punishing. If it is rewarding for the acting individual, under similar situation the actor would most likely repeat the same behaviour. On the contrary, if the impact is painful and unrewarding such an action will not be resorted to by the individual again. In simple terms, the past consequences of a given behaviour largely shape up our present behaviour (Ritzer 1996).

More specially, psychological behaviourism of B. F. Skinner of Harvard University had a direct influence on the development of social exchange theory. In his attempt to make social theories more empirically grounded and concrete, Skinner emphasized upon the study of behaviour and its consequences. An assessment of the past consequences would tell us about whether such similar behaviours would be repeated in the present. The idea of 'reinforcement effectiveness' is important according to Skinner (Martindale 1988). Reinforcement effectiveness is a sort of positive response that an environment imparts an individual behaviour, which encourages reinforcement or strengthening of similar behaviour. The stimulus–response cycle is the basic idea behind such psychological behaviourism. Both imitation and willingness to follow instruction are the basis of such positive repetition of behaviour. Skinner cited the language learning process of a child to elicit the way reinforcement acts as the backbone of social exchange.

Finally, it is the rational choice theory which provided the basic model for the development of social exchange theory in sociology. It is the principle of utilitarian economics which prompted George Homans and others to theorize on human behaviour as one dictated by profit maximizing decisions on a rational basis. Here, human behaviour is taken as an intended act which combines ends and means in the best possible way. One purposefully operates within the constraints of scarcity of resources as well as that imposed by social institutions. Debra Friedman and Michael Hechter have outlined the premises about individual psychology that the market-oriented economists like Adam Smith or David Ricardo had worked with to propose a utilitarian economics. An application of these premises on the study of social behaviour is what social exchange theory relied on. Like what human beings do while engaging themselves with goods and services in a free market, in the society too the same behavioural intent could be observed. In social exchange, people as acting individuals participate with a variety of interests or values (material as well as non-material rewards). All self-interest-driven individuals would maximize pleasure avoiding pain. This utilitarian approach that ensures greatest good for the maximum number of people in turn leads to a balance between all the different individuals thereby fostering a group equilibrium. Social exchange theory heavily adopted such an idea of group equilibrium as the salient feature of human society.

GEORGE C. HOMANS (1910–89)

A Biographical Sketch and Intellectual Influences

George Homans is credited as the pioneer in establishing social exchange theory as a major sociological perspective. In his own admission, he became a sociologist as a matter of accident (Homans 1984). He was born in 1910 in Boston, United States. He had an early interest in academics. He was privileged with a household library, from which he benefitted most. Homans joined Harvard and earned his bachelor's degree in 1932 with English literature as major. However, his sustained interest in sociology began in 1933 at the Harvard Business School in the association of Professors Laurence Henderson and Elton Mayo. Both were into behavioural psychology and Mayo guided Homans to the anthropological works of Malinowski, Radcliffe-Brown and Raymond Firth. Through an acquaintance with the classical anthropological works Homans was more into an understanding that instead of cultures being unique, human nature is universally similar under similar situations.

As far as common human behaviour and psychology is concerned, Homans was impacted upon by Vilfredo Pareto's psychological treatment of basic human behaviour. In fact, along with Charles Curtis, he co-authored *An Introduction to Pareto (1934),* which helped him to get a position in the sociology department at Harvard. During World War II, he served the navy, and while on duty at sea he reflected on the vast material of 'field' studies of small human groups, both modern and pre-modern. And then and there he could conceive of fitting those detail studies in a conceptual framework which would be common for all human groups. The result was his first major work. *The Human Group* (1950), which he developed after returning from the war duty to Harvard.

Homans was closely associated with the leading theorist Talcott Parsons in Harvard. He considered Parson's grand theories as just conceptual schemes which failed to offer proposition which could relate the concepts to one another and have reference with a low order of generality. Thus, in *The Human Group,* Homans stated such propositions and analysed the structures and processes of small human groups. His next major work is *The Nature of Social Sciences (1967)*, where he elaborated why the general propositions need to account for individual human beings as numbers of a species. As he thought that all human behaviours could be explained by basic psychological principles. Essentially, Homans went against the functionalist perspective prevalent in the 1950s and 1960s in the US universities, by emphasizing the psychological drives of human behaviour, which was a result of his acquaintance with field and experimental studies in social psychology.

Homans' interests on small-group studies were a result of influences from various disciplinary sources. Disciplines like behavioural psychology, functional anthropology, utilitarian economics as well as biochemistry impacted upon his thinking process. While it is true that, his first major work, *The Human Group,* belonged to the same tradition of the functional school of British anthropology, but subsequently such a framework was dismissed by him. This was due to Homans' coming in touch with the leading psychological behaviouralist B. F. Skinner.

Skinner as a professor of psychological behaviourism was dismissive of all social theories as being mystical which were for removed from concrete behaviours of active human beings. Instead, he proposed the study of operant behaviour — the framework was that of the notion of a stimulus–response dyad. Applying this to study pigeon behaviour, he suggested that both human and animal behaviours are governed by the fact when a subject was presented with a stimulus, a response would automatically follow, and that, a *desired* behaviour could then be generated there by reinforcement of such desired behaviour. Without equating animal and human behaviour, Homans adopted Skinner's theory and combined it with utilitarian cost-benefit economic perspective to develop his exchange theory.

> We begin at what may seem a long distance from human social behavior — at the behavior of individual animals. And a long distance it is: not for one moment do we imply that the behavior of men and the behavior of animals is the same. But if they are not the same they may yet be similar and similar in just those ways that will most interest us. (Homans 1961: 17)

Also, being influenced by George Simmel, Homans' theory was to look for fundamental nature of human life. Simmel's idea of reciprocity that marks every human interaction actually shaped small-group research of Homans. He effectively combined the rationality principle of utilitarian economics with behavioural psychology and thereby promoted small-group researches.

Human Behaviour in Homan's Scheme

In simple terms, self-interest is considered by Homans as the governing principle of human behaviour. In terms of the returns from every interaction human beings universally modify and shape their behaviour. A rational calculation of benefits and costs governs human society, which is constituted by interacting individual beings. The foundation of social exchange theory of Homans rests on a set of five general propositions of all human behaviour. Gathering insights from everyday social interaction, he theorized that a sociology could be developed on such basic principles of human behaviour which would be sufficient to explain all social behaviour (Homans 1984).

The five propositions are:

i. The success proposition
ii. The stimulus proposition
iii. The value proposition
iv. The deprivation–satiation proposition, and
v. The aggression–approval proposition.

Success Proposition

Homans from his small-group interactive studies gave the example of the success proposition with reference to an office situation. A person asks for good advice from others only when s/he realizes that in the past on similar situation such advices bore fruit for him/her. Thus, the more the incidence of useful advice in the past, the more is the likelihood of such advices being sought in the future. This works for both the giver and taker of such advices.

In other words, the success proposition works on the principle of reward, that is, if an activity was rewarded in the past and if the reward was quick then, such activity will be repeated in the future. Human behaviour is principally thought to be guided by a desire to secure project. A project is nothing but rewards minus the incidental costs. Cost is a negative value; every activity while striving for a reward also incurs a cost, and hence we have alternative rewarding activities as well. The best possible activity then is ensured, also on the count that a regular interval of reward followed by a repetition of the same activity might elicit monotony. Such satiation is often overcome by investing in activity which results intermittent rewards. Homans made it obvious that,

> . . . we define psychic profit as reward less cost, and we argue that no exchange continues unless both parties are making a profit. Even the pigeon, when it finds its rewards and costs nicely balanced, may try to get out of the situation or indulge in emotional behaviour rather than continue its exchange with the psychologist. But our argument is more familiar in the field of human buying and selling. (Homans 1961: 61)

Basically, Homans was interested in exemplifying how the basic principles of utilitarian economics are fused with entire social behaviour.

Stimulus Proposition

The same stimulus results in similar response. Homans explained this proposition very lucidly by stating, 'A fisherman who has cast his line into a dark pool and has caught a fish becomes more apt to fish in dark pools again' (Homans 1974: 23).

In other words, it works on the principle of experience. Simultaneously it puts forward the process of generalization, i.e., one tends to extend the behaviour to other similar circumstances on the basis of successful experience. Generalization works at different levels. From the example of fishing, one level of generalization would prompt one who is successful in fishing in dark pools to move to any pool with any degree of shadiness. At a higher level of generalization one may move from one kind of fishing or even to another kind of fishing or even to other similar kind of activity.

Similarly, an individual actor's sensitivity and alertness to stimulus or set of stimuli allow him or her to discriminate also. *Discrimination* means that even if there is success with a particular stimulus, the same behaviour might not be repeated if the conditions under which such an accomplishment occurred appear to be complicated enough.

Value Proposition

To appreciate the outcome of a behaviour Homans introduced the idea of both reward and punishment. Rewards are understood to be associated with actions which are endowed with positive values. On the other hand, punishments are actions with negative values. The value preposition works on the principle of reward and punishment. Quite obviously, any increase in positive acts, acts as an incentive to engage in the same desired behaviour.

Also, rewards vary by degree of value, which allows an individual to indulge in making a rational choice between alternative actions. Along with the first two propositions, Homans used a third proposition concerning reward and punishment to explain how an individual weighs between alternatives to secure favourable outcomes. A person chooses the one for which, as perceived by him/her at the time the best not only in terms of absolute positive value attached to the activity but also with a calculation of the probability of securing favourable rewards. Reward with a high probability, even with a relative low positive reward value might be preferred by an individual (Homans 1961).

Deprivation–satiation Proposition

Directly borrowed from principles of economics Homans proposed this deprivation–satiation as the principle of diminishing returns. As he stated, 'The more often in the recent past a person has received a particular reward; the less valuable any further unit of that reward becomes for him' (Homans 1974: 29).

To explain this proposition, Homans used the concepts of cost and profit. Profit in any interactive situation is calculated as that unit of reward which is over and above the cost. Obviously, any behaviour entails a cost, which is the unit of reward lost in selecting a particular line of action foregoing the other alternatives.

Social exchange involves human activities. Thus the human element in it allows for a variation in action–reward situations. Social exchange thereby is not a fixed, standardized interaction. It is rather that differentially placed individuals always change their choices to maximize profits and rewards. If the rewards become too regular and abundant, then as a result of over-satiation the motivation towards such an activity gets lost.

Behavioural psychologist Skinner's study of pigeon's behaviour had a direct bearing on Homan's present proposition. Thus, when a pigeon has an abundance of food, its need to engage in pegging at the target to secure food automatically goes down. This animal behaviour was applied to human society by Homans, but with a qualification. In relation to the time, context and precise nature of the object of satisfaction, the principle of diminishing return is actually operationalized. For some rewards like money or power the reward may never reach a point of satiation. However, for rewards like food and sex, it may reach such a point but is also capable of a recovery of the value after a time gap.

Aggression–approval Proposition

This proposition of Homans is based on the principle of distributive justice. As in most of his theories, here too Homans is influenced by Skinner's pigeon study. He wrote:

> when a pigeon pecks but gets no grain, although the stimulus-conditions resemble those under which it was previously rewarded for pecking, the pigeon displays what looks to a human observer for all the world like anger and frustration: it turns away from the target, flapping its wings and cooing hurriedly. (Homans 1961: 72–73)

In simpler terms, a person gets angry when his/her expectation from a particular activity are not met and are instead rewarded negatively. This leads to aggressive behaviour. Such aggressive performance is then considered as rewarding. If this behaviour could be termed as negative emotions, the contrary is also plausible, that is, it is quite possible that a person's action fetches more reward than what was expected out of it in the first place. Or, that s/he does not receive any punishment when expected. Such approving behaviour then would be highly valued and the person will most likely to engage himself/herself in such approving behaviours.

In all the above propositions, Homans relied heavily an behaviourism. He also fused the rationality principle of economics with psychological behaviourism. The rational choice theory overall governs Homans' understanding of human social exchanges. Human society as one constituted of actors who act in accord with the rationality proposition are intrinsically maximizing their utilities. Thus, in the last count Homans' individual is an actor who is essentially a rational profit seeker. Homans suggested a sociology which would attempt to understand elementary social behaviour comprehensively in order to generalize and theorize for large-scale structures. It is only that at the societal level the nature of exchanges are made up of complex processes.

Homans focused on individual exchanges. However, he was clear about the constitution of the human group. The group is understood to be a result of activity, interaction, sentiment and norms. The emphasis on the face-to-face situation, however, remains the starting point of social exchange theory of Homans. In the very opening page of *The Human Group*, it is emphasized, '… a number of persons who communicate with one another often over a span of time, and who are few enough so that each person who is able to communicate with all the others not at secondhand, through other people, but face to face' (Homans 1961: 1).

PETER BLAU (1918–2002)

A Brief Biographical Sketch

Peter Blau is credited with developing George Homans' scheme of social exchange from its application to elementary form of social life to an analysis of complex structures. In simple terms, he qualified the theory of social exchange beyond its original micro roots. Peter Blau's contention involves as to how at the higher levels social life is organized into more complex structures out of the association among wo/men. Blau's ideas are useful for a sociological understanding of the intricate relation between organization, power and bureaucracy. His *Exchange and Power in Social life* (1964) stands out as the major sociological work based on the theory of social exchange.

Peter Blau is a doctorate from Columbia University (1952) and completed his undergraduate sociology from the little known Elmhurst College, Illinois. He was born in Vienna, Austria in 1918 and later migrated to the United States. His school days were interrupted by World War II. He taught at many of the US universities and became a Professor of sociology in Columbia University. Later on, he shifted to the University of North Carolina at Chapel Hill.

In the sociology syllabi across the world, Peter Blau mainly figures for his study of the *American Occupational Structure* (1968) and his theory on occupation and social stratification. However, his major contribution remains in his effort to theoretically integrate small-scale issue with large-scale sociological theories. He has also contributed to the development of the structured theory. In fact, he collaborated with advanced functionalist Robert king Merton to coauthor *Continuities in Structural Inquiry* (1981). Blau has authored many articles and books mainly on the themes of organization and modern society.

Sociological Theory and Social Exchange

In this book *Exchange and Power in Social Life* (1964), Peter Blau makes clear his chief goal, '... an understanding of social structure on the basic of an analysis of the social processes that govern the relations between individuals and groups' (Blau 1964: 2). Against any project of developing grand schemes of sociological theory, he was more into an empirical bent. Accordingly, he opted for such a theory which could be tested empirically. Face-to-face micro studies, as suggested by Homans, is not discarded by Blau, but he views this as the means to gain insight to move beyond the behavioural level of social exchange. The nature of sociological theory is proposed by him as, 'A formal theory from which empiral predictions can be logically deduced plays the dominant role in research that is designed to test the prediction and thereby indirectly the theory' (Blau 1973: 45).

Apart from George Homans, Peter Blau is indebted to both Simmel and Emile Durkheim. For Simmel, the basic motive that drives individuals to associate with others is to satisfy individual needs. In such associations, individuals do not always enjoy rewards as per expectation but the expectation that marks such interaction makes them all social exchanges. Thus, social exchange is taken as the axial principle of social life. For Blau, the principle holds true for both individual as well as group behaviours. On the other hand, while theorizing on the structure of social associations, Blau takes recourse to Durkheim's understanding of society as more than just a summation of individuals — that as a social fact, society is a result of an association, and association acts an integrative factor to give rise to social behaviour. More in a Durkheimian way, he envisages social exchanges as creating associations and as well giving *rise* to social position and statuses.

Following Homans, Blau builds up the process of social association starting with at least two persons engaged in an exchange of social activity. Such social activity intrinsically involves both rewards and costs, either manifested or latent. The social anthropological insights are also invoked by Blau to see such exchanges as creating not only bonds between participants but also the nature of such exchanges establish differential statuses for the participants.

As long as the exchange process benefits the participants the process continues. A sort of cost–benefit assessment between the exchange partners as well as the social context of the exchange process gives rise to a complex at the societal level.

As commented upon by George Ritzer, Blau's scheme of social exchange starts with interpersonal exchange and ends with social change (Ritzer 1996). The scheme involves a four-stage sequence:

i. Interpersonal exchanges
ii. Status and power differentiation
iii. Legitimization and organization, and
iv. Opposition and change.

Each of these stages leads to the next stage. Social associations are a result of interaction between people who due to variety of reasons come together. After the initial ties are secured, on the basis of variability of rewards that accrue to the exchanging persons, the subsequent stages unfold. Rewards, as long as they satisfy expectations between the interactive persons and so long as they enhance the bonds, lead to a stable organization. On the other hand, due to insufficient rewards oppositional forces emerge which provide incentives for change. Quite obviously, mostly interactive parties cannot share rewards out of social exchange in equal terms; such inequality leads to power differences within a society.

Blau comprehensively adopts Homans' elementary forms of behaviour to explain higher level social structures. He is clear with his understanding that the exchange processes at the individual level can be fully appreciated by contextualizing them within the social structure that surrounds them. As noted before, the Durkhemian influence is prominent in Blau's theorization. While it is true that the social structure arises out of the social interactions/exchanges, but once they are constituted, they attain a life of their own. In turn they then affect the process of interaction.

Group Formation and Cohesion

Social groups provide the very basic site of social interaction. As social exchange is always directed towards other people, a social group is a pre-condition for such an interaction to take place at the first instance. Moreover, people are always drawn to those groups which offer them better exchanges. Thus, in order to get accepted as new members, people indulge in impressing the existing group members. Of course, such exercise come at a cost but an expectation of reciprocity balances the exchanges towards a stable stage of equilibrium. In simpler terms, the group formation takes place as those which promise greater rewards are the most sought out ones. Individuals flock to those and engage in such exchanges which allow them to get absorbed as successful group members.

In *Exchange and Power in Social Life* (1964), Blau discusses the integrative bonds that develop within a group. The integrative bonds that contribute to the cohesive character of a group are in the form of:

i. Impressing others
ii. Social approval
iii. Attractiveness, and
iv. Love.

Initially one indulges in various strategies of impressing others in order to get accepted in a group. Strategies are adopted with respect to specific social situation, which may range from taking risks to exhibiting ease.

Another integrative bond is social approval. When an individual undertakes social exchange, s/he expects that his/her activity would receive approval from the other participating individuals. Thus, the approving agreement of others helps one to gain confidence in one's decision, opinions and actions. It serves as a crucial element of any social grouping process.

Attractiveness is simply the appeal of association shared by participants in social exchange. It follows from social approval that it generates attractiveness amongst the individuals. As under normal conditions, people tend to interact and associate with others who agree with their actions and decisions. Quite obviously, any conflict of opinions if continues for a long term would lead on the contrary to a lack of attraction and result in rejection. Fleeting impression or bluffing through first impression as a mechanism for generating attractiveness in the final count are self-defeating in creating cohesion in any group.

Finally, Blau talked about love as that selfless devotion by one to those they love. Such intrinsic attraction, however, cannot be fully selfless. It rests on an expectation of maintaining the other's love. Love relationship is a unique kind of social exchange where the rewards are not so specific as in other social exchanges. Interestingly, in such relationships there is an asymmetry whereby the one who is 'less in love' gains more power and manipulate the exchange in his/her favour drawing more rewards. Thus, love is such a delicate integrative bond whose unrestricted rewards diminish its worth and value.

Such social integration by implication rests on shared values amongst the group members. Consensus on normative standards at the operational level not only leads to a strengthening of the group cohesion but also invokes informal sanctions on individual actions which are on the contrary.

Complex Organization and Bureaucracy

Although Blau adapted the elementary forms of social exchange to explain complex social structures, he was aware of the distinct nature of complex large collectivities. In his *Bureaucracy in Modern Society* (1956), he establishes how one needs to qualify the use of elementary face-to-face individual exchanges to account for such large impersonal social structures:

> The complex social structures that characterize large collectives differ fundamentally from the simpler structures of small groups. A structure of social relations develops in a small group in the course of social interaction among its members. Since there is no direct social interaction among most members of a large community or entire society, some other mechanism must mediate the structure of social relations among them. (Blau 1964: 253)

Blau's contribution to the sociology of *bureaucracy* is immense. He explains bureaucracy as one organization which accomplishes large-scale administrative organization tasks. Such a complex administrative organization also works on the principle of social exchange but rests also on the principle of increasing rationalization of society. However, the lack of a personal face-to-face situation so necessary for social exchange to take place is accounted for by Blau. In dealing with such large complex, he reiterates the role of value consensus that marks a society.

As large organizations like bureaucracy are marked by indirect exchanges, alternative mechanisms come into play to substitute for direct exchanges. The norms and values mediate among social structures and facilitate social exchange. Instead of interpersonal exchange, such organizations are marked by collectivity-individual exchanges. He examines organizations by focusing on the role of organizational sub-structures and confirms that the same basic principle holds true for such organizational functioning too. They exist and perform on the basis of cost and rewards.

> Commonly agreed upon values and norms serve as media of social life and as mediating links for social transaction. They make indirect social exchange possible, and they govern the processes of social integration and differentiation in complex social structures as well as the development of social organization and reorganization in them. (Blau 1964: 255)

Blau, therefore, is attentive to the problem of developing theoretical orientation beyond the face-to-face exchange theory of Homans to account for the macro structures. Blau develops such theoretical formulation as a complement to the original social exchange theory of Homans. The primary small-scale exchange theory of Homans is taken by him as a premise to build theories of organization which are large-scale. He attempts to integrate the small-scale and large-scale sociological issues theoretically.

SUMMARY

George Homans founded the unique perspective of social exchange in sociological theory. Human beings indulge in social exchanges in terms of rewards and punishments. The image of the human being here is that of a rational being who is competent to make rational choice. Primarily an individual being is driven by self-interest. Homans heavily relied on behavioural psychologism to develop a micro-oriented exchange theory.

Peter Blau takes the micro-oriented conceptualization of social exchange to a higher plane to account for macro social structures. To build sociological theory in order to study large-scale organization, he focuses on the role of norms and values. According to Blau, when one moves beyond the face-to-face human interaction, one realizes that social exchanges occur between individuals who need not be all too consistent and be driven by a singular goal. Moreover, the rational choice theory of economics need not be absolutely implanted on social behaviour, because a total and complete knowledge about alternative course of action/choices is quite an improbability for human beings.

Blau's theory has been instrumental in sociology for developing important theories of organization and bureaucracy. Understanding of group behaviour has been enhanced by social exchange theories and the perspective has been furthered by many other contemporary theorists.

KEY WORDS

- *Group Formation*
- *Psychological Behaviourism*
- *Rational Choice Theory*
- *Social Exchange*
- *Utilitarianism*

GLOSSARY

Rational Choice Theory: Attempts to explain social phenomenon in terms of how self-interested individuals make choices under the influence of their preferences. It treats social exchange as similar to economic exchange where all parties try to maximize their advantage or gain, and to minimize their disadvantage or loss.

Social Behaviourism: An approach in social sciences which seeks to provide an objective, quantified approach to explaining and predicting social behaviour. It is associated with the rise of the behavioural sciences, modelled after the natural sciences.

Social Exchange Theory: Based on the assumptions of rational choice theory it explains social change and stability as a process of negotiated exchanges between parties.

Utilitarianism: States that humans act rationally to maximize their benefits through relations with others. In relation to social exchange theory, people try to maximize the profit and rewards they receive in an interaction by making choices that will benefit them.

Discussion Points

- The intellectual premise of Social Exchange Theory.
- Human behaviour as utility-driven in Homan's Model.
- Understanding group through Social Exchange Theory.

10

Phenomenology and Ethnomethodology

As a philosophical movement, phenomenology is a product of the early twentieth-century intellectual fervour in the Western world. The social crisis between the two world wars generated fresh thinking on the society. Max Weber's interpretive sociology has had already put sociological thinking on a subjective mould. The idealist current in the German intellectual thought continued to probe into the problem of 'objective' knowledge of the society. The central question for sociological method and theory remained — whether it is valid to understand and explain the world from the perspective of the observer.

Edmund Husserl (1859–1938), the German philosopher, founded phenomenology as that philosophy which could further the cause of probing into the subjective world. Husserl posited phenomenology both as a philosophical perspective and as a theory of knowledge. There is no a priori reality per se; instead it is always given form and meaning by humans who experience it. Husserl insisted on studying phenomena not as they 'appear' to an observer's (analyst) consciousness, but to any consciousness whatsoever. At the turn of the twentieth-century, the entire baggage of classical sociological thinking and theories were subjected to critical thinking. Compounded with the rapid socio-political upheavals, the world of sociology took a turn towards a 'new' philosophy. Taking philosophy as a 'rigorous science' sociological theories started questioning the taken-for-grantedness of the world of experience.

The spirit of the time was to question the certainty assumptions of social scientific researches, that is, every certainty is questionable. If we intend to appreciate the basic thrust of the phenomenological school of thinking, we need to acknowledge that against 'objectivism' — a distinct way of looking at the reality marked the early decades of the twentieth-century. It was a turn towards a philosophical sociology which could place the world of conscious experience as its subject matter. We can see in this attempt a Weberian influence, as it prioritized the point of view of the acting subject. Thus, understanding social behaviour was premised not from the angle and perspective of the social scientist, but from the ways as experienced by the people who constitute the social reality.

We have already noted that Weberian sociology tried to account for the elements of motives, values and judgments involved in social interactions. In the similar spirit, Edmund Husserl tried to come up with a philosophy which could account for the conditions for an objective study of the subjective world. Consciousness and the content of conscious experience were fore-grounded in this new project. The fundamental idea of Husserl was to organize a systematic reflection on and analysis of the structure of consciousness.

Subsequently, ethnomethodology as a distinct school of sociological thinking developed in the Western world. The bearing of phenomenology on ethnomethodology is quite obvious. Ethnomethodology also questions the 'facticity' of the social order for granted. Traditional sociology, according to ethnomethodologists, has analysed the society with less attention and the procedures by which a particular society is being ordered. For a correction, ethnomethodology emphasized the procedures by which a social order is sustained. We can sense, therefore, that in both phenomenology and ethnomethodology the striving was to take account of the subjective world of the people constituting the social reality. Simplistically, the ethnomethodological thinking was to account for the methods that ordinary people employ to make sense of their world. The foremost thinker who introduced the ethnomethodogical school of sociological theory is Harold Garfinkel (1917–2011). In ethnomethodology, we find an interesting blend of the Parsonian emphasis of 'social order' with the classical Weberian insistence on 'interpretation' of human actions which give rise to social interaction and, thereby, a social order.

EDMUND HUSSERL

A Biographical Sketch and Influences

The philosophy of phenomenology was formulated by Edmund Husserl, the early twentieth-century German philosopher and social thinker. Husserl was fortunate to enjoy best schooling during his younger days. Born into a rich Jewish family, he went to school in Vienna. At the age of 10, in the year 1869, he started his German classical education. In 1876, he graduated and went to Leipzig University (then a part of the Austrian Empire). Thereafter, he went to Berlin. During that time his subjects were mathematics, physics and philosophy. Interestingly his doctoral work was in mathematics from Vienna. Husserl took up teaching positions first at Halle University, and then at Gottingen. Finally he served as a professor for the period between 1916 and 1928 at Freiburg. It was at Freiburg that Husserl developed his philosophical thinking.

We can note that the essential ideas of phenomenology were the product of that intervening year between the two World Wars. It was an anxiety about the future which formed Husserl's search for the phenomenological approach. It was a search for a deeper understanding of the essence of phenomena. For him, the task was to penetrate beyond the taken-for-granted world of experience (*Lebenswelt*) through a bracketing procedure to arrive at a deeper understanding of the essence of phenomena.

The classical thinkers who influenced Husserl were Descartes, Hume and Kant. Naturally, the phenomenological approach was embedded in the idealist German philosophical tradition. Although the English-speaking world realized Husserl's unique philosophy in the 1960s, the main ideas and concepts of it were to be found in his early lectures in Gottingen in 1907. He tried to assimilate ideas from the three great philosophers mentioned above.

It was Descartes who had a profound bearing on Husserl. It was Husserl's reading of Descartes that prompted him to conceive of the world as one essentially reflected upon and as experienced upon by people. David Hume's 'phenomenism' too had its place in Husserl's early interests. But he was sceptical of absolute 'phenomenism' — that, appearances reveal nothing about which appears. He was against the idea that appearances provide no knowledge about phenomena that appear because such a position would lead to a rejection of any theory of knowledge. For Husserl, these appearances are all that important to theorize on knowledge. The way such appearances are re-constructed by individuals in their own consciousness, the meanings of such appearances of 'things' are the bases of theory. Finally, Husserl realized the crucial difference that the realm of culture enjoys from the realm of nature from Immanuel Kant — that, active individuals act on the reality by imposing their thought categories to comprehend and construct their world. These thought categories are the a priori essential constituents, the framework into which the real world is conceptualized. Recognizing this subjective nature of the realm of culture and society, the phenomenological approach of Husserl put consciousness as the 'absolute' being, whereby, he strived for a science of essential being and not just a science of facts.

Early Phenomenology: Facts and Essences

The emphasis on the difference between facts and essences is fundamental in any phenomenological method of study. How do we realize facts? Rather, what is a fact? A fact is something real which enjoys a time and space and therefore has a temporal entity. We experience such facts through our cognitive faculty, that is to say, what is 'real' is actually experienced as 'real' through the mediation of our cognitive faculty. According to Husserl, an essence on the contrary is premised on consciousness which is essentially intentional, that, it refers beyond itself to things other than itself. A man is an embodiment of self-consciousness and since consciousness is always intentional, everyone by dint of this power stands beyond oneself. The datum of this essential intuition is essence. He emphasized essence, in so far as he maintained that pure essence was exemplified in the data of experience (Husserl 1967: 57). An essence, therefore, is to be understood as an essential possibility and not just an empirical possibility.

Beyond the scope of objectivity, phenomenological method is an attitude of mind that underscores a philosophical method. An orthodox practitioner of sociology would put phenomenology and sociology as two distinct pursuits. Sociology, traditionally, would study the perspective of the other and collect them in the form of data. It is in this way that a sense of order is placed on the reality. But instead of gathering data of the behaviour of others or the perspective of others, phenomenology would emphasize the ways through which individuals perceive and construct the world around them in their own consciousness. Simplistically, the emphasis here is on the reflexive experience of the individuals and the ways it shapes one's consciousness.

But the growing uncertainty about the possibility of an 'objective' sociology in the early twentieth-century opened up a whole range of reflexive sociology. From a high pedestal of 'science', sociology directed itself more towards the ordinary life and the common sense world. Thus, phenomenology could suggest the coming of a sort of creative sociology; creative in the sense that it attempted to understand and explain the world from the 'others' perspective, relegating the overriding scheme of thought of the analyst. Thereby, phenomenology puts a question mark on the supposed 'objective' world. It replaced the notion of 'natural order' of the society to an understanding of the 'social construction' of the reality. Expectedly, the heavy reliance on facts and empirical verification of theories on the basis of facts, which is highlighted by science, was scrutinized.

Does this make Husserl interested in the metaphysical world? Not only did Husserl develop his method with a critique of psychologism, he focused on individual consciousness to dismiss any metaphysical bearing. He was against the view that philosophy is reducible to a factual science. And, obviously he could see that, psychologism reduces the fundamental laws of logic and mathematics to psychological generalizations about the way an individual thinks. George Nakhnikian in his introduction to *The Idea of Phenomenology* (Husserl 1964:) puts across this methodological stance of Husserl in no uncertain terms: 'Husserl's phenomenology is an out growth of his attack on psychologism. Psychologism is a species of the view that philosophy is reducible to a factual science, in this case to psychology. Husserl is just as strongly against 'biologism' and 'anthropologism' as he is against psychologism' (Husserl 1964). Also, the emphasis of Husserl on individual consciousness saves phenomenology from being metaphysical.

Evidence is what is being offered by consciousness, and hence phenomenology does not conform to a science of facts, but suggests a science of essential being. Thus, when it studies the way people reflect and conceive the reality, such personal reflection is not a psychological activity of consciousness. Instead, such reflection is crucially linked to an objective structure as an ideal act of consciousness. Husserl suggested a notion of eidetic science, trying to put phenomenology as a 'science' that strives to push for a knowledge of essences rather a 'science' of essential being (Husserl 1965).

PHENOMENOLOGICAL METHOD

What is central to Husserl's method is the distinction that he made between 'essence' and 'existence'/facts. Again, 'essence' can be 'bracketed' as distinct from 'existence'/facts which is to say that, we may speak about any one of them, while suspending all statements about the other. However, Husserl made an attempt to relate them together. Without dismissing the empirical world of facts it is possible to 'bracket' the essential being. We could appreciate that for Husserl, the world of essence as 'bracketed' may be incompatible with the world of facts; yet the latter may remain side by side with the former. This is so, because Husserl considered the world of corporeal existents to be the empirical counter part of the world of essence. Accordingly, pure essence is exemplified in the concrete existents (Husserl 1957). Therefore, the real being of a concrete existence lies, not in its corporeality, but in its essence.

Such a method of study is a direct fall out of Husserl's skeptical attitude towards naturalism as promoted by orthodox scientific method. The cognitive approach of science was questioned by Husserl as he held that philosophical thinking is inevitably shaped by one's position towards the reality that one is attempting to cognize. 'Bracketing' the 'given' of the natural order is the plinth of phenomenology. Thus, even if objectivity is the goal of science, such a goal is always circumscribed by one's perception of the reality. Objective perception is a matter of lived experiences. It is temporal and yet related to the part time in terms of memory and the retention of it. The past subjective realities as retained in memory shape one's perception, immediate reflection and interpretation of events. Husserl proposed such a method which could view humans acting in accordance with both past behaviours and current situations. The bearing of memory as subjective reality has a crucial consequence in one's consciousness. Moreover, assigning agency to the actors, Husserl confirmed that all present acts are subject to modification on behalf of individual perceptions which allows alteration of perceived events. Proposing such a link between the past and the present, between time and consciousness, Husserl would state:

> All the essential characteristics of experience and consciousness which we have reached are for us necessary steps towards the attainment of the end which is unceasingly drawing us an, the discovery namely, of the essence of that 'pure' consciousness which is to fix the limits of the phenomenological field. Our inquires were eidetic; but the individual instances of the essences we have referred to as experience, stream of experience, 'consciousness' in all its senses, belonged as real events to the natural world. (Husserl 1957: 125–26)

Such a proposal allows continuous flow of perceptual patterns to exhibit an objective 'flow of time' and a true knowledge of time. Thus, through an imaginative method Husserl suggested that one could probe the rudimentary structures and processes of experience.

ALFRED SCHUTZ (1899–1959)

Titled *The Phenomenology of the Social World* (1967), Alfred Schutz's seminal text actually placed phenomenology as a distinct school in sociological theory. The decade of the 1960s was all important for the development of phenomenological sociology precisely because Schutz's text was translated for the English-speaking world in 1967, although the original German text was out in 1932. The phenomenological philosophy of Edmund Husserl was adopted by Schutz to give it a more vigorous sociological turn. He laid the foundations of social constructions for a wide range of social, cultural and feminist studies.

Biography and Influences

Born in 1899, Alfred Schutz enrolled himself at the University of Vienna, Austria. In fact, he hailed from Vienna and had the opportunity of studying law and social sciences. Sociologist, Othman Spann at Vienna introduced him to the works of Max Weber. Weber's methodological treatise interested Schutz, as he too endeavoured to seek a basis for an interpretative sociology.

Schutz adopted the Weberian school of thought that understanding social action was the methodological and epistemological foundation of sociology. But his was a critical acceptance of Weber's approach, and for a consistent theory of meaning (which was supposed to be distinctive of human action) he looked forward to Husserl's ideas.

The original German text of *The Phenomenology of the Social World* (1967), a result of a rigorous research for twelve years, was published in 1932. Between Husserl and Schutz, there had been a great deal of deliberations after Schutz dedicated a copy of the text to Husserl.

Finally, Schutz headed for the United States after spending a brief period in parts of France, to escape the Nazi Occupation of Austria. He prospered academically as he joined the New School for Social Research in New York City. Subsequently he was involved in the establishment of the International Phenomenological Research. He collaborated with Thomas Luckmann for his last work *The Structures of the Life-World*, which was published posthumously in 1973. Schutz died while working on this text in the year 1959. Summarily, we can say that Schutz was drawn primarily towards Weber's interpretative sociology and tried to enrich it by a critical adaptation of Husserl's transcendental phenomenology. While accepting Husserl's notion of the everyday world of experience characterized by the natural attitude of uncritical acceptance, Schutz accounted for social reality as one in which people cognitively suspend doubt.

BEYOND WEBER'S NOTION OF SOCIAL ACTION

According to Max Weber, who is to be credited for making sociology sensitive to subtle subjective ways of social life, the unit of sociological subject matter is social action. Action is social in so far as and by virtue of the subjective meaning attached to it by the acting individual/ individuals, it takes account of the behaviour of others. Thereby, it is oriented in its course. Schutz made a qualification to this act of reflection. Accordingly, while it is correct to say that we perform a reflective act of attention when we observe our own lived experiences, it is also true that observing others it is not at all necessary to live their experiences. As we accept our own existence, we accept the existence of others as well. Thus, we can only observe their experiences. A social action cannot orient itself simply by taking account of the behaviour of others, but it is a case of 'intentional conscious experiences directed toward the other self' (Schutz 19677: 144).

Sharing the same experiences does not automatically result in sharing the same consciousness. We can only say that, one's stream of consciousness can be in simultaneous relation to others' stream of consciousness. One attends to all other parallel streams of consciousness. It is not simply an act of experiencing them but a reflection in the everyday life of behaviours of fellow human beings. The realm of inter-subjectivity suggests that the social world exhibits both unity and inner differentiation. If it is divided on the basis of individual experiences/interpretation of events, it is united on one's conscious awareness of the streams of consciousness; sharing the same world assures the sharing of the subjective meanings attached to our experiences.

However, such interpretation of other's experiences may not always be accurate. Such misinterpretation of the interactions among the people — the possibility of it — was admitted by Schutz. This is the reason why he emphasized on 'intentional conscious experiences directed toward the other self'.

> Conscious experiences intentionally related to another self which emerge in the form of spontaneous activity we shall speak of as social behaviour. If such experiences have the character of being previously projected, we shall speak of them as social action. Social behaviour so defined will embrace all specific -Ego-Acts (Ich-Akte) which are intentionally directed upon a Thou as upon another self having consciousness and duration. Here we include experiences such as feelings of sympathy and antipathy, erotic attitudes, and feeling-activities of all kinds. (Schutz 1967: 144)

The element of choice is also highlighted by Schutz in the context of social action. One may or may not always act purposively. Also, one's intentional acts of consciousness directed toward others, when reciprocated, give rise to social relationship.

In Schutz' phenomenological sociology, the notion of the 'significant other' is in-built. It is important in this scheme of phenomenological understanding to appreciate social action as a lived experienced. A 'significant other' is one with whom one shares a common space and time of community. In other words, such a 'significant other' pre-supposes a face-to-face situation. Such face-to-face situations involve all acts of reflection and other-orientation. This inevitably leads to simultaneity of separate streams of consciousness. According to Schutz, shared lived experience is then marked by the subject's spontaneous activity which is unique from all other lived experiences by the fact of intentionality.

To satisfy the condition of objectivity, Schutz suggested that there are alternative ways for an observer to ascertain and interpret the motives/experiences of others. One can fall back upon one's own memory for similar actions of his/her own. Second, in case of an absence of such a direct reference, one can take recourse to one's own knowledge of the customary behaviour of the observed person. Finally, in the absence of the both, one interprets an action in terms of the effect which it actually has and assumes that the effect is what was intended. Yet, it is being easier suggested than actually accomplished. In one way or the other, in order to understand observed social relationships an observer must take recourse to one's own experiences of such relationships. The notion of stock of knowledge is relevant here to appreciate that, it is not only the specialist observer/researcher but also all individuals who are caught in the web of interactions in a social setting, who draw upon past experiences to interpret the present.

Schutz, therefore, invoked the notion of 'stock of knowledge' to account for the repository of experiences that an individual falls back upon to indulge in inter-subjective understanding. Quite obviously this stock of knowledge is a result of one's diverse life experiences and awareness of events. The more diverse it is, the richer is the stock of knowledge. Schutz talked about different categories of stock of knowledge, of which the *habitual knowledge* was more important for his analysis. It is that type which offers us definitive solutions to problems, which are organized in the flow of lived experiences. This type brings us closer to the notion of common sense. But Schutz would hold that even that which appears 'common' in everyday life is more than a simple sense presentation. Instead, he said:

> It is a thought object, a construct of a highly complicated nature ... in other words, the so-called concrete facts of commonsense perception are not as concrete as it seems. They already involve abstractions of a highly complicated nature, and we have to take account of this situation lest we commit the fallacy of misplaced concreteness. (Schutz 1962: 3–4)

Hence, it is quite possible that the commonsense knowledge is a sort of taken-for-granted, which could be relevant only among those who actually share the same life-experiences. Thus, quite possibly all individuals may not share the same commonsense as they differ in their life-experiences. Again, there may be people who would regularly defy the commonsense, which brings us to the proposition that any understanding of reality is a continuous process as we grasp only certain aspects of it at a time.

The everyday-life world is all that important for Schutz, whose last work is the *Structure of the Life-World* (1973).This text is co-authored by Thomas Luckmann and was actually finished by him. For every individual the primary reality and all his/her activities are actually played out in this primary reality. This primary reality is a construct of both-the natural elements and the social elements. This life-world is actually inter-subjective and it is the very context of where social actors act. Schutz and Luckmann attempted a comprehensive examination of the nature of social reality:

> The everyday life-world is the region of reality in which man can engage himself and which he can change while he operates in it by means of his animate organisms.... Only in this realm can one be understood by his fellow-men, and only in it can he work together with them. Only in the world of everyday life can a common, communicative, surrounding would be constituted. The world of everyday life is consequently man's fundamental and permanent reality. (Schutz and Luckmann 1973: 3)

It was in this way that Schutz tired to sort out the problem of inter-subjectivity. The life-world itself appears meaningful in one's consciousness. As it is constituted of many such individuals, social action is therefore embedded in such meanings and context, and is subjectively motivated and articulated purposefully as per the structured interests and possibilities. Schutz, therefore, laid bare the structure of the life world in terms of typifications that people make in everyday life with respect to their familiarity and strangeness with life experiences and shared consciousness.

Taking the cue from Husserl, Alfred Schutz problematized the very nature of day-to-day perception. According to Schutz, Husserl's idea of the everyday world of experience is characterized by the natural attitude of uncritical acceptance. Instead, he accounted for social realities as one in which individuals cognitively suspend doubts. Commonsense does include many misunderstandings and misinterpretations in the taken-for-granted world, which does not suggest that understanding of reality is an improbable task. Rather it prepares us to be ever doubtful and be confident of capturing a part of reality at a time.

PETER LUDWIG BERGER (1929-)

A Biographical Sketch and Influences

Peter Berger, born in 1929, is an American sociologist. He was born in Vienna, Austria and later shifted to the United States after World War II. The trajectory of this early life was akin to that of Alfred Schutz. For his post graduation he studied in the New School for Social Research, New York. He secured his doctoral degree from the same in the year 1954. While in the New School, Berger came under the direct influence of Alfred Schutz. Obviously the phenomenological approach was embraced by Berger.

Primarily, Berger was interested to introduce a sociology of knowledge perspective to any analysis of the social world. The human consciousness is a result of his/her social being. Berger acknowledged the fundamental contribution of Karl Marx on this proposition. Also, the classical thinkers, whose theories had a bearing on the sociology of knowledge perspective, were reflected upon by Berger. Thus, we see the multiple influences of the theorizations of Emile Durkheim, Max Weber, Karl Manheim and Talcott Parsons on him.

Initially, Berger worked for a couple of years in Bad Boll, Germany. Subsequently, he joined the University of North Carolina. He was also an associate professor at Hartford Theological Seminary from 1958 to 1963. Thereafter, he joined the New School for

Social Research, New York as a professor. Since then, he has served many other colleges and universities.

Co-authored with Thomas Luckmann, *The Social Construction of Reality* (1966) stands as the most influential text of Peter Berger till date. He also covered a wide span of subjects confronting the modern society with various other authors. Some important books by him are: *A Rumour of* Angels (1969) and *Movement and Revolution* (1970), both co-authored with Richard Neuhaus; and *The Homeless Mind* (1973), co-authored with Brigitte Berger and Hansfried Kellner. He also co-authored books like *Facing Up to Modernity* (1977), *The War Over the Family* (1983) and a few more with his wife Brigitte Berger.

Social Reality: A Form of Consciousness

Peter Berger and Thomas Luckmann were both students of Alfred Schutz. Through their book *The Social Constitution of Reality* they did their best to integrate the phenomenological thoughts of Schutz with the mainstream sociological theories. Central to their endeavour was to examine the individual–society relationships.

Society is both an objective as well as a subjective reality. This is the cornerstone of Berger's analysis of social reality. This analysis of society as a subjective reality examines the process by which an individual's conception/experience of reality are generated as a result of his/her interaction with social structures. Again, Berger focuses on the process of objectification, that is, how the new ideas and concepts of individuals become a part of their reality.

A sociology of knowledge perspective has to address the question of how reality is socially constructed. This has been the primary question for Berger and Luckmann. For them, it is the knowledge that governs our conduct in everyday life as the plinth of reality.

> Everyday life presents itself as a reality interpreted by men and subjectively meaningful to them as a cone vent world. As sociologists we take this reality as the object of an analysis. With in the frame of reference of sociology as an empirical science it is possible to take this reality as given, to take as data particular phenomena arising within it, without further inquiring about the foundations of this reality, which is a philosophical task.... The world of everyday life is not only taken for granted ad reality by the ordinary members of society in the subjectively meaningful conduct of their lives. It is a world that originates in their thoughts and actions, and is maintained ad real by these. (Berger and Luckmann 1966: 19)

Social reality is constructed through a triadic scheme of subjectification, objectification and socialization. As we have already noted, social reality is subjective as its construction is accomplished by individuals as a result of their past behaviours which have a constant interface with present activities which allows its modification and re-creation. Simultaneously, the process of objectification tells us how the same individuals tend to view everyday-life world as a given and ordered reality independent of the actors' agency.

At this point, Berger underscores the important role played by language in effecting the integration of everyday reality. Language is the most important sign system of human society. It links up commonsense knowledge with finite provinces of meaning. The crucial role played by language lies in its capacity of being the objective repository of vast accumulations of meaning and experience. This repository is preserved in time and as well as transmitted to following generations. Finally, internalization is the third point of this triadic scheme. Evidently, it connects individuals to society. As members in a community, individuals share the same normative order as well as behavioural expectations and thereby, they share a similar social reality. It is this socialization process that finally explains the intricate locking of the individual, norms and society.

Related to the process of objectification, that is, the process of acceptance of the constructs of the subjective consciousness as something of a pre-arranged order independent of the actors, is the process of reification. Reification denies human beings the self-knowledge. It negates human beings the knowledge that this social world is actually human-made; that the world inhabited by human beings is a creation of the same human beings is obscured by the process of reification, which in turn leads to alienation. It is a case of acute objectification in which *thing-hood* attains the pedestal of objective reality.

Espousing the cause of sociology of knowledge, especially in modern times and its technological growth, Berger had to address the question of reification in specific. Any sociology of knowledge that attempt to account for consciousness cannot overlook the huge impact of technology. How such technological advancement has aggravated the process of reification and consequently individual consciousness, has received analysis in Berger's *The Homeless Mind*, which is co-authored with Brigitte Berger and Hansfried Kellner. It examines how the level of technological knowledge affects the individual's everyday life and thereby, his/her consciousness.The ideas of Schutz were taken up by Peter Berger, his student. Along with Thomas Luckmann, Berger puts the phenomenological perspective into regular sociological theories that attempt to explain the individual–society relationship. The role of culture, social expectations and social institutions are acknowledged by Berger to account for how this social reality is constructed. It is being constructed as a result of the everyday interactions of individuals who are all implicated in social institutions. Invoking the twin processes of subjectification and objectification; and recognizing the process of socialization, Berger and Luckmann put phenomenology as an important school which emphasizes micro-oriented Sociological Theory. It allowed a wide application in sociological research because of its focus on the everyday aspects of human existence.

HAROLD GARFINKEL (1917–2011)

Ethnomethodology, simply put, is the study of the methods that people employ regularly to make sense of their world through interactions. It is quite distinct from phenomenology, but somewhere their thrust area is common, that is, put the ordinary members of society in the everyday situations on the foreground of sociological investigation. It is not so surprising to note that the founder of ethno-methodological perspective, Harold Garfinkel was taught by Alfred Schutz at the New School for Social Research, New York.

A Biographical Sketch and Influences

Harold Garfinkel, an American sociologist was born in New Jersey, 1917. He started off as a student of economics in 1935 at the University of Network, New Jersey. After his graduation, he joined the University of North Carolina in 1939. He studied Sociology which was more directed at accomplishing public works.

Obtaining his Masters in 1942, Garfinkel had to serve the military for a short while before joining Harvard University. At Harvard he came under the influence of the greatest functionalist sociologist Talcott Parsons. Immediately after obtaining his doctorate degree from Harvard, Garfinkel involved himself with studying day-to-day deliberations of juries in Winchita, Kansas. The study influenced him to coin the term 'ethnomethodology', which he introduced in the American Sociological Association meetings in 1954. Subsequently, he moved to the University of California at Los Angeles as a teaching faculty and continued with his work on developing ethnomethodology as an important tool for micro-sociology.

It is quite obvious that, Garfinkel was influenced by phenomenology. But, as admitted by himself, Parson's work was instrumental in shaping him as a sociologist who looked for precise and practical reasoning to account for the nature of social consensus and order. Interestingly it was at Parsons' insistence that Garfinkel visited and studied with Alfred Schutz at the New School for Social Research, New York. In a way, Parsons introduced him to the theories of Edmund Husserl and Alfred Schutz. Apart from that, Garfinkel's ethnomethodology was also impacted upon by concepts from symbolic interactionism, linguists and anthropology.

Garfinkel differed with Parsons on the question of treatment of the ordinary and the mundane. Mundane social action does not find much attention in Parsons's Theory of Social Action. The more general and regular social action that actors engage in through internalization of norms was not sufficient for Garfinkel to explain social order. Yet, he was influenced by Parsons' *The Structure of Social Action* to develop a distinct method which could account for the production and relevance of immortal, ordinary society (Garfinkel 1988). Finally, it was Schutz's phenomenological ideas of the constitution of the commonsense world and the related concepts that shaped ethnomethodology largely.

Problem of Order

From Parsons, Garfinkel realized the significance of normative order as a sustaining force of social reality. But the problem for him was to search for the process by which, not just the grand process of all too familiar norm internalization, the mundane and the ordinary maintain order and meaning in their lives. It is an attempt to look beyond the comfort zone that orthodox sociology always sought to indulge in. According to Garfinkel:

> Ethnomethodology's fundamental phenomenon and its standing technical preoccupation in its studies is to find, collect, specify, and make inscrutable observable the local endogenous production and natural accountability of immortal familiar society's most ordinary organizational things in the word, and to provide for them both and simultaneously as objects and procedurally, as alternate methodologies the identity of objects and methodologies is key. (Garfinkel 1996: 6)

Literally, ethno methodology would mean the methods of ordinary people that are used on a daily basis to satisfy the order of social reality. Actually as we have noted before, while studying the jurists at Kansas, Garfinkel was interested to theorize on how people come to see the world. While researching on the deliberations of the jurists, he realized that they were indulging in their deliberations with a self-certificate of doing the job of jurists. Thus, in their decision-making process; the jurists were dependent on a taken-for-granted world. Hence it was a case of the jurors doing their own methodology while being involved in decision-making process (Wallace and Wolf 1999).

The cornerstone of ethno methodology is the ordered social reality and that order is a resultant of actors indulging in exchanging accounts of their interactions. This way it attempts to explain the subjective nature of human interactions, which have an underlying goal of striking a consensus. As Garkinkel makes if clear, 'I use the term "ethno methodology" to refer to the investigation of the rational properties of indexical expressions and other practical actions as contingent ongoing accomplishments of organized, artful practices of everyday life....'(Garfinkel 1967l).

In every interactions actually the actors account for their actions that is they explain specific situations and contexts, and by 'indexical expressions' he refers to the fact that ordinary descriptive terms are powerfully influenced whenever they are being contextualized. To explain the 'order', the stable features of everyday life, sociologists usually select familiar settings and subjects. In the process many all-too-familiar, rather 'expected' features of reality are ignored. But ethnomethodology would focus on that 'taken-for-granted' and problematize it. There lies the immense potential of studying how people make sense of the commonsense world.

Tools of Ethnomethodology

Breaching experiments and conversation analysis are considered to be the two most useful tools that Garfinkel suggest to apply in order to account for the ways that people employ in their day-to-day life to make sense of the world of order. Ethnomethodology is always searching for the 'unaccounted' for in the familiar. Thus, while studying the ways people account for their ways of looking and doing things in the world, one need to intentionally disrupt the process of such accounting for the order. This is to suggest that, while actors negotiate and construct meaningfully their reality, there remains normally hidden methods of negotiation. By breaching one can disturb these normal situations of interactions, whereby one can unearth the hidden, unattended, possibly taken-for-granted acts.

Breaching experiments help a sociologist to break the everyday rules so that the hidden comes out, that is, quite often being unaware people indulge in actions that leads to interactions; that the social life is not always a result of any methodical procedures and production. Related to this technique of disrupting the normal, is the focus on conversation analysis in ethnomethodology. The mundane, day-to-day conversation is a primary focus of any ethnomethodological study. Human communication is that crucial act with the help of which human beings interact. Words are used as a means of interactions, interactions in order to clarify and reconstruct social order. Garfinkel is of the opinion that, what is being spoken or said is far less important than, what is being left out of conversation.

In our day-to-day conversation, much of the deliberations is again taken-for-granted. On the basis of past knowledge and past interactions much of the present conversation rests on anticipatory knowledge, that is, there was an area of nonverbal communication. Thus, the spoken world is marked by an appearance of consensus which is shared by all involved in any interaction. By looking beyond and searching the unstated sociology could gain crucial insights into such interactions.

Ethnomethodology, by focusing on these tools of breaching experiments, and conversation analysis basically points out how a person understands the world in their everyday life. Generally speaking, this method falls outside the scope of traditional sociology. It is so because with its focus on the mundane it stands in opposition to the scope of mainstream sociology. Mainstream sociology have deliberated a great deal and theorized on grand social structures engaging in methods of abstractions. Ethnomethodology has paid little attention to such abstracted social structures in themselves; instead the interest of ethnomethodologists is in the way that people make sense of these grand structures in their daily life.

SUMMARY

Phenomenology as a distinct philosophical method was established by Edmund Husserl. Husserl was essentially an intellectual product of the great idealist tradition of German philosophy. His analysis was based on a task of the philosopher to look beyond the taken-for-grantedness of the world of experience. Such penetrative exercise only allows a deeper understanding of the essence of phenomena. Thus, one needs to examine the phenomena of consciousness and bracket them in order to test their truth.

This is to say that, the conscious experience of the individuals constitutes the subject-matter for phenomenologist. Hence, the day-to-day routine life, common sense and conscious experience are all important for building such sociology of everyday life.

Phenomenology emphasizes that our perceptions are influenced by memories, conscious experience and recollections. According to Schutz, all of these impact upon our ways of perceiving social situations and others. Past experiences, moreover, allow us to bracket possible courses of action in the everyday-life world. As an extreme micro perspective in sociology, ethnomethodology, on the other hand, is concerned with the organization of the everyday world. Being critical of conventional sociology, it focuses on studying what people actually do, instead of imposing the theorists' sense of reality upon them.

Key Words

- *Enlightenment Ideals*
- *Frankfurt School*
- *Human Practice*
- *Ideal Speech Situation*
- *Life-world*
- *Mass Culture*
- *Neo-Marxist*
- *Public Sphere*
- *Social Criticism*
- *Technological Rationality*

Glossary

Alienation: The process whereby human beings develop a sense of separation from themselves, their activity, fellow human beings and the world of nature.

Critical Theory: Designates several generations of German philosophers and social theorists in the Western European Marxist tradition known as the Frankfurt School. It may be distinguished from a traditional theory according to a specific practical purpose — a theory is critical to the extent that it seeks human emancipation, to liberate human beings from the circumstances that enslave them.

Culture Industry: The term developed by critical theorists to refer to industries such as movies and radio that were serving to make culture a more important factor in society than the economy.

Enlightenment Ideals: Ideas which humans develop through the use of their reason. Individuals can seek knowledge and use their own reason rather than be told how to think by the church or the state.

Ideal Speech Situation: Developed by Habermas as a situation where communication between individuals is not bound and governed by institutional coercions, but when speeches are governed by basic — but required and implied — rules which are generally and tacitly accepted by both the communicating parties.

Life-world: May be conceived as a universe of what is self-evident or given a world that subjects may experience together. For Habermas, life-world is more or less the 'background' environment of competences, practices and attitudes representable in terms of one's cognitive horizon.

Mass Culture: The culture (such as entertainment media) that has been made available to, and is popular among, the masses.

Mass Society: A society resulting from and mass culture as entirely new forms of social domination that could not be adequately explained within the terms of traditional Marxist sociology.

Neo-Marxism: The concept arose as a way to explain questions which were not explained in Karl Marx's works. By drawing upon elements from other intellectual traditions like psychoanalysis and existentialism, it attempts to explain inequality moving beyond the narrow economic sphere.

Reification: In Marxist terminology, reification is a specific form of alienation in which the consciousness of the individual is so overwhelmed by his/her identification with the means and fruit of production, and the artificial designation of value that the dialectical process of identity is arrested.

Technological Rationality: An idea postulated by Herbert Marcuse, which posits that rational decisions to incorporate technological advances into society can, once the technology is ubiquitous, change what is considered rational within that society, by creating false needs.

Discussion Points

- The importance of culture in Critical Theory.
- Critical Theory as against science and reason.
- Moving beyond Marxist Theory.
- Habermas on communicative action.

11

Critical Theory

Critical theory is synonymously known as the Frankfurt School perspective in sociology. Essentially, it is a collective coinage for the works of a number of German social thinkers of the first half of the twentieth-century. All the thinkers have drawn their intellectual inspiration from the work of Karl Marx. As they belong to the same tradition of critiquing the society like Marx, they are being called as critical theorist. And the conglomerates of such theories are popularly known as constituting the Critical School. If Marx made a scathing criticism of the capitalist order — the social system that was emergent and a marker of his times — the thinkers of the new century responded to their specific historical setting. In the heyday of industrial capitation, Marx's attention was drawn to the economic structure of the society. Over the next fifty years and more — the point of emergence of Critical School — the capitalist system had undergone critical changes; dramatically more than the economic control measures ideology and culture emerged as far more effective device to dispossess people and 'pauperize' them from their species being. The centre of critical theory was at Frankfurt, Germany. As an autonomous research centre in 1923, the Institute of Social Research was founded in Frankfurt initially to study and explore the possibilities of classical Marxist texts and at the same time contest Semitism.

INTELLECTUAL AND SOCIAL BACKGROUND

Technically, the starting point of critical theory was in 1923 with the establishment of the Institute for Social Research in Frankfurt. The encyclopaedic work of Karl Marx formed the backdrop of such an independent initiative by a group of German scholars to refresh the tenets of Marxism. At a philosophical level it was an attempt to reinterpret and revise Marx's materialist conception of history. There were many such prolific theorists who worked with the same spirit. Georg Lukacs, Max Horkheimer, Theodor Adorno and Herbert Mercuse were the leading figures, also known as neo-Marxist. Another towering figure of the neo-Marxist school was Jurgen Habermas who joined the institute late and is known for his use of critical Marxism to develop a very distinctive sociological theory on modernity and nationality. If critical theorists are to be understood as neo-Marxists, then there is another variant of neo-Marxists who featured in the French intellectual world. They are the structural Marxists who revitalized the Marxist theory in a different way. It simultaneously works against reductionism prevalent in orthodox Marxism as well as the idealist bent in Critical School approach. The main proponent of structural Marxism was Louis Althusser.

Originally the Frankfurt school was characterized by an orthodox approach towards Marxism. Overall, Marxism provided the theoretical inspiration behind the setting up of the institute. Carl Grunberg was the leading figure in the institute till 1929 and exposed a scientific Marxism. Max Horkheimer took charge of the institute in 1930 and was instrumental in initiating research beyond the dogmatic position in Marxism. Apparently, the failure of the revolutionary class movement across Europe and the rise of the fascist regimes formed the background for a fresh look at the basic tenets of Marxism. The Nazi capture of the institute forced the theoreticians of the institute to flee to Germany and the institute was relocated to Columbia University in the United States in 1934.

The period was marked by an overall critical approach towards all that were orthodox. The prevalent rise of anti-democratic forces and the decadence of soviet Marxism prodded the group of German theorists to immigrate to the United States to develop the idea of critical theory. They drew their insights by arguing that the young Marx was less a reductionist materialist. They traced the Hegelian strains in Marx's initial theorizations to establish their position against any world view which had a slightest inkling for positivist explanation. Many of the theorists were absorbed in the various Universities in the United States, while some returned to Germany much after the end of World War II. In the post-war scenario the Frankfurt school was reconstructed in Germany by 1953. Interestingly although Marxism provided the basic for the Critical School, the pioneers of the critical thinking tried to energize it with inputs from the more idealist sociologist Max Weber. One can actually trace the legacy of German idealism in the major works of the critical theories.

Quite obviously, it was George Hegel's philosophy which prompted the critical theorists to reinterpret Marx. A fresh interpretation of Hegel's *The Phenomenology of Mind* (1931) revealed to them that Hegel sought to show how philosophical critique spills over into social theory, that the concept of 'negation' in Hegel is intrinsically critical in content. The self examination and realization of the sources of domination is an act of consciousness in its striving to seek absolute knowledge. Not only from the illusory coercive forces that human beings need to be liberated, but also from the social forms through which the coercive illusions operate in order to realize human beings' full capability of thought and action. From Hegel an image of human being as a subject was formed by the critical theorists. As a subject who is continuously creating, negating and recreating oneself as well as the objective world (Antonio 1983). Thus the Critical School is a product of the social and intellectual churning that marked the European history in the intervening years between the two world wars.

CULTURE INDUSTRY

A major focus of all critical theorists is to re-theorize the concept and role of culture. This follows from their criticism of traditional Marxian theory. The economic determination in Marx is questioned and the prime importance is given to the economic structure as a determinant for all other aspects of social life is abandoned. The popular arrangement of the two metaphors of *base* and *superstructure;* superstructure as constituting of the political–legal–cultural realm of a society whose base is the mode of production (economy) is thought to be mechanistic and simplistic. Instead the critical theorist point out at the overwhelming dominance of entertainment media like movies, radio etc. in advance capitalist societies over the basic economy. As a result culture has emerged as an industry by itself and not just a mere reflection of the economic base. The culture industry and all those who own and control it are significantly autonomous and independent of the economic structure and therefore are in a position to hegemonize people's mind and thought. In fact they are more effective under advanced capitalism to subjugate the mass. The role of culture is more powerful than that of economic forces.

Related to this pre-eminence of *culture industry* is the concept of *mass culture*, which holds that, the culture industry has given rise to a mass culture. The newspapers, magazines, entertainment package through various mass media disseminate a culture which engulfs the masses off guard. The mass is taken in by such dissemination which actually creates a singular conforming culture. The impact of such culture is much more pervasive than that of capitalist logic of production at the work level. Without realizing the role of such cultural dissemination in controlling and dominating them, people strive for more such mass culture. Thus, people are being controlled in a more complicated and deceiving way. Maintenance of capitalist order at an advance stage is actually the work of the culture industry, which makes them gullible consumers of the capitalist cultural codes and products without resistance. The critical theorists' chief achievement was to demystify the culture industry and after the forms of the Marxist theory of society.

Apart from interrogating the culture of modern capitalism, the object of criticism for different critical theorists were the growing technology backed by modernity and the overdose of 'scientism' in social thinking, especially sociology. As such the dominance of rationality principle in social life and thinking was under severe scrutiny by the leading critical thinkers. The liberating notion of science, technology and rationality were critiqued by many of them and a grim picture for the future of the modern world is drawn to a large extent.

GEORG LUKACS (1885–1971)

Georg Lukacs is credited with his attempt to free Marxism from economic determinism. He accomplished this by pointing to the Hegelian roots of Marx's theory. Lukacs indicated that the works of Marx could be divided into a young Marx and a matured Marx. Instead of realizing Marx only through his later economic works, if one pays attention more to his *The Economic and Philosophic Manuscripts* (1844), an early work, one can better appreciate Marxism. Lukacs did that and as a Hegelian Marxist tried to see the dialectic between the subjective and the objective realms of society.

The Frankfurt school at its formative years was to a large extent shaped by Lukacs. His major work is *History and Class Consciousness* (1923) where he comprehensively explained the subjective aspect of Marx's own understanding of commodity and reification — that, class consciousness is not an automatic formation out of material condition but much depends upon free-action of the proletariat itself. Thus, emancipation from the capitalist order is quite not an automatic consequence of material conditions alone.

It is not only that Lukacs tried to trace the Hegelian side of Marx but while acknowledging the fetish character of commodity as advanced by Marx, he infused it with Max Weber's understanding of rationality as all encompassing; that, with the coming of the modern society, the relation between people are dominated by rational calculations with money and market at the centre of exchanges. This is a result of the demise of human communication between individuals to secure social integration. In his *History and class consciousness,* Lukacs re-examined the central importance of commodity in a capitalist society. Through his treatment of the process of reification, Lukacs put the issue of ideology at the forefront of social theory. In fact, the insistence of the Critical School on the overwhelming role of ideology in modern society is largely due to Lukacs' theory.

Commodity production is the defining character of capitalism. It actually involves the relationship between living human being as products of their creative labour. Under generalized commodity production commodities take the form of a thing and develops an objective form independent of the actual producers. Fetishism of commodities is a condition analysed by Marx as a condition caused when the producer assumes that the commodity produced has an objective reality of its own. They lose sight of the fact that they are the actual producers of these commodities. Thus, the producers fail to recognize their role as the creator of the value of the commodities. Instead such value is seen to be the products of the market. From such a fetish character of commodities as theorized by Marx, Lukacs developed his concept of reification: reification as pervasive in all spheres of social life and not just restricted to the economic realm only. All aspects of social life under capitalism is characterized by a reified existence — the social structures which are the actual result of people's relationships emerging with an objective reality as people themselves think that such structure have a logic of their own existence. As he put:

> Man in capitalist society confronts a reality 'made' by himself (as a class) which appears to him to be a natural phenomenon alien to himself; he is wholly at the

> mercy of its 'laws'; his activity is confined to the exploitation of the inexorable fulfillment of certain individual laws for his own (egoistic) interest. But even while 'acting' he remains, in the nature of the case, the object and the subject of event. (Lukacs 1922/1968: 135)

Lukacs' concept of reification addressed the experiences of the European societies especially after World War I. It tried to address the crises of orthodox Marxist theories which failed to inspire socialist movement. Failed revolutionary movements in Hungary, Germany, Italy and Austria and the parallel the tendency of the Russian communist party to develop Marxism into a closed system of thought and practice called for a reinterpretation of the basic philosophical premise of Marx's theory of class consciousness.

In other words, against a deterministic version of Marxism, Lukacs looked for a more self reflexive version of Marxism. More than the politico-economic angle of the revolutionary struggle, an ideological plane of struggle was emphasized. Lukacs proposed instead a philosophy of praxis stressing the importance of subjectivity, culture and action. The philosophy of praxis stands opposed to orthodox Marxist positions for which the 'economic laws' and objective social conditions are of primary importance. Instead, it is interested to appreciate the unity of theory and practice — a more action-oriented approach — which puts human subjectivity at the centre of history-making (Kellner 1989).

Moving beyond the confines of the economic structures of society, Lukacs introduced a more subjectivist application of Marx by adopting Weberian sociology of rationality. This expanded the scope of commodity fetishism to include every other aspects of contemporary capitalist society.

> We are concerned above all with the *principle* at work here: the principle of rationalization based on what is and *can be calculated....* Rationalization in the sense of being able to predict with ever greater precision all the results to be achieved is only to be acquired by the exact breakdown of every complex into its elements and by the study of the special laws governing production. (Lukacs 1922/1968: 214)

Actually, one can observe that, Lukacs was instrumental in introducing totalizing categories in critical thinking to account for society, state, culture, economy and everyday life in one sweep. This laid the foundation of a critique of instrumental reason which figured prominently in the writings of subsequent critical theorists.

MAX HARKHEIMER AND THEODOR ADORNO

The publication of the co-authored *Dialectic of Enlightenment* by Max Harkheimer and Theodor Adorno in 1947 was a watershed in the history of Critical School theories. On one hand the experience of exile by the critical thinkers, being forced to the flee to

Germany due to Nazi assault, allowed them to see the trajectory of modernity and its discontents beyond the confines of particular social system. On the other hand, the socio-historical transformation of capitalism and its success in creating a consumer society prompted both Horkheimer and Adorno to engage in a critique of the very philosophy of enlightenment. Also, as a consequence of the above 'new experience', critical theory moved ahead of just critiquing modernity as dictated by techno-rationality. As such critical theories took a turn towards understanding human nature by an all encroaching techno-rational worldview, which is not just associated with the political economy of the capitalist system.

Short Biographies

Max Horkheimer (1895–1973) was a German philosopher who controlled the Institute for Social Research, Frankfurt from 1930. He secured his doctorate for his work on the German idealist philosopher Immanuel Kant in 1922 from Frankfurt University. In 1925, he joined the Frankfurt school, the popular coinage for the Institute for Social Research, as a lecturer. In 1930 he became the director of the institute. He promoted multidisciplinary approach in the institute and given his background as a philosopher, he advocated a fusion of the reflective capacity of philosophy and the rigorous methodological procedures of sciences in social theory building exercise. After the Nazi occupation of the institute, Horkheimer along with other fellow theorists had to seek refuge in the United States and only returned after the end of the World War II. But he did not travel to Washington to work for the United States government. In his early scholarship he was a sympathetic supporter of the Russian Revolution but he was never an uncritical defender of soviet communism. The events of the failures of socialist movements in Europe, the turbulent year of the World War II, and the flourishing of the consumer society in the United States — all shaped up his subsequent thought processes and committed himself to theoretical work. He essentially strived to see critical theory as competent to infuse ideology with criticality necessary to examine the gap between ideas and reality; that concepts are interdependent and irreducible aspects of the total societal process (Held 1980).

Theodor Adorno (1903–69) was from a successful Jewish merchant family and was born in Frankfurt. Like his colleague Horkheimer, he also studied philosophy and wrote his thesis on Husserl's phenomenology. He secured his doctorate from the University of Frankfurt in 1924. In 1931 he became associated with the institute. Like Horkheimer he too relocated himself in the United States after a while. He collaborated extensively with Horkheimer to espouse the theoretical cause of the Critical School. However, he was more philosophical and research-oriented than Horkheimer.

During his stay in the United States as a theorist in exile, Adorno wrote *Minima Moralia*. It was written from 1944 through 1947, while he was in California. The text reveals that the starting point of his critical inquiries of social life was the embodied experiences of the 'intellectual in emigration'. From the vantage point as a European refugee, Adorno could see the novel conditions of contemporary capitalism and how if differed from the earlier orthodox stage of capitalism. Such a novel reality demanded from Adorno to break away from orthodox way of understanding capitalism or the structure of society. Thus, he worked to develop a 'critical social consciousness' to show how philosophy embodies objective structures the same way art expresses social contradictions in a mediated from.

Critique of Science and Reason

Dialectic of Enlightenment (1947) is the combined work of Max Horkheimer and Theodor Adorno, which carries the grand statement against the emancipatory project of European Enlightenment. It is a philosophical critique of culture at the same time subjecting the celebration of science and reason to fresh inquiry. The publication of *Dialectic Enlightenment* signalled a new direction in critical thinking. This shift from earlier theorization on the vacuity of politico–economic approach to a philosophical approach towards the grand schemes of science and reason was conditioned by the historical reality of weakening of socialist revolution across the world. The spread of fascist ideas, the events of World War II and the dispersion of the Institute's multidisciplinary group in the United States — all combined to influence both Horkheimer and Adorno, while in virtual exile, to engage in a theoretical probe into the trajectory of modern science and its relationship with human nature (Kellner 1989).

Distancing themselves from both Fascist tendencies and the project of communism (as exemplified by Bolshevik system of the Soviet), Horkheinmer and Adorno located the interlocking of the techno-scientific temper with the apparatus of rule in modern society. Their main contention was that science and reason have lost their liberating potential and have growingly become formalist and instrumental in character. Instead of being a weapon of critical inquiry into the travails of social life, they have become conformist and have determining role in the apparatus of domination. This is so, as science, scientific reason and technology are an integral part of the modern mode of production, which is oppressive not only economically but as such a dehumanizing enterprise. *Dialectic of Enlightenment* stands as a critique of modern science and more as a mistrust of the promise of the Enlightenment ideals.

The Enlightenment ideals were grounded in emancipatory principles to rescue human civilization from the hold of blind faiths and mysticism. The rational thought and strength of scientific reason was supposed to help human beings to take control of nature in turn. Thus, the element of domination was ingrained in the very ideals and the supposedly national thoughts and enlightened ideals actually contain mythical ideas and breed irrationality. This is the dialectic of enlightenment according to Horkheinmer and Adorno. The ideals of such Enlightenment are to be traced from the Baconian scientific temper which is based on a desire to dominate nature by valourizing a mode thought which relies on the criteria of utility, verifiability, efficiency and success.

According to Horkheimer and Adorno, the scientism of the Enlightenment principles is actually totalitarian in that it exclusively strips human life and thought from all kinds of subjectivity, feelings, aesthetics and quality. Instead it fosters a spirit of conformism by restricting human thought and knowledge to technical principle of calculation, efficiency and systematization. The social implication of such restricting ideals is to give rise to a mind set which foregoes liberty in favour of greater control and administration. An administrated society is therefore a logical outcome of the Enlightenment principles. The Enlightenment thought logically proceeded from the principles of dominating nature to becoming a tool of dominations of human beings. The totalizing principles of universal truth of science logically create a society without differences but of similitudes, i.e., a *mass society*. The techno-rational governed administered society is a mass society. Overall speaking, Horkeimer and Adorno theorized an image of modern society where the forces of science, technology and instrumental rationality dehumanizes species character of human beings. In defense of his argument Horkheimer wrote:

> In a historical period like the present true theory is more critical than affirmative, just as the society that corresponds to it cannot be called "productive". The future of humanity depends on the existence today of the critical attitude, which of course contain within it elements from traditional theories and from our declining culture generally. Mankind has already been abandoned by a science which in its imaginary self-sufficiency thinks if the shaping of practice, which it serves and to which it belong, simply as something lying outside its borders and is content with this separation of thought and action ... the self-definition of science grows ever more abstract. But conformism in thought and the insistence that thinking is a fixed vocation, a self-enclosed realm culture within society as a whole, betrays the very essence of thought. (Horkheimer 1972: 243)

Adorno on Culture

The central role of culture and ideology in advance capitalist societies directed critical theories to cultural criticism. Theodor Adorno took a lead role and a deep interest in making a systematic inquiry into the nature and function of culture in contemporary societies. By contextualizing culture within social developments, Adorno, as well as other critical theorists, formulated a close association between social theory and cultural critique.

The juggernauts of science and rationality structure every aspects of social life. Cultural realm is not left aside from the encompassing rationalization and standardization techniques of instrumental rationality. Culture no longer remains the repository of beauty, truth and individuality; instead it becomes a zone of social life where individuals are homogenized and made to conform to the existing social order. Thereby, culture plays a deciding a role in promoting conformity, which is so essential for the functioning of an administered society. Adorno was instrumental in forwarding a critique of culture which made the Critical School best known for its concept of culture industry. But Adorno emphasized that while privileging culture as an important tool for creating mass society, one must not overlook culture as the source of social knowledge and as a potential form of social criticism. As Adorno is quoted by D. Kellner:

> The task of [cultural] criticism must be not so much to search for the particular interest groups to which cultural phenomena are to be assigned, but rather to decipher the general social tendencies which are expressed in these phenomena and through which the most powerful interest realize themselves. Cultural criticism must become social physiognomy. The spontaneous elements, is socially mediated and filtered, is 'consciousness', the more it becomes 'culture'. (Adorno 1967: 30)

Adorno's critique of culture was in tune with the Critical School's analysis of the spread of rationalization and reification into every sphere of human society. He wrote consistently from 1932 (*on the social situation of music*) on various forms of mass culture and popular music. The loss of aesthetic quality from mass culture was analysed by Adorno using mainly the concepts of fetishism, commoditization, rationalization and reification. As against the loss of aesthetics he promoted the idea that only genuine experience could provide the space for individual freedom as well as resistance. Hence, art was considered as an instrument for emancipation. Aesthetic experience could provide critical consciousness for an individual. Such necessary awareness was thought to be crucial as it explored the existing reality and reiterated the need for social transformation. However, the culture industry played a dubious role. Instead of its cardinal role of promoting individual creativity it created a mass society like capitalist mass production industry. It acted as an extension of ideology of domination. A mass deception was carried out as a result, which effectively manipulated the people in order to seek consent to the prevalent mode of economic and political domination. Adorno had been prolific to champion the cause of a cultural critic.

> The position of the cultural critic, by virtue of its difference from the prevailing disorder, enables him to go beyond it theoretically, although often enough he merely falls behind. But he incorporates which he seeks to leave behind and which itself need the difference in order to fancy itself culture. Characteristic of culture's pretension to distinction, through which it exempts itself from evaluation against the material condition of life, is that it is insatiable... the cultural critic makes such distinction his privilege and forfeits his legitimation by collaborating with culture as its salaried and honoured nuisance. (Adorno 1967: 19)

In a way Adorno promoted a dialectical view of culture. His theoretical reflections on culture suggested both — either culture could be used as a device of manipulation and generating conforming, or it could be used as a force of opposition. Adorno strongly opposed the mechanically mediated works of mass culture as conformist, while he promoted those works of culture which resisted commoditization and mechanical reproduction. Such a criticism of culture by Adorno possibly remains as the most lasting legacy of the Critical School till date.

HERBERT MARCUSE (1898–1979)

The overall project of critical theory was to investigate the dialectics of the history of modernity. It will not be an overstatement to see the critical theory as an attempt to rediscover human freedom by sorting out the matrix of progressive and regressive forces bound up with the coming of modernity. Given the unfolding of capitalist system in advance stage it tried to update the Marxian theory with a multidisciplinary approach. The contribution of Herbert Marcuse to the Critical School embodies this very guiding spirit of the critical theory. He consistently examined, defended and reconstructed the Marxist enterprise. Unlike many of his colleagues from the Critical School, Marcuse stood by the emancipatory potential of socialism. He promoted the critical approach to society to see the emancipation of consciousness.

A Biographical Sketch

Coming from a prosperous Jewish family of Berlin Marcuse served the German army in World War II. Subsequently, he became a part of the revolutionary Soldiers Council in Berlin as a member of the Social Democratic Party. Soon he left the party and studied philosophy at the universities of Freiburg and Berlin. In 1923 he secured his doctorate on literature. He returned to Freiburg to study the philosophers Edmund Husserl and Martin Heidegger.

Like many of his compatriots, Marcuse too left Germany during the Nazi rule. He landed in the United States to join the Institute for Social Research, which was relocated from Frankfurt to New York, at Columbia University from 1934 to 1940. Marcuse was academically as well as politically active. He actively worked with the office of secret services to free Germany from the Nazis. He taught at Columbia and Harvard universities. Later, he joined Brandeis University as a Professor of political science. Marcuse was a prolific writer, academic and an orator, which made him the most conspicuous figure of the new left movement in the 1960s.

Best known for his most popular treatise *One-dimensional Man* (1964), Marcuse wrote several others thought provoking books. Some of them are *Reason and Revolution* (1941), *Eros* and *Civilization* (1955) and *Negations: Essays in Critical Theory* (1968).

Critical Theory

Herbert Marcuse was not an orthodox Marxist even though he was deeply grounded on a theory which acknowledges a potential in humans which is yet to be realized. Thus, reworking the Marxist tenets, he could still work towards the defense of utopian objectives. Apart from Marx, Georg Hegel's dialectics heavily influenced Marcuse. He was instrumental, along with Georg Lukacs for a reinvention of Hegel in European thought in the early twentieth-century. Like Hegel, he placed great value on reason and was impressed with Hegel's objection to Kant's theory. He felt that if 'things-in-themselves' are beyond the capacity of reason, reason will remain a mere subjective principle without relevance to the objective structure of reality. Philosophy for Marcuse should have an objective referent; as a praxis it needs to combine both theory and practice (action). The role of reason in social criticism is stated by Marcuse most sharply:

> Reason is the fundamental category of philosophical thought, the only one by means of which it has bound itself to human destiny. Philosophy wanted to discover the ultimate and most general grounds of being. Under the name of reason it conceived the idea of an authentic being in which all significant antitheses (of subject and object, essence and appearance, thought and being) were reconciled.... Reason represents the highest potentiality of man and of existence; the two belong together.... (Marcuse 1989: 58)

Unlike Horkheimer and Adorno, Marcuse was more inclined towards classical Marxism. As an astute student of German philosophy he found the sources of his critical theory primarily in Marx's early writing's like *Economic and Philosophical Manuscripts* (1844) although he shared the critique and transcendence of reification with Adorno. With Horkheimer he agreed on the unconcluded nature of the dialectic and the centrality of human practice in the constitution of knowledge. However, Marcuse was keen to engage himself in revisions of Marx's theory to develop his critical theory. As he consistently held that such a theory is imperative not only to comprehend the new stage of capitalism but also to transform it to realize full human potentiality. The uniqueness of Marcuse lies in his attempt to reconstruct the Marxist method of analysis. Thus, he did not hesitate to infuse the basic transformative content in Marx's method of study with ideas from Hegel and even with that of Sigmund Freud's psychoanalytical categories.

> Critical theory of society is essentially linked with materialism ... the theory of society is an economic, not philosophical system. There are two basic elements linking materialism to correct social theory: concern with human happiness, and the conviction that it can be attained only through a transformation of the material condition of existence. The actual course of the transformation and the fundamental measures to be taken in order to arrive at a rational organization of society are prescribed by analysis of economic and political condition in the given historical situation. (Marcuse 1989: 58–59)

For one thing, unlike most of the critical theorists Marcuse was not led to despair and hopelessness with respect to the possibility of a better future. It was quite in line that he emerged as the cult figure during the renewed period of radical movement in the 1960s among the young generation. Whereas most Marxists as well as critical theorists often failed to clearly theorize the link between individual consciousness and culture, Marcuse took recourse to Freudian categories for a critical interpretation of culture. To integrate the individual level of consciousness (the unconscious as well) the Freudian psychoanalytical categories proved to be useful for him. Thereby, he could analyse the process by which sexual and aggressive instincts are repressed and channelled into socially necessary labour, so necessary for the generation of surplus value under a dehumanized capitalist mode of production. The collective nature of the repressive organization of the instincts was analysed by him to account for human alienation. This critique of technology actually shows Marcuse's radical orientation to social theory.

Alienating Technology

The repressive character of modern industrial society has been a central focus in Marcuse's social theory. He was a critic of repression of whatever form, be it capitalist or the Soviet system and traced the source of it in the logic of technology driven modernity. Modern technology as an alienating instrument has been the target of his criticism — a theme that runs through all his works but best captured in his *One-dimensional Man* (1964).

Marcuse's attack on modern technology is intrinsically linked to the tradition of Critical School's critique of the culture industry. He adapted the Freudian notion of 'repression' to account for the rise of the mass media. He explained the catapultion of individuals to the overarching role of technology directed mass media by referring to the transformed nature of socialization in advance capitalism.

> The repressive organization of the instincts seems to be collective, and the ego seems to be prematurely socialized by a whole system of extra-familial agents and agencies. As early as the pre-school level, gangs, radio, and rebellion; deviation from the pattern are punished not so much in the family as outside and against the family. The experts of the mass media transmit the required values; they offer the perfect training in efficiency, toughness, personality, dream, and romance. With this education, the family can longer compete. (Marcuse 1955: 97)

According to Marcuse, with the displacement of the family as the primary agent of socialization, mass media has assumed the role of the principle agent. Mass media has effectively controlled the mind and instinct to the extent of narcotizing individual initiatives and freedom. It is a sort of manipulation by the gigantic complex of entertainment and information imparting mass media which essentially numbs the individuals. Advanced industrial society is thereby essentially alienating and the defining character of such society is the total reliance on technology. Such techno-rational mass media create false needs amongst individuals who are in effect stripped of their authentic culture and oppositional thought. They all become 'one-dimensional' in thought and action. The repressive technology operates with a face of being pleasant and entertaining. It is a case of deceit and deception that makes individuals 'happy' and in the process they lose the most important human faculty of criticality.

Technology is not neutral in modern industrial society. It is an instrument of domination as long as it is an expression of formal rationality. It only gives an impression of being neutral and thereby becomes more effective in manipulating the mind of people, while at the same time repressing their creative instincts. However, Marcuse did not pronounce the abolishing of technology per se. He is critical of the way it is being used in modern industrial society. He wrote, 'Technology, no matter how "pure", sustains and streamlines the continuum of domination. This fatal link can be cut only by a revolution which makes technology and technique subservient to the needs and goals of free men' (Marcuse 1969: 56).

By critiquing the concept of technological rationality, Marcuse showed his willingness to extend the scope of Marxian criticism of capitalist logic to include Weber's idea of rationalization. The ever increasing rationalization process in modern society is a process of growing regimentation of social life. Despite the seeming rationality of modem life, in essence it is irrational. Governed by the principle of formal rationality technology, mass media, popular culture — all are promoting a mode of thought and living which is alienating. The reification of the social structure is the result of such rationalization process. Against such an alienating experience Marcuse promoted an ideal world where people would be able to relate to the larger structures like technology in a meaningful way. In such a possibility people would be creative while fulfilling their needs and employ appropriate technology to realize their ability. Such a dialectic relationship between people and technology was envisioned by Marcuse.

JURGEN HABERMAS (1929-)

Jurgen Habermas represents the second generation of critical theorists after Horkheimer, Adorno and Marcuse. He is the most prolific commentator and theorist of the neo-Marxist tradition. Although he joined the Critical School and is considered as a part of it, over the years he expanded his scope of social inquiry by fusing Marxian theory with theories from phenomenological school of thought to develop a distractive theoretical tradition.

A Biographical Sketch and Influences

Jurgen Habermas was born in a small town in Germany, in 1929. He was a doctorate in philosophy. He earned his degree from Bonn in 1954. He associated himself with the Institute for Social Research in Frankfurt and worked with Theodor Adorno. In 1964 he took over Horkheimer's chair in philosophy at the Institute. Meanwhile he also secured his second doctorate at Mainz and taught for some time in Heidelberg. His most significant works are *Communication and the Evolution of Society* (1962), *Knowledge and Human Interests* (1968), *The Theory of Communicative Action* (1989), *The Philosophical Discourse of Modernity* (1987).

Habermas acknowledges the transformative potential in Marx's writings but energized it with the contemporary theories of social interaction, phenomenology and theories of communication. While accepting the Weberian analysis of rationality as insightful he tries to improve upon it by dismissing the pessimistic view of future society ingrained in it. Self-emancipation of human beings is indicated by Habermas as the process by which subjective consciousness can be transformed. Heavily drawing upon phenomenological and interactionist theories he developed his famous theory of communicative action. By communicative action he described structure of action and structures of mutual understanding which result from intuitive knowledge of competent members of modern society. The liberating notion of communicative action stems from Habermas's conviction of combining critical thought with practical action. In fact, such a standpoint earned the displeasure of Horkheimer in the Frankfurt school.

Habermas's insistence on the coupling of thought with practice is rooted in his fascination for classical Greek and German philosophy. The classical thought emphasized the inseparability of facts and values (Held 1980).

Critique of Culture and Communicative Action

Like his predecessors in the Critical School, Habermas critiques the rise of cultural industries in contemporary capitalist societies. But he made a historical analysis to chart out the way the public sphere of free debate and opinion has shrunk over the years. In his analysis he has shown the transition from a form of liberal capitalism to a form of monopoly capitalism. Liberal capitalism allowed a democratic public sphere in which 'public opinion' was formed by debate and consensus. Such a public sphere was liberal to the extent that it allowed an educated and competent public to critically discuss socio-political issues unhindered. Whereas the transition from the liberal to the monopoly stage of capitalism altered the very character of their public sphere. The sphere has shrunk as no longer through open debates are public opinions formed. It is the mass media which has usurped this sphere and shapes public opinion. Instead of an active participation in culture, the public has become a passive consumer in a cultural industry (Kellner 1989).

How the emergent media has impacted upon culture negatively is brought out sharply by Habermas:

> With the shift from writing to images and sounds, the electronic media — first film and radio, later television — present themselves as an apparatus that completely permeates and dominates the language of everyday communication. On the one hand, if transforms the authentic content of modern culture into the sterilized and ideologically effective stereotypes of a mass culture that merely replicates what exists: on the other hand, it uses up a culture cleansed of all subversive and transcending elements for an encompassing system of social controls, which is spread over individuals, in part reinforcing their weakened internal behavioral controls, in part replacing them. (Habermas 1987: 389–90)

As a counter to the situation of mass culture, Habermas talks about an *ideal speech situation*. It is a notion of free and open communication. An ideal speech situation is free from the distortion and manipulation which are regularly implemented by power holders. In contemporary world communication is largely distorted as power decides which argument would win. In such a scenario consensus is generated by power but not arrived at through the strength of evidence and argument. Habermas' communicative action promotes an idea of consensus out of a contest between differing ideas and opinions which are freely expressed. Thus, truth is not simply a matter of what is given, but has to emerge out of such consensus.

For Habermas, a just society is one where people are free to assemble and communicate openly. The mode of communication and the understanding of language are the keys to comprehend knowledge. Extending Marx's conception of species-being to account for the changes that mark contemporary society, he added language to labour as a marker of such species-being. Rejecting a reductionist materialist position of orthodox Marxism, Habermas sees communication action as not simply a mirror reflection of the economic forces but places it as a constitutive force of history. The use of language as a significant aspect of human development is theorized by Habermas and consequently he sees the foundation for emancipation of individuals in undistorted communication.

We find a very precise understanding of Habermas' communicative action in his words:

> Under the functional aspect of mutual understanding, communicative action serves to transmit and renew cultural knowledge; under the aspect of *coordinating action*, it serves social integration and the establishment of solidarity; finally, under the aspect of *socialization*, communicative action serves the formation of personal identities. The symbolic structures of the lifeworld are reproduced by way of the continuation of valid knowledge, stabilization of group solidarity, and socialization of responsible actors. The process of reproduction connects up new situations with the exiting conditions of the lifeworld; it does this in the *semantic* dimension of meanings or contents (of the cultural tradition), as well as in the dimensions of *social space* (of socially integrated groups), and *historical time* (of successive generations). Corresponding to these processes of *cultural reproduction, social integration*, and *socialization* are the structural components of the lifeworld: culture, society, person. (Habermas 1987: 137–38)

On Rationality

Unlike most of his predecessors of the Critical School of thinking, Habermas does not unequivocally condemn rationality of the modern would as dehumanizing in the absolute sense. He realizes that be it capitalist or socialist, all modern industrial societies have reduced the human world to a form of technocratic and economic efficiency only. But the rationality principle is more than a principle of strategic calculation of matching the ends with most efficient means. Rationality implies the capacity to think logically and analytically. It serves the human beings and is a crucial ingredient in understanding others in communicative situations. Instead of condemning contemporary forms of modernity, Habermas considers modernity as an unfinished project of human civilization. He extends the scope of critical theory beyond the concerns of its first generation scholars. Adorno, Horkheimer and Marcuse attempted to revise and reinterpret Marx's theory to account for the eventful social history of twentieth-century Western world. Overall there was a sense of despair with the emergence of advance capitalist system and its concomitant culture which scuttled every socialist aspiration. On the other hand, at the philosophical level, too, the French based post-modernist thinking promoted the demise of any foundational knowledge for society. A continuous dispersal of meaning created a decentred notion of knowledge and thought. Habermas, while working within the Critical School takes on such post-modernist attack on modernity, as the post-modernist attack on modern thinking at a general plan denied any comprehensive system of emancipatory thought. Habermas sees such attempts as rooted in counter Enlightenment ideologies. He posits modernity as a project which has emancipatory potential (Kellner 1989).

Habermas' understanding of modernity holds clue to his attempt to see rationality beyond its contemporary application. Essentially he adopts Weber's interpretation of modernity as a process of differentiation of functional systems such as the state and the economy. The process of differentiation engulfs all other spheres of society, be it culture, religion, philosophy and so forth. Habermas contends that since the fifth century every new epoch of consciousness claimed itself to be modern. The term modernity therefore is problematic. As he says,

> The word "modern" was first employed in the late fifth century in order to distinguish the present, new officially Christian, from the pagan and Roman past. With a different content in each case, the expression content in each case, the expression 'modernity' repeatedly articulates the consciousness of an era that refers back to the past of classical antiquity precisely in order to comprehend itself as the result of a transition from the old to the new. (Habermas 1997: 39)

Modernity then is a continuous process which distinguishes itself from the old by the fact that it opens itself to the future. At every moment of history, as long as it offers something 'new' it is modern — it is therefore characteristic of historical consciousness.

To analyse the advance modern societies Habermas uses the concepts of *life-world* and shows how it is being increasingly colonized (Ritzer 2007). Life-world as a concept refers to the everyday life of a society in phenomenological social theories. Alfred Schutz used it to refer to the inter-subjective relations that govern the world of everyday life. For Habermas the inter-subjective relations are characterized by interpersonal communication. Free and open communication means the rationalization of communication within the life-world, whereas, the process of rationalization of the society increasingly differentiates the structures of the society. The rationalization of the system (society) makes it more complex and it takes a different turn from the rationalization of the world. It thereby intrudes upon the life-world — the sphere of free interpersonal communication. Thus, rationalization in effect destroys the life-world by colonizing it.

The destructive character of rationalization of the system (those structure over above the everyday life of people) is seen by Habermas as a fallout of 'technocratic consciousness' that marks advance modern societies. Instrumental reason is the guiding spirit of such technocratic consciousness. The crisis of modernity is thus commented upon by Habermas:

> The paradoxes of planning rationally can be explained by the fact that rational action orientations came into contradiction with themselves through unintended systemic effects. These crisis tendencies are worked through not only in the subsystem in which they arise, but also in the complementary action subsystem into which they can be shifted. (Habermas 1987: 385)

In Habermas' theory, the criticism is more directed at the ever expanding structures of rationally organized administrative system. As capitalism grows, the system of such techno-rational administration spreads its reach to usurp even the private sphere. Such a process is complemented with the growth of scientism. Thus a critique of positivism is utmost necessary in Habermas's scheme. Knowledge is identified with science as positivism governs the mode of inquiry. Positivism thereby objectifies knowledge and has become the sustaining strength of technocratic consciousness. Habermas' critique of modernity is linked to his dismissal of the positivist view to objectify knowledge. A world cannot be understood in terms of facts and laws. A successful critique of modernity (as given) then has to be a subject-centred philosophy.

SUMMARY

It is difficult to characterize critical theory by a particular methodology or theoretical proposition. Yet, it is a coherent approach to study social reality. The heart of critical theory is its criticality of inquiry by breaking away from established social theories. Essentially it examines the way in which modern industrial societies give an expression of 'pleasant' life while distorting the authentic life and culture. The central role of power and its diverse use in modern societies is a running subject-matter for all critical theorists. Culture has been the primary theme for analysis by almost all thinkers. It is simply because in advance capitalist societies more than the economic structures, the cultural and ideological apparatuses play a lead role in controlling human beings. The assault on the thought process by the ever growing rationality governed social structures is under severe criticism from the Critical School.

The critical theory started off with an orientation to review and revise Marx's writings in order to account for the 'new' social situations that Marx could not foresee in his time, for example, the rise of the middle-classes, the growth of mass media and an increasing conformity with the capitalist order. Later thinkers are more philosophical in their approach to direct their attention to the very project of rationality. Critical theory no doubt re-energizes Marxism and infuses a new reflexive criticality in social inquiry.

Key Words

- *Bracketing*
- *Ethnomethodology*
- *Everyday-life World*
- *Habitual Knowledge*
- *Knowledge of Essences*
- *Psychologism*
- *Phenomenology*
- *Significant Other*
- *Sociology of Knowledge*

Glossary

Bracketing: A term that stands for the act of suspending judgement about the natural world that precedes phenomenological analysis. It involves setting aside the question of the real existence of the contemplated object, as well as all other questions about its physical or objective nature.

Breaching Experiments: A method for revealing or exposing the common work that is performed by members of particular social groups in maintaining a clearly recognizable and shared social order.

Ethnomethodology: Coined by Harold Garfinkel, ethnomethodology is a study of the methods that individuals use in daily life to construct their reality, primarily through intimate exchanges of meanings in conversation.

Life-world: The world as immediately or directly experienced in the subjectivity of everyday life, as sharply distinguished from the objective 'worlds' of the sciences. It includes individual, social, perceptual and practical experiences.

Phenomenology: The philosophical position adapted by sociologists to promote an understanding of the relationship between states of individual consciousness and social life. As a sociological perspective, phenomenology seeks to reveal how human awareness is implicated in the production of social action, social situations and social worlds.

Discussion Points

- The influences on early phenomenology.
- Schutz's treatment of everyday-life world.
- Social construction of reality: Contribution of Berger and Luckmann.
- Garfinkel's insistence on ethnomethodology.

12

Post-modern Theory and Post-structural Sociology

Sociological theories right from functionalism to ethnomethodology have studied modern society from various perspectives and with different methodological tools. Such theories helped to organize sociology as a discipline which attempts to explain the functioning of modern industrial society. Such analyses helped to see the transformations associated with modernity. All such theories (except some of Critical School theorists) are united in the sense that they took modernity as a liberating condition for human society. The Weberian thought, however, carried with it an element of scepticism about the future prospect of rational–legal social forms. However, the idea progress of human society was central to all the traditional and mainstream sociological theories. It is only with the coming of the critical school that the very premise of modernity was problematized. The concurrent socio-political events acted as an impetus for critical theorists to critique the premise of modernity. The metamorphosed face of society gave rise to such theories of society which questioned the worth of objective knowledge and instead asked for a reflexive social research which heavily draws upon subjectivism.

Advance industrial capitation defied many of the projections of traditional social theories. Critical theories were a strong reaction to that particular historical setting of Western industrial societies of the first half of the twentieth-century and a little beyond. But the subsequent development and unfolding of industrial societies provided an altogether different mode of social life. Understanding that shift of industrial society actually foregrounds the strivings for a fresh look at society. Beyond the paradigm of modernity post-modernist thinking mainly originated in the field of philosophy, literature and culture.

Such themes worked on the idea of not exactly on the end of modernity but more on the premise of exhaustion of all modernist projects and thought process. Coming from divergent disciplines the post-modernist thinkers approach the issue in as many divergent ways. It is difficult to define post-modernism, as it has been variously used — as a philosophy, as a method, as a condition of social life and even as a critique of modernity. The common thread that runs through various post-modernist works is their disdain and refutation of the conceptual systems of Western culture and knowledge. To appreciate the rise of post-modern theories an understanding of the transition of the industrial society is imperative.

DANIEL BELL'S POST-INDUSTRIAL SOCIETY

In his *The Coming of Post-Industrial Society* (1973), Daniel Bell charts out a theory of the great sweep of recent history. The focus of the study is to identify the conditions that mark the passing of the classical industrial society. Although he has examined the transition from the very pre-industrial stage of society, the contrast between industrial and post-industrial society is underscored to understand the structural change of contemporary society.

By post-industrial society Bell meant a change from the industrial society at various levels of its structure. Primarily, at the level of economy it signals a change from a protectionist economy to a consumerist economy. The new economy is geared more towards the service sectors with a less emphasis on production of goods. This fundamental transition from goods production to the provision of services (right from health, education, research, government services etc.) has implication for the occupational structure. It marks a dwindling of the manual workers and a parallel growth of white-collar workers. A more heterogeneous society follows as a result with the demise of a clear-cut capitalist-workers contradiction. And such a society is marked by an enhanced importance of professionals, service holders etc. Another important implication of the transition is felt in the knowledge system. Instead of empirical knowledge a more theoretical and codified knowledge becomes dominant. The focus becomes more on theoretical know-how as scientific research gets more institutionalized to foster a fusion of science and innovation. The ramification of these changes is ultimately felt at the cultural realm. Bell argues that two different principles govern the social structure and the culture in such post-industrial society. While the social structure is shaped by growing rationality and efficiency, culture is dominated more by irrationality, self-gratification and self-realization. A sort of hedonistic principle comes to shape the cultural life of post-industrial society against the ideas of self-discipline and restraint of industrial society. In Bell's theory of post-industrial society there is a clear disjuncture between social structure and culture (Ritzer 2007). The rise of consumer society occasioned by such transition serves as a prelude to acknowledge the social milieu that fuelled post-modernist thinking, especially in the field of culture, art, literature and philosophy.

POST-MODERN THEORY

With less precision the concept of post-modern has been widely used. This is partly due to the valid ways in which different post-modernist thinkers have approached the issue of 'post-modern'. The concept of post-modernity essentially seeks to describe the contemporary epoch, the contemporary being contrasted with modernity. The watershed at the ground level is the coming of the new economy accelerated by the development of information technologies and the end of mass markets. The events of the world wars fractured the concept of a universal 'we'. Thus the rational pursuit of truth and enlightenment, defining feature of modernity is revised with the end of such meta-narrative. The utopian vision of a united future and identity is being replaced by petit-narratives or identities of nation, gender, sexuality or ethnicity. A post-modern theory then is an explanation of such post-modern condition. Post-modernists like Fredric Jameson with Marxist leanings would prefer to call post-modernism as the cultural logic of late capitalism. (Jameson 1991)

At the philosophical level it forsakes the view that science is built on a firm base of observable facts. It argues against any form of 'foundational' knowledge. From the philosophical point-of-view, Jacques Derrida therefore repudiated logo-centrism — the mode of thinking that applies truth claims to universal propositions. While Jean Baudrillard as a radical post-modernist social philosopher opens up the debate between the cultural and the social. Considering post-modernism as a cultural and intellectual phenomena entailing production, consumption and distribution of symbolic goods, Baudrillard points at the cracks between instrumentality (which governs the markets and corporations) and culture (domain of subjective meanings which are not shared) and thereby, there is a loss of social reference. Post-modern themes seek to account for the 'loss' of the social. Growing fragmentation of the social world and rampant differentiation inform post-modern theories to abandon modes of analysis which marks mainstream sociology, as the 'present' is marked by continuous shift in power balances and societal ties are unbound and rebound.

Post-modern thought is mainly contributed by thinkers who were not disciplinarily bound by sociology. The prominent figures are Jacques Derrida, Jean-Francois Lyotard and Fredric Jameson. Importantly, there is a debate over whether there can be a post-modern sociology. Terminologically itself such an exercise would be self-defeating as it would then forsake by definition the formative questions that lay at the foundation of the very discipline of sociology. Instead, sociology can incorporate and be informed by post-modernist ideas to develop sociology of post-modernity. In league with modern sociology, it can then explain the process and structure of post-modern society as a type which is distinctive and unique. This is basically the contention of Zygmunt Bauman. Apart from Bauman, the other sociologist who enriched the discipline of sociology with post-modernist ideas is Jean Baudrillard. Pierre Bourdieu's basic ideas (as a post-structural theorist) are to be dealt in this chapter at the end, as he offers a very powerful and distinct theoretical perspective for doing sociology in contemporary society.

BASIC THEMES IN POST-MODERN THOUGHT

With the emergence of the 'new' social life marked by both differentiating and differentiated social structures, the subject matter for social theory undergoes a change. The reality is less represented than being replicated. The overwhelming dominance of technology and networks allows a free play of signs and symbols to the extent that more than the signified, the signifier takes the central stage in social forms. Post-modern thinking is an intellectual response to such a reality. The 'reality' itself is in question; the post-modern thought can be appreciated as a debate about reality. To begin with, it is all about modernity. The gradual rationalization of every aspect of social life leading to a liberating condition premised on conclusive theories of society is subjected to scrutiny.

As the traditional notion of space and time gets undermined by an exponential growth of technology and communication, the modernist paradigm of centred notion of social, cultural and political takes a backseat. Rather the continuous, crisis-crossing flows of people, data, images and capital constitute new patterns of social identity. Post-modern thinkers address this 'new' condition focusing more on the cultural and symbolic undercurrent of social life. The consumer society which foregrounds every thing for the public image and show draws the primary attention of post-modernist thinking. Consumption practice, more than that of production, is thought to be the central clue for the emerging social condition. The basic conditioning of post-modern thought emerges from such a 'loss of reality'.

As the confidence of a better, unified and just society is being replaced by a growing scepticism and ambivalence towards the promise of science, reason and rationality, the French intellectuals advanced theories that address such a changed scenario. The intellectual legacy of anti-Enlightenment philosophers like Friedrich Nietzsche (1844–1900) and Martin Heidegger (1889–1976) have largely impacted upon post-modern thoughts.

Nietzsche's philosophy centred on exposing the hollowness of Enlightenment hopes, as his famous phrase goes 'nihilism stands at the door'. This concept of nihilism governs post-modernist thinking on reality and the loss/multiplicity of realities. The anchorless conceptualization of reality questions the value of reason and truth resulting from such assertions, rather than persuasion of reason.

The other philosophical input comes from Heidegger, whose philosophy centred on examining the nature of thought in existing human beings. He takes a step forward from the Nietzschian philosophy to suggest that instead of truth the concern of philosophy should be Being. Humanism is at stake which is caused by the displacement and replacement of God by humanity at the centre of the universe. According to him, crisis is a result of attempts by humans to consider themselves as the measure of all things. Instead he emphasizes the difference of Being. By putting humans at the centre stage, technology has assumed the dominating dimension. As such he does not consider humanism as opposed to technology; rather the crisis as perceived in Western rational thinking acts as an occasion for rebuilding (Lyon 2002).

The major contribution to post-modern thought comes from Jacques Derrida and Michel Foucault, both French intellectuals. However, the term 'post-modern' shot into prominence and popular usage after the proposition of Jean-Francois Lyotard in his book *The Postmodern Condition* (the original French edition appeared in 1979, the English translation was published in 1984). Commissioned by the University of Quebec, Lyotard examined the 'new' condition of advance/late capitation and termed it as 'post-modern'.

MICHEL FOUCAULT (1926–84)

Michel Foucault is primarily a historian of social ideas. As a grand theorist Foucault worked on areas which are of significant importance for sociologists. His seminal research works covered analysis of knowledge-system, prisons, asylums, medicine and sexual practices. While there is a debate as to frame Foucault in any particular school of thought, the fact that he introduced a new style and method of writing history is beyond doubt.

Foucault's history is unique in the sense that he differs from most of the grand theories. Unlike other grand theories he dismisses the uni-linear continuities over time. History, for him is not an unfolding of events over a continuous and uni-linear time frame. This marks him as a forerunner of post-modern social theory (Ritzer 2007). Instead of searching for the source or origin of any social practice or institutions, he seeks to describe such practice or institution at various points of history great detail and analyse them.

The twists and turns, the ebbs and flows of history are more important for Foucault than the modernist concern for coherence and unidirectional flow of historical development. By emphasizing on discontinuities and ruptures in history, Foucault all the more influences subsequent post-modernist thinking in the French academic and intellectual circles. His major texts like *The Archeology of Knowledge* (1969), *The History of Sexuality* (1976) and *Discipline and Punish: The Birth of the Prison* (1977) bear testimony to basic methodological insistence that human sciences can only be treated as autonomous systems of discourse.

By the notion of discourse, Foucault means that while meaning is seen to be generated only from the abstract system of language and we can apprehend the world only through language system, the fact remains that the resources of language are always subject to the historical developments and conflicts of social relation in general. Thus, the notion of power is inevitably fused with discourse. In Foucault's theory power and knowledge are intertwined. The basic method of reading history shapes the post-modernist style of looking for an anchorless reality to a large extent.

JACQUES DERRIDA (1930–2004)

French philosopher and essayist Jacques Derrida has been a forerunner in post-modernist thinking. His employment of deconstruction as a strategy of analysis of such wide areas of literature, linguistics, philosophy, law and architecture has been of crucial significance for the development of post-modern theories. Through such a mode of analysis Derrida emphasizes the primacy of the words we use, the concepts they embody and the rules that develop within a group about what are the appropriate ways of talking about things. He promotes a discourse analysis that sees discourse as mediating between us and reality (Wallace and Wolf 1999).

Deconstruction for Derrida is a repudiation of the logo-centric construction of grand narratives. Logo-centrism refers to a mode of thinking that apply truth claims to universal propositions. He refutes the paradigm of knowledge of the social world which is grounded in a belief that one makes sense of the ever-changing and highly complex social reality by referring to certain unchanging fixed principles. Such an epistemology runs through the three basic texts of Derrida, all published in 1967. They are *Speech and Phenomena*, *Of Grammatology* and *Writing and Difference*. The post-modernist scepticism and refutation of the Western philosophical tradition is rooted in Derrida's criticism of grand narratives. He effectively contributes to the blurring of the traditional distinctions between logic and rhetoric, literal language and metaphor, and finally argument and narrative. Proposing a hermeneutical method he rejects the authority of canonical interpretations which characterize modernist thinkers. As he writes, '... the necessity of gaining this understanding before submitting the first reading to a symptomatic and historical interpretation regulated by other axioms or protocols, before and in order to destabilize, wherever this is possible and if it is necessary, the authority of canonical interpretations' (Derrida 1997: 61).

JEAN-FRANCOIS LYOTARD (1924–98)

Along with Michel Foucault and Jacques Derrida, Jean-Francois Lyotard was the leading proponent of the post-modernist school. Championing an interdisciplinary discourse he covered a wide range of themes which include treatise of post-modern conditions, art, architecture, language, knowledge, communication, meta-narratives and legitimization. In fact, Lyotard is to be credited with popularizing the term 'post-modern'. It all started with the publication of the *Postmodern Condition: A Report on Knowledge* (1999), which was first published in French in 1979.

Commissioned by the Canadian Government, *The Postmodern Condition* is actually a status report on the change in knowledge structure in the advanced societies. Impacted upon by the globalized high technology the advanced societies provided Lyotard the right subject matter to examine the viability of the promise of emancipation as projected by the Enlightenment ideals. The plinth of such ideals is the faith in science — science legitimizing itself as the bearer of emancipation. The grand narrative of modernity is that as we understand our world better we will be freed; that knowledge liberates while science is defining the character of such knowledge. All legitimate knowledge has to be scientific. But Lyotard is sceptical about such claims as he sees that in advanced societies the growing field of science and technology no longer shows its assumed unity. As a unified enterprise science no longer legislates. This prompted Lyotard to analyse the growth of knowledge as a social and cultural process.

KNOWLEDGE AND POST-MODERN CONDITION

In his study Lyotard covered everything from macro-level studies of complication of the military with major techno-science projects, to micro-level studies of how scientific decisions are actually implemented in designated laboratories. Such social conditioning and inter-institutional influence upon science basically undermines the rational and objective claims of science.

Lyotard indicates at a managerial society where the rationale of knowledge is sought only in the immediate. There is no intrinsic or grand purpose of knowledge and the emphasis is more on efficiency and 'performativity'. The post-war development of resurgence of liberal capitalism and the simultaneous waning of communist ideology has created the spirit of individual enjoyment. Lyotard calls it 'atomization of the social', which has lain to rest any universal theory of liberation.

The tendency among social scientists to move away from their traditional reliance on universalism prompted Lyotard to see such a condition as post-modern knowledge. In most highly developed societies such a condition of knowledge prevails, as he writes:

> The object of this study is the condition of knowledge in the most highly developed societies. I have decided to use the word postmodern to describe that condition.... It designates the state of our culture following the transformations which, since the end of the nineteenth century, have altered the game rules for science, literature, and the arts. (Lyotard 1999: xxiii)

For Lyotard the pace of development of any society is contingent upon the growth of technological knowledge. Advanced technology and exponential growing of computer technology propels a society faster towards a knowledge-based society. As knowledge becomes the principal motor of production, it has ramifications in other spheres of the society. There is a growing disjuncture between knowledge and science, as science becomes only a type of knowledge.

As the advancement of knowledge excludes positivist assumptions, only a post-modern approach to the study of society is possible. Rhetorically, he considers that searching for certitudes and proofs in turn leads to inventing counter examples of the same. In consequence, he dismisses all kinds of orthodoxies, or truth claims. Such analysis of post-modern condition of knowledge is a cornerstone of post-modern theories. The question of legitimation is central to post-modern theory, and Lyotard calls legitimation as:

> ... the process by which a 'legislator' dealing with scientific discourse is authorized to prescribe the stated conditions determining whether a statement is to be included in that discourse for consideration by the scientific community ... For it appears in its most complete form, that of reversion, revealing that knowledge and power are simply two sides of the same question: who decides what knowledge is, and who knows what needs to be decided? (Lyotard 1999: 8)

According to Lyotard, positivists' knowledge has lost their claims of legitimacy. Tradition resting on positivistic grand narratives has undergone a rupture under post-modern condition. Narratives as integral aspects of culture have a direct impact on the language of any society. Language is not only a requirement for a society to exist but can also be a tool of emancipation. It is then imperative to theorize on communication in order to understand social relations. Such a theorization entails a theory of language games. In *The Postmodern Condition* Lyotard describes language games by focusing on the effects of different modes of discourse or what he calls the various categories of utterances. Each category of utterance stands for specific rules and properties, and the uses to which they can be put.

Lyotard uses the term 'metanarratives' and its loss to define post-modernism.

> Simplifying to the extreme, I define postmodern as incredulity toward metanarratives. This incredulity is undoubtedly a product of progress in the sciences: but the process in turn presupposes it. To the obsolescence of the metanarrative apparatus of legitimation corresponds, most notably, the crisis of metaphysical philosophy and of the university institution which in the past relied on it. (Lyotard 1999: xxiv)

Using the concept of narratives, language and legitimation, Lyotard succeeds in explaining how and why the grand narratives of knowledge have lost their appeal to truth — the condition for such a loss is post-modern.

ZYGMUNT BAUMAN (1925–)

There is a direct link between Lyotard's contentions of the end of meta-narratives with Zygmunt Bauman's understanding of post-modernity. Bauman does not see the demise of universalizing meta-narratives as inherently crippling. As a Polish sociologist, Bauman is in fact opposed to the idea of post-modern sociology because such insistence on the non-rational and a sceptic attitude towards seeking explanations of any formation, according to him, would destabilize the discipline of sociology itself. Thus, a preferred term could be 'sociology of post-modernity' for him. It can retain the disciplinary gird, thereby, by developing a model of post-modern society employing the rational and systematic discourse (Rifer 2007).It can explain post-modern society as a distinct type and not just an aberration. As a prominent sociologist Bauman abundantly used theoretical categories from varied perspectives to emerge as a perceptive analyst of contemporary society.

Modernity and Ambivalence

Post-modernity for Bauman is the end of certitudes that modernity offered. However, it does not mean a complete chaos for him; instead he takes such a condition as a challenge to live with ambivalence. Post-modernity means coming to terms with the ambiguities of meanings. The indeterminacy of the future as emphasized by many post-modernist thinkers is taken as an occasion to accept and celebrate differences. The bottom-line for Bauman is that the tolerance of differences prompted by post-modernity can be used as life-enhancing although the negative side is that of a life lived without guarantees. Bauman is also aware that universalizing certitudes promoted by modernity has often given rise to totalitarian power in the past.

Bauman has written a large number of books addressing the question of modernity and ethics. As a sociologist he engages himself with the complex and unpredictable nature of post-modern world. Two of his best known works are *Modernity and Ambivalence* (1991) and *Modernity and Holocaust* (1989).

In *Modernity and Ambivalence*, Bauman introduces the allegorical figure of 'the stranger' to invoke the life-situation is post-modern world. The stranger is the society's undecidable. Drawing ideas from Simmel and Derrida, he describes the stranger as the person who is present, and yet unfamiliar. The sociological idea behind this use of allegory is to characterize the defining feature of post-modernity as that of ambivalence.

Bauman understands post-modernity as opposite to modernity. As against the universalizing propositions of modernity certifying and commanding truths, post-modernity is marked by a lack of goal-setting organization. As a result the existential situation of agents is quite fluid. Ambivalence, therefore, is a singular marker of post-modernity. Such ambivalences indicate differences in post-modernity, and to live with differences in turn promotes tolerance. But the other danger remains, where such differences collapse into indifference. Justice may suffer as a result of indifference, when inequality might as well be passed and unattended.

> Like all other human conditions, postmodern tolerance and diversity has its dangers and its fears. Its survival is not guaranteed- not by God's design, universal reason, laws of history, or any other supra-human force. In this respect, of course, the postmodern condition does not differ at all from all other conditions; it differs only by knowing about it, by its knowing of living without guarantee, of being on its own. This makes it exceedingly anxiety-prone. And this also gives it a chance. (Bauman 1999: 355)

By not imposing order on it post-modernity promotes messiness of the world. By accepting the stranger post-modernity fosters tolerance but it shares a fear of the void with modernity. Bauman examines in his book the different approaches that post-modern society takes towards the issue of ambivalence. There are two sides to it. Examining the dominance of consumer society in the post-modern world, Bauman finds that as far as the consumer society is concerned the 'stranger' and unfamiliar is always enticing. For example, in styles of food, in different fashions and in tourism it is possible to experience the allurement of what is unfamiliar, whereas on the negative side exhibits that the stranger is unpredictable and, therefore, an object of fear for the society. One who is outside the society's boundary and expected ways is constantly threatening. Thereby, post-modernity is both exhilarating and worrying, rolled into one.

Post-modernity as a result of ambivalence is still marked by popular disaffection and discontent, although it offers hope against ambivalence. It does not control such discontent, and thus Bauman sees such scattered ambivalence as the opportunity which can be used to help society reproduce itself (Ritzer 2007). The cruel side of post-modernity too is diagnosed by Bauman as the tolerance for differences does not automatically lead to greater solidarity in a post-modern world. As he writes:

> Postmodernity is a chance of modernity. Tolerance is a chance of postmodernty. Solidarity is a chance of tolerance. Solidarity is a third-degree chance. This does not sound reassuring for one wishing solidarity well. Solidarity cannot draw its confidence from anything remotely as solid and thereby as comforting as social structures, laws of history or the destination of nations and races from which modern projects derived their optimism, self-confidence and determination. (Bauman 1999: 355–56)

While coercion-supported dictatorship or ideological indoctrination is not required in post-modernity, the privatization of ambivalence deflects aspirations of human liberty from the management of collective life. The prosperity of consumer freedom adds to the situation by orienting life towards market-organized commodities. As a corollary it precludes the crucial freedom from market. Freedom exists everywhere except that from the choice between standard market-decided commercial products. All possible collective dissent is thereby depoliticized beforehand. The scenario of post-modernity is then for Bauman a retreat into personal anxiety and concerns. Removed from the centres of societal power one is deflected into increased fascination with the world of commodities. In his analysis Bauman shows the void of collective action under post-modernity. Thus, post-modernity acts both ways — by allowing de-centredness it offers a site of opportunities, and by negating collective formations it acts as a site of danger as well.

JEAN BAUDRILLARD (1929–2007)

Perhaps the most enchanting post-modern sociological theories are offered by the French sociologist, Jean Baudrillard. He is a doctorate in sociology being tutored by Henri Lefebvre. He was a trained sociologist but his work is quite diversified and his theoretical thrust kept changing as he grew intellectually.

Some of Baudrillard's lasting contribution to the world of sociology are *Systems of Objects* (1968), *Consumer Society* (1970), *Critique of the Political Economy of the Sign* (1972), *Symbolic Exchange and Death* (1976) and *On Seduction* (1982). In his formative years he was against the traditional sociological thought. He was a critic of the consumer society during the heydays of neo-capitalism in France in the 1960s. Influenced by Marxist ideas he studied the consumer society, media, fashion and sexuality. The rise of the electronic mass media and the aggressive expressions of the consumer society drew his critical sociological attention.

In 1970 with the publication of *The Consumer Society* we discover a different Baudrillard. From his earlier theoretical positions of being a structural Marxist, Baudrillard shifted away to post-modernist ideas. He was influenced more and more after the 1970s by linguistics and semiotics. The all important dominance of the cultural world in the following decades in Western capitalist world in controlling the public sphere and every day life drew his attention more towards the world of signs and symbols. As against his earlier concern with the material world, the world of the symbolic order became his principal scope of doing sociology. The concurrent post-modernist ideas engulfed him and he enriched it further through his path breaking analyses of the emergent dominance of the cultural and symbolic world on human life.

Post-modernity and the Age of Simulation

The Consumer Society marks a shift in Baudrillard's theoretical position from orthodox Marxism. Away from the sphere of production he focuses on the consumption sphere to understand class domination. Monopoly capitalism and its accomplice, consumer society mobilizes people as consumers. The need to consume becomes as essential, if not more, as their labour power. More than the consumption of material goods, it is the symbolic significance of consumption behaviour which becomes important. More than commodity exchange the symbolic exchange of the consumer order, according to Baudrillard attains importance as the real basis of radical critique of capitalism (Baudrillard 1981).

In a post-modern world the empirical object is a myth. Signs no longer represent something real; instead they themselves become 'real'. In fact, they refer to little more than themselves. In a way signs have become self-referential. Being encouraged by linguistics Baudrillard goes on to view consumption practices as different from his earlier Marxist productionist angle. He considers consumption of objects as a kind of language. Like a system of language, each consumer object has a sign associated with it. Thus, when we consume we also purchase the sign as much or more than our actual act of consuming an abject. Consumption is most importantly about signs and not goods.

With the coming of post-modernity the distinction between what is real and what is fabricated is blurred. Thus, the distinction between signs and reality has imploded. For Baudrillard, the shift from a modern to a post-modern world is signalled primarily by a shift from explosion of the production process to an implosion of the symbolic consumption. In a post-modern world, signs no longer are for real but are manufactured; thereby the symbolic meaning is all that is important. In a genuine cultural world, symbolic exchange can be real, but in contemporary world symbolic exchanges are characterized by their lack of genuineness. This is called 'simulation' by Baudrillard. Simulations are deceptive and Baudrillard envisions a world increasingly dominated by them. Simulations lead to the creation of simulacra — the reproductions of objects or events in post-modern world.

Employing post-modernist perspective Bourdieu believes that the new technical world of objects causes changes in values, modes of behaviour, relations to objects and to other people. The new technical advancements have affected all other aspects of society, while people have adapted to a new world — a world which is not 'real'. As Baudrillard says,

> We live in a hyperreal world where signs have acquired a life of their own and serve no other purpose than symbolic exchange. Symbolic exchange involves the continuous cycle of taking and returning, giving and receiving, a cycle of gifts and counter gifts. (Baudrillard 1975: 83)

The intrinsic use value of the objects then in reality is that of merely 'sign exchange value'. Thus, the emergent society can only entail a hyperreal world which lacks any empirically referential reality. The contemporary culture in advance industrial societies are saturated by the media, entertainment and new information systems. These triangular structures combinedly have actually created this hyperreality.

Baudrillard offers a grand theory of the change witnessed by the contemporary world, mainly at the sphere of consumption. For him, an unreal world dominated by simulations is moving in an extraordinary direction. His influence is not restricted to social theory and many fields of humanities are influenced by him. Baudrillard has disdain for the post-modern label, yet his concepts and theories are very much a part of post-modernist thinking. He has influenced not only further post-modern theories of the social but also other sociological perspectives which are more mainstream.

PIERRE BOURDIEU (1930–2002)

Born in 1930 in a small rural town in France, Pierre Bourdieu grew up in a lower middle-class family. He studied in the prestigious Ecole Normale Superieure, Paris. He held the prestigious chair in sociology at College de France. As a powerful intellectual and a dominant sociologist he addressed a varied range of subjects — anthropology, education and sociology.

Bourdieu is considered as the most prolific sociologist of the last half of the twentieth-century. The range of themes addressed by him made him almost a cult figure in Western intellectual field and with the English translation of his works, the rest of the world discovered another encyclopaedic thinker to offer sociological theories to examine the methodological issues as well as the question of how society and culture is being reproduced in contemporary times. The important concepts of Bourdieu that have been introduced in sociology are that of *habitus*, *field* and *symbolic capital.*

Outline of a Theory of Practice (1977)) was first published in French in 1972. This is a major text of Bourdieu as it settles the issue for an appropriate sociological method. It accomplishes the task by questioning both — 'who reflect on the social sciences without practising them and those who practice them without reflecting on them'. Theoretically, Bourdieu tries to overcome the oppositions that have characterized social theory traditionally. The fundamental opposition is that between science and its object. He tries to build a reflexive science of society by transcending this basic opposition and problematizing scientists and science as part and product of their social universe.

Symbolic Capital

The important concept that marks Bourdien's sociology is that of symbolic capital. Bourdieu describes power in terms of symbolic capital. It signifies the amount of honour and prestige possessed by an actor. Symbolic capital comes with social position and it accords prestige. Bourdieu's use and analysis of symbolic capital signals his departure from Marx and comes closer to Weber. However, under a closer scrutiny it shows his theoretical acumen to extend the scope of Marx's understanding of capital. It shows his resolve not to get swayed away by the proliferation of signs and symbols that mark the advance/post industrial societies and land up with post-modernist thought of dismissing everything which is foundational. The notion of capital and power associated with it remains central in Bourdieu's sociology. The idea of symbolic capital is, of course, drawn from the economic sphere. He talks about four different and distinct types of capital — the economic capital, the cultural capital, the social capital and finally, the symbolic capital. As the advance industrial society gets more and more differentiated such differentiation of capital is all but obvious.

To account for the advance stage of capitalist society, Bourdieu theorizes beyond economic capital which simply refers to the economic resources possessed by an actor. By cultural capital Bourdieu means the various kinds of legitimate knowledge possessed by an actor, while social capital is the valued social positions enjoyed by an actor. To top them all is the symbolic capital, the culmination of all such positions and capital to signify honour and prestige possessed. The economic, cultural and social capitals have their surpluses and their own storage and can be traded to accumulate symbolic capital.

According to Bourdieu, economic capital can be converted into symbolic capital in order to gain sufficient obligation back and create relationships of dependence from lower social classes. Moreover, economic capital can be deferred via symbolic capital.

Bourdieu gives the example of the education system in consumer society to establish his idea of symbolic capital. Education and knowledge of higher order can be purchased with money. Thus, for one's offsprings one spends money but is rewarded at a later stage by the process of reproduction as the symbolic value of higher educational possessions ploughs back high status position for the family. On the other hand, cultural capital works via superior aesthetic tastes which relates to social position. In his empirical study of tastes among different social classes, Bourdieu demonstrates the importance of cultural and symbolic order in modern consumer society over the material order (Bourdieu 1984). He views culture as a kind of economy or market place. In this marketplace it is the cultural goods/capital which is utilized for social placements rather than economic goods/capital. This capital is expressed symbolically, but is an expression of one's social class origin as well as their educational possessions. While studying differential tastes, Bourdieu asserts that actual preferences relate to social status. By examining the different categories and forms of capital, and showing their derivative character he basically confirms that capital is a form of social relation.

Habitus and Practice

Bourdieu's usage of the concept of habitus is central to his sociology. Through the concept of habitus he seeks to transcend the theoretical oppositions as subjective/objective, culture/society and structure/action. Against both objectivism and subjectivism he suggests 'practice' as an organizing concept in social research. Neither objectivism nor subjectivism can explain social life fully, which needs to be understood in terms of both the objective structures of the society and the constituting practices and experiences of individuals and groups.

Objectivism essentially has given a theoretical and ontological primary basis to social structure — that, the institutions and norms exclusively shape and govern the actions of individuals in society. On the other hand, subjectivism confers on human beings an agency. As volitional agent human beings are seen as being capable of making a difference in and changing the social systems they inhabit. For Bourdieu, if subjectivism suffers from methodological individualism, objectivism gets trapped in methodological holism. 'Practice' can neither be seen as constituting social structure (Phenomenological School) nor as being constituted by social structure (structuation and variants structural functionalism).

Bourdieu appreciates that human beings as agents act within socially constructed ranges of possibilities durably inscribed within them as well as within the social world in which they operate. As such, the relationship between the agent and social world is a relation between two dimensions of the social and not two separate sorts of living. The image of social life drawn by Bourdieu is unique. He understands social life as a mutually constituting interaction of structures, dispositions, and actions as a result of which social structures and embodied knowledge of these structures produce enduring orientations to action which, in turn, are constitutive of social structures. Thus, these orientations are at once 'structuring structures' and 'structured structures'. Simultaneously they shape and are being shaped by social practice. Practice results from a process of improvisation, while at the same time is structured by cultural orientations, personal trajectories, and the ability to play the game of social interaction (Calhoun 2000). The capacity for structured improvisation is what Bourdieu characterizes as the habitus. Therefore, the habitus produces and is produced by the social world. With the concept of habitus Bourdieu resolves the opposition between subjectivism and objectivism.

As a system of dispositions habitus is both subjective and objective; and as a system of general generative schemes it is durable, as inscribed in the social construction of the self, and transposable from one *field* to another. For Bourdieu, field is a network of relations and by definition, as an arena of struggle and battle with people occupying positions within fields and oriented, either as individuals or collectivities. Such orientations are aimed at consolidating their positions or improving them. With the concept of habitus, along with the concept of field, Bourdieu analyses the behaviour of agents as objectively coordinated and regular without being the product of rules, on the one hand, or conscious rationality, on the other. With the help of these concepts Bourdieu emphasizes upon the practical mastery that people have over their social situation, while grounding that mastery itself socially. The habitus is the key which provides the principle by which people make choices and choose their appropriate strategies to make sense of their world. Interestingly, Bourdieu has moved away from the modernist world-view of considering human beings as rational, the habitus indicates that people are practical than being rational. In their agency there is reason, the reason of practical sense. The logic of practice governs them — *practice* as the outcome of the dialectical relationship between structure and agency (Ritzer 2007).

The way Bourdieu analyses the issue of revolutionary collective actions makes clear his understanding of habitus as the product of history as well as producing history in accordance with the schemes engendered by history. Collective actions are imbricated within conjunctures and still crucially dependent on the same habitus which has hitherto organized reproduction. Thus, revolutions do not mark a break with the habitus, but are based on it, even though they break the pattern of stable reproductions.

> It is just as true and just as untrue to say that collective actions produce the event or that they are its product. The conjuncture capable of transforming practices objectively co-ordinated because subordinated to partially or wholly identical objective necessaries, into collective action (e.g. revolutionary action) is constituted in the dialectical relationship between, on the one hand, a habitus ... and on the other hand, an objective event which exerts its action of conditional stimulation calling for or demanding a determinate response.... (Bourdieu 1977: 82–83)

Bourdieu's sociology in defence of 'practice' challenges the structuralist elimination of agents and also takes guard against subjectivism which imagined that agents are not decided upon by their backgrounds/situations, that actions originate within choices among abstractly conceived possibilities. In fact, he extends his methodological stance to the practice of the discipline of sociology as well. His program for a reflexive sociology is in consonance with his concepts of habitus and practice. The tools for better understanding of social life need to be simultaneously adopted by sociologists with respect to their own work. His call for a reflexive sociology alerts the practitioner to be aware of the external social and intellectual acting on them. The impact of such influences on their research would then be realized and such realization could help to make sociology a self-conscious discipline. 'Using his own terminology, Bourdieu would favour examining the habitus and practices of sociologists within the fields of sociology as a discipline and the academic world, as well as the relationship between those fields and fields of stratification and politics' (Ritzer 2007: 177).

While it is true that structuralist perspective influenced Bourdieu, he realized that objective structures are confining human thought, action and interaction. The way people represent the world affect the objective structures as well. Without succumbing to the determination of the large-scale structures, he analysed the way people, governed by the habitus and the field they encounter, perceive and construct the world. Artistically such perceptions and constructions are both animated and constrained by the objective social structures. Thus, a structuralist constructivism marks his sociology. Hence, Bourdieu's towering influence in sociology is due to his grand efforts to synthesize many theoretical ideas to move beyond structuralist perspective. At the same time when post-modernist thinking in sociology almost questioned the viability of any objective explanatory scheme of thought, Bourdieu brought the two extremes of subjectivism and objectivism together. The interplay between the internal cognitive structures through which people negotiate the social world (habitus) and the external structure of differentiated power positions (field) explains social life better. Assuredly, Bourdieu stands tall among all of his contemporaries, as he stands against the grain — the sweep of post-modernist thinking to account for the dramatic changes of the economy and society. At best he could be credited with coming up with a sociology of post-modern society, Nevertheless, the term post-modern remains contentious.

SUMMARY

Overall speaking, post-modern social theory successfully brings in the contrast of the present with the immediate past. The phenomenal rise of information and technology and the parallel shrinking of mass production based industries have given rise to new social conditions of existence. The socio-historical events of dying down of organized mass movement against a surging neo-liberal world economy has also provided a set up for a fresh and new thinking on society. A palpable disenchantment with the promise of science and claims of truth (ideology) make thinking along anti-foundational knowledge quite obvious. The new domains of social life — the ever expanding zones of consumer practice, the role of technology, knowledge system and its relationship with the modern, are all subjected to insightful analysis by the post-modernist thinkers. While popularly acknowledged as a poststructuralist, Bourdieu's sociology tries to overcome objectivist – subjectivist dilemma in sociological tradition. By offering the *concept* of practice, he establish the dynamic relation between in the two.

Key Words

- *Ambivalence*
- *Discourse*
- *Habitus*
- *Hyperreal World*
- *Legitimation*
- *Logocentrism*
- *Post-industrial*
- *Post-modern Conditionl*
- *Symbolic Capital*

Glossary

Habitus: A concept developed by Bourdieu to refer to the set of socially learnt dispositions, skills and ways of acting, that are often taken for granted, and which are acquired through the activities and experiences of everyday life.

Hyperreal: A condition in which 'reality' has been replaced by simulacra. While simulacra are sign systems which have no relation to reality; they simulate simulations.

Logocentrism: A term used by Jacques Derrida to designate the desire for a centre or original guarantee of all meanings, which in Derrida's view has characterized Western philosophy since Plato. The Western science and philosophy traditionally situates the logos, 'the word' or the 'act of speech', as epistemologically superior in a system.

Metanarrative: A philosophical term which attempts to give a totalizing, comprehensive account to various historical events, experiences and social, cultural phenomena based upon the appeal to universal truth or universal values.

Post-industrial Society: A society characterized by the centrality of theoretical knowledge as the source of innovation and policy formation for the society. A society no longer dominated by a manufacturing-based economy and moves on to a structure of society based on the provision of information, innovation, finance and services .

Post-modernism: A philosopohical perspective that stands against the viewpoint of modernism. More specifically it is a tendency in contemporary culture characterized by the problem of objective truth and inherent suspicion towards foundational knowledge. It suggests that many, if not all, apparent realities are only social constructs, as they are subject to change inherent to time and place.

Post-structuralism: A perspective that attempts to look beyond the structuralist method of arriving at secure knowledge through the charting of differences within structures. The basic theme of all varieties of post-structuralist theory include the rejection of the self-sufficiency of the structures that structuralism posits and an interrogation of the binary oppositions that constitute those structures.

Practice: The concept used by Bourdieu to suggest that actions are the outcome of the dialectical relationship between structure and agency, i.e., human actions are neither objectively determined, nor do they result from free will of individuals.

Simulation: A post-modernist term used by Baudrillard which suggests a circular world in which the 'sign' is not exchanged for meaning, but merely for another sign.

Discussion Points

- The premise for the coming of post-modern theories.
- The possibility of post-modern sociology.
- Bourdieu's attempt to resolve subjectivism and objectivism.

13

Conclusion

Sociology as a discipline is a product of modern society. Sociological theory, therefore, endeavours to account for modern society. This is true for all the classical statements about the emergence and transformation of human society more or less between the period of the French Revolution of the later half of the eighteenth-century and the end of Word War I. It was a period that saw a dramatic change in people's lives and social living. A liberal, modern, bureaucratic nation-state grew in this period in the West, breaking away from the rural, conservative, theology-inspired feudal States. Classical sociological theory is exclusively an intellectual response to theorize on the problems and issues associated with the emergence of the modern period.

Beyond the classical period sociological encyclopedic theory moved away from grand theorization to the task of applying the insights drawn from the great classicists to address more contemporary issues. Here, the question of self and methodology figured prominently. Various schools of thought have prospered, being inspired by contesting traditions of sociology, which carry forward the task of authorizing the practice of sociology as an autonomous discipline. More and more finer methodological issues have been deliberated upon, yet the core concern of all sociological theory continue to revolve on the question of individual–societal relationship. The nature of social organization and the place of an individual in such an organization continue to be the rallying point for sociological theories. The root of such theorization lies, as we have noted before, in the socio-historical context of the origin of the discipline. The new way in which the subjects viewed the social world and their place in it, was first stimulated by the events of the late eighteenth-century. And it continued for more than a century whereby all the salient features of a modern age were fully established. The changing subject-position vis-à-vis the social world, however, continued with the proliferation and dramatic changes of technology along with widespread societal changes which mark contemporary social life. Modern theories are just logical responses to such a scenario.

The spirit of science governed the embryonic stage of sociology. The classical theories reflect, however, that such theorists have simultaneously tried to make sociology both objective and value-orienting. This is best exemplified by the works of Max Weber. But to start with the foremost theorist Karl Marx, we understand that although he was not a professional sociologist, his profound thought has been the most important influence on the subsequent emergence of sociology as an academic discipline.

INDIVIDUAL AND SOCIETY

The idea of progress and the role of individuals in the development of society dominated classical thinkers like Marx, Durkheim, Weber et al. The idea of progress and seeking for a more appropriate social order took shape to counter the dwindling individual–social ties, growing pauperization of industrial workers, social disorganization and problems associated with the decline of traditional religious ways of life. Marx with his unique method of dialectically applying materialism saw the historical process as one created by active human beings. A predetermined state of being is refuted in favour of human agency. Capitalism for him was a necessary step forward in human history. Marx related the enforced and dehumanized division of labour to the question of material ownership of means of production. Progress for him was transcendence from such a state of society to a state marked by social ownership of means of production and socially directed division of labour.

Dialectical thinking is the essence of Marx's writings; while asserting the creative potential of individual beings he held that freedom can only be accomplished within the confines of particular and historically variable types of society. Demystifying the illusion of freedom offered by capitalism, Marx tried to drive home the conception of the individual as a being who could attain self-determination only in association with others at particular junctures of history, defying the logic of private appropriation.

For Marx, alienation was integral to the expansion of the division of labour and he treated the abolition of it as synonymous with the abolition of private property relations. According to Marx, emergence of class societies in history is dependent upon the growth of the specialization of tasks made possible by the existence of surplus production. In contrast, for Durkheim, the growth of the division of labour represented the integrating consequences of specialization rather than in terms of the formation of class systems. Durkheim, too, recognized the alienating character of the division of labour, but his proposals for the eradication of this dehumanization of the worker were based upon the moral consolidation of specialization in the division of labour.

As a direct bearer of the spirit of positivism as formulated by Comte and Saint-Simon, Durkheim advanced the idea of scientific study of social facts. Subsequently, he suggested that human progress was directly linked to the successful discovery of the laws found in society. As against pathologic and anomic conditions of division of labour, for Durkheim a normal solidaristic social system in modernity would require norms and laws which would define the relational conditions of reciprocity and cooperation among differentiated elements in the larger social context.

Max Weber, on the other hand, represented an altogether different tradition in sociological thought. Weber carried the neo-Kantian idealist tradition in his sociological theorization. He adopted a historical and ideographic approach in order to grasp the subjective realm of human society, to be precise, the cultural reality. Weber had an overriding interest in the unfolding of the rational modern order, but he theorized the overarching forces of instrumental rationality as a deterrent for any realization of human freedom. He studied the rationalization of culture and of everyday life by emphasizing that rationalism was the defining feature of contemporary Western civilization. He went on to conclude that there is an inherent ambivalence and tension in the modern world. Modern societies have replaced substantive meanings by formal rationality. The formal rationality being empty of any orientations towards things of ultimate significance relies on only instrumental effectiveness.

The emergent modern world for Weber is an ensemble of pursuits of instrumental efficiency. Hence, despite the feeling of mastery over the world, contemporary modern individuals would contemplate a universe that has become indifferent to humanity and lacks meaning. Weber was not different from Marx in conceiving the fate of the individual under advanced industrial societies. But he, unlike Marx, did not envision a possible form of social arrangement where the individual and society could exist in perfect harmony. The predicament of the modern individual was located in the encompassing techno-rational bureaucratic order. Unlike Marx, Weber could not theorize an emancipatory condition of the inhuman rationalizing trends.

Vilfredo Pareto, too, adopted a pessimistic view about the individual's place in a modern society. He saw a growing incapacity of the individual to take rational control of destiny. In his sociology, human nature is seen as relatively immune to the effects of social and historical change. Taking an anti-Enlightenment stand Pareto refuted the progressive march of human society in terms of rationality principle. The dead weight of sentiments, essentially psychologically derived, was Pareto's central emphasis in theorizing upon the stability of society.

The events of World War I, too, impacted upon sociological theory. Apart from the rise of Marxian practice across the world, the emergence of the United States as a global power led to an accompanying development of its sociology departments. The leading figure in this initiative was Talcott Parsons who treaded the tested path of the great European thinkers to develop a grand theory of society in systemic terms. As against the revolutionary overhauling of post-War societies inspired by Marxist theories of change, Parson's theory tried to synthesize the classical sociological theorists of Europe to reconcile social action and social structure. The idea was to offer a view of society as a system, the stability of which is ensured by an underlying pattern of value consensus that was beyond individual choice.

Under the leadership of Parsons, functionalism tried to understand society in terms of its systemic features. The integration of individual beings with the social system was theorized in terms of an interacting and inter-penetrating sub-system of personality, culture and society, each considered as quasi-autonomous systems. In terms of motivations, orientations and situational constraints Parsons used his general theory of social action to highlight system equilibrium. The image of society developed thereby rested on a macro-analysis of the parts of society and the various actors. The place of individual human agency and the scope for social change was minimally treated, although subsequently Robert Merton attempted to make the perspective more dynamic. But the emphasis on structure neglected the dimension of process in such structural–functional theorizations.

As against the consensual view of society inspired by the functional school of thought, the mid-twentieth-century saw a rise of conflict approaching the society. Theorists like Coser, Mills and Dahrendrof advanced an alternative image of society. That society is coordinated as a result of power struggles and power differentials. The existence of power differentials and interest groups make conflict an inevitable feature for all societies to come. If the consensus theorists exaggerated on the shaping of a normative order, the conflict theorists went to the other extreme of explaining only the constraining aspects of a society always caught in power struggles.

The central position of the individual in sociological theory, without ignoring the social structure was accorded by symbolic interactionist school, while the social exchange theorists posited an image of individual who is rational in calculating pleasures, profits and pains. Hence, a society is the result of such interacting individuals. However, group structure and corresponding interactions are theorized more at a micro-level ignoring large-scale structures. Symbolic interactionists like George Herbert Mead, on the other hand, analysed how the individual 'Being' and the 'Self' result from social processes. Focusing on the aspects of the symbolic order it is being shown how an individual is fitted into the large patterns of social interaction. To be fair, these perspectives throw less light on society, and instead engage us rigorously on understanding human behaviour. In an emergent world of growing exchanges between variously placed cultures such micro-perspectives on human behaviour and social exchange are useful to study how people use different non-verbal signs and align themselves spatially in different ways during interactive situations.

Away from the project of classical sociological thinkers, more and more sociology during the later half of the twentieth-century delimited its scope to the micro aspects of social living. Given the growing scepticism with objective mode of analysis of varied social phenomena, more rigorous attempts were made at the methodological issues. The ethnomethodologists attempted to probe into human behaviour by examining the methods that people themselves employ to make sense of their world. As against traditional sociology, which studies society as reality without and a priori, the ethnomethodological perspective tried to construct an image of society through the everyday practices of the people who constitute such a society. Phenomenologists in a somewhat similar vein made the conscious experience of individuals as its subject matter. The everyday taken-for-granted approach that people invoke in their perceptions of the social world is the primary focus of such sociological theory. Such perspectives are to be credited in making Sociology a reflexive science of society.

The events leading to World War II and the failures of orthodox theories of progress and human emancipation resulted in the appearance of the critical school of sociological theories. The experiences of totalitarian dictatorship enjoying popular support created a great disillusionment with the promises of modernity. The age of overwhelming bureaucratic control and dominance of mass media prompted thinkers like Adorno, Horkheimer and others to indict capitalist modernity. The social and psychological dimensions of suffocating individual self-expression and personality were probed to unmask the techniques of mass deception and manipulation. Reinvesting individual consciousness with critical creative agency, critical theories foresaw the coming of post-modern theory. In essence, critical theory offered a view of modern society in which growing rationalization turned against reason. It laid threadbare the face of such society which reduces human choices to consumer options, and in turn lacks the capacity to transform and liberate social institutions.

The debacle of the promise of rationality and reason in organizing a just and fair society led to an altogether rejection of modernist thinking by post-modern thinkers like Lyotard, Baudrillard and others. With multi-faceted development of contemporary societies in the post-industrial phase of development, the idea of a single coherent reality is being questioned. No longer is a foundational theory of society tenable for such a post-modern society. Hence, all the grand theorizing and narratives that mark traditional sociological theories are led to rest in favour of a theory that insists on continuous deferrals of meanings and ever shifting positions of individual identity in a world designed more by a virtual reality. Here the society is bereft of the 'social', and is instead bombarded with a hyperreality at the behest of the mass media. Amidst such pronouncements of the eclipse of the 'social', post-structuralist thinker Pierre Bourdieu offered a methodologically strengthened understanding of the relation between human agency and social structure. Adopting an idea of relationality, Bordieu depicted an image of society where cultural production and its products are situated as well as constituted in terms of a number of processes and social realities. By using the concept of habits he showed the objectification of social structure at the level of individual subjectivity. Thereby, he attempted to resolve the perennial debate between subjectivism and objectivism in sociological theory.

Finally, theory is not an axiom. It is a continuous process of seeking explanation of events surrounding respective theorists. Sociological theory has gained from ideas from the ancient world, thoughts of great philosophers of antiquity and observations of a great many social reformers. Only in the nineteenth-century sociological theory gained autonomy and as such, its subject matter kept on evolving with twists and turns in tandem with the metamorphosis of human society. It might have started with a mission to seek for 'laws' of society but such 'laws' are at best tendential in character. All sociological theories are built or inspired upon preceding thoughts, ideas and theories, which actually make them provisional in spirit and aspiration. What is constant in the history of the discipline is the quest for understanding the intricate relation between individual and society. Related to this central query is the question of settling the issue of creative human agency vis-à-vis the stable social structure. From time to time, sociological thinkers have attempted to answer this fundamental issue of social life.

SUMMARY

Sociology as a discipline developed in the historical context of fundamental changes in society affecting the social (class), industrial, political and cultural relations. The decline and rise of social groups, and changes in the economic and social structures were accompanied by complementary cultural changes. Classical sociological theories attempted to explain such sweeping changes. The initial theorizations on the relationship between individual and society by and large resulted in the theoretical treatment of the relationship between action and social structure. The overbearing importance of social structure continued in sociological theories, till a substantial shift from structural matters to cultural matters allowed a new theoretical development. The new focus has been on areas of identity, communication and consumption. Such a shift in subject matter changed the very discipline of sociology in the last few decades of the 20th century. The impact and influence of post-structuralism and postmodernism on sociological thinking, one can say, is a result of a fundamental alteration in the very image of society.

Bibliography

Adams, Bert and R. A. Sydie. 2001. Sociological Theory. Thousand Oaks, CA: Pine Forge Press.

Adorno, T. W. 1967. 'Cultural Criticism and Society', in *Prisms*. London: Neville Spearman.

Antonio, Robert J. 1983. 'The Origin, Development, and Contemporary Status of Critical Theory'. *Sociological Quarterly*, 24 (Summer): 325–51.

Baudrillard, Jean. 1970. *The Consumer Society*. London: Sage.

———. 1975. *The Mirror of Production*. St. Louis: Telos Press.

———. 1981. *For a Critique of the Political Economy of the Sign*. St. Louis: Telos Press.

Bauman, Zygmunt. 1989. *Modernity and the Holocaust*. Ithaca, New York: Cornell University Press.

———. 1999. *In Search of Politics*. Cambridge: Polity.

Bell, Daniel. 1973. *The Coming of Post-Industrial Society: A Venture in Social Forecasting*. New York: Basic Books.

Berger, Peter, Brigette Berger and Hansfried Kellner. 1973. *The Homeless Mind*. New York: Random House.

Berger, Peter and Thomas Luckman. 1980. *The Social Construction of Reality*. New York: Irvington.

Blumer, Herbert. 1954. 'What Is Wrong with Social Theory?', *American Sociological Review,* 19(1): 3–10.

———. 1969. *Symbolic Interaction.* Englewood Cliffs, NJ: Prentice Hall.

Bourdieu, Pierre. 1977. *Outline of a Theory of Practice*. Cambridge and New York: Cambridge University Press.

———. 1984. *Distinction: A Social Critique of the Judgment of Taste*. London: Routledge.

———. 1990. *Reproduction in Education, Society and Culture* (Theory, Culture and Society Series) with J.-C. Passeron. New Delhi: Sage Publications Limited.

Calhoun, Craig. 1993. 'Habitus, Field, and Capital: The Question of Historical Specificity', in C. Calhoun, E. LiPuma and M. Postone, eds, *Bourdieu: Critical Perspectives.* Chicago: University of Chicago Press, pp. 61–88.

Comte, Auguste. 1957 [1849]. *A General View of Positivism* (J. H. Bridges, trans.), New York: Robert Speller and Sons.

Cooley, Charles. 1964. *Human Nature and the Social Order.* New York: Schocken.

Coser, Lewis. 1956. *The Functions of Social Conflict.* New York: Free Press.

———. 1972. 'The Alien as a Servant of Power: Court Jews and Christian Renegades', *American Sociological Review*, 37(5): 574–81.

Crunden, Robert M. 1982. *Ministers of Reform: The Progressive Achievement in American Civilization, 1889–1920*. New York: Basic Books.

Dahrendorf, Ralph. 1959. *Class and Class Conflict in Industrial Society.* Stanford: Stanford University Press.

———. 1968, *Essays in the Theory of Society*. Standford: Standford University Press.

Derrida, Jacques. 1997. 'To Do Justice to Freud: The History of Madness in the Age of Psychoanalysis', in Arnold I. Davidson, ed., *Foucault and His Interlocutors.* Chicago: The University of Chicago Press, pp. 57–104.

Durkhiem, Emile. 1964 [1893]. *The Division of Labour in Society* (G. Simpson, trans.). New York: Free Press.

———. 1965 [1912]. *The Elementary Forms of Religious Life*. New York: Free Press.

———. 1973 [1914]. 'The Dualism of Human Nature and its Social Condition', in Emile K. Bellah, ed., *Durkheim: On Morality and Society*. Chicago: University of Chicago Press, pp. 149–63.

———. 1984 [1893]. *The Division of Labour in Society* (W. D. Halls, trans.). New York: Free Press.

———. 1982 [1895]. *The Rules of Sociological Method and Selected Texts on Sociology and Its Method* (Steven Lukes, ed.; W. D. Halls, trans.). New York: Free Press.

———. 1951. *Suicide* (A. Spaulding and G. Simpson, trans.). New York: Random House.

Engels, Frederick. 1974 [1883]. Dialectics of Nature. Moscow: Progress Publishers. 1975

———.[1892]. *Socialism: Utopian and Scientific*. Peking; Foregin Langnge Press.

Garfinkel, Harold. 1967. *Studies in Ethnomethodology.* Englewoods Cliffs, NJ: Prentice Hall.

———. 1988. 'Evidence for Locally Produced, Naturally Accountable Phenomena of Order, Logic, Reason, Meaning etc. In and as of the Essential Quiddity of Immortal Ordinary Society (I of IV): An Announcement of Studies', *Sociological Theory*, (1): 103–09.

———. 1996. 'Ethnomethodology's Program', *Social Psychology Quarterly*, 59(1): 5–21.

Goffman, Erving. 1959. *Presentation of Self in Everyday Life.* Garden City, NY: Anchor.

———. 1961. *Encounters: Two Sides in the Sociology of Interaction.* Indianapolis: Bobbs-Merrill.

———. 1963. *Stigma: Notes on the Management of Spoiled Identity.* Englewood Cliffs, NJ: Prentice-Hall.

———. 1974. *Frame Analysis: An Essay on the Organization of Experience.* New York: Harper Colophon.

Habermas, Jurgen. 1987a. *The Philosophical Discourse of Modernity* (Frederick Lawrence, trans.). Cambridge, MA: The MIT Press.

———. 1987b. *The Theory of Communicative Action,* Vol. II. Boston: Beacon.

———. 1997. 'Modernity: An Unfinished Project', in Maurizio Passerin and Seyla Benhabib, eds, *Habermas and the Unfinished Project of Modernity*, Cambridge, MA: The MIT Press, pp. 38–55.

Held, David. 1980. *Introduction to Critical Theory*. Berkeley: University of California Press.

Hobsbawm, Eric. 1964 [1857–58]. *Karl Marx: Pre-Capitalist Economic Formations*, intro. and ed. New York: International Publishers.

Homans, George. 1950. *The Human Group*. New York: Harcourt & Brace.

———. 1961. *Social Behavior: Its Elementary Forms*. New York: Harcourt, Brace and World.

———. 1967. *The Nature of Social Science.* New York: Harcourt, Brace and World.

———. 1984. *Coming to My Senses: The Autobiography of a Sociologist.* New Brunswick, NJ: Transaction Books.

Horkheimer, Max. 2002 [1972]. 'Traditional and Critical Theory', in Craig Calhoun, Joseph Gerteis, James Moody, Steven Peaff, Kathryn Schmidt and Indermohan Virk, eds, *Classical Sociological Theory.* Massachussetts : Blackwell Publishers Inc.

Horkheimer, Max and Theodor W. Adorno. 1944. *Dialectic of Enlightenment*. New York: Continuum.

Husserl, Edmund. 1964. *The Idea of Phenomenology* (William P. Alston and George Nakhnikian, trans.). The Hague: Martinus Nijhoff.

———. 1957. *Ideas* (Boyce Gibson, trans.). London: George Allen & Unwin Ltd.

———. 1965. *The Phenomenology of Internal Time-Consciousness*, Martin Heidegger, ed. Bloomington, IN: University Press.

Jameson, Fredric. 1991. *Postmodernism or The Cultural Logic of Late Capitalism.* Durham, N.C.: Duke University Press.

Lukacs, Georg. 1923. *History and Class Consciousness.* Berlin: Malik Verlag.

Lyotard, Jean-Francois. 1979. *The Postmodern Condition: A Report on Knowledge*, Minneapolis: University of Minnesota Press.

———. 1999. *The Postmodern Condition: A Report on Knowledge.* Minneapolis: University of Minnesota Press.

Marcuse, Herbert. 1956. *Eros and Civilization.* England: Routledge and Kegan Paul Ltd.

———. 1969. *Essay of Liberation.* Boston: Beacon Press.

———. 1989. 'Philosophy and Critical Theory', in Stephen Eric Bronner and Douglas Kellner, eds, *Critical Theory and Society.* New York: Routledge, pp.58–74.

Martindale, Don. 1988. *The Nature and Types of Sociological Theory.* Prospect Heights, IL: Waveland Press.

Marx, Karl.1964. *The Economic and Phiolosophic Manuscripts of 1844* (Dirk Strunk, ed.). New York: International Publishers.

———. 1976 [1845]. Theses on Feuerbach, in Karl Marx and Frederick Engels, eds, *Collected Works, Vol. 4.* Moscow: Progress Publishers.

———. 1973 [1847]. *The Poverty of Philosophy.* Moscow: Progress Publishers.

———. 1932 [1848]. *The Communist Manifesto.* New York: International Publishers.

———. 1968 [1859]. 'Preface to a Contribution to the Critique of Political Economy', in Karl Marx and Frederick Engels, ed., *Selected Works.* Moscow: Progress Publishers.

———. 1967 [1867, 1885. 1894]. *Capital*, Vols I, II and III (S. Moore and E. Aveling, trans.). New York: International Publishers.

Marx, Karl and Frederick Engels. 1972 [1845–46]. *The German Ideology* (C. J. Arthur, ed.), New York: International Publishers.

———. 1976. *Marx and Engels, Collected Works.* Moscow: Progress Publishers.

———. 1974 [1883]. *Dialectics of Nature.* Moscow: Progress Publishers.

Mead, George Herbert. 1934. *Mind, Self, and Society* (Charles W. Morris, ed.). Chicago: University of Chicago Press.

———. 1938. *The Philosophy of the Act.* Chicago: University of Chicago Press.

Merton, Robert King. 1968 [1949]. *Social Theory and Social Structure.* New York: Free Press.

———. 1996 [1994]. 'A Life of Learning', in Piotr Sztompka, ed., *Robert K. Merton: On Social Structure and Science.* Chicago: Chicago University Press, pp. 339–59.

Mills, C. Wright. 1956. *The Power Elite.* New York: Oxford University Press.

———. 1958. 'The Structure of Power in American Society', British Journal of Sociology, 9(1) : 29–41.

———. 1959. The Sociological Imagination. New York: Oxford University Press.

Nisbet, Robert A. 1967. *The Sociological Tradition.* London: Heinemann.

Pareto, Vilfredo, 1963 [1916]. *The Mind and Society: A Treatise on General Sociology* (2 vols), Arthur Livingston, ed., and A. Bongiorno and A. Livingston, trans. New York: Dover.

———. 1980. *The Other Pareto,* (Bucolo Placido, ed. and trans.). New York: St. Martin's Press.

Parsons, Talcott. 1949 [1937]. *The Structure of Social Action.* Glencoe, IL: Dorsey Press.

———. 1951. The Social System. Glencoe, IL: Free Press.

Ritzer, George. 1996. *Modern Sociological Theory.* New York: The McGraw-Hill Companies, Inc.

Schutz, Alfred. 1962. *Collected Papers.* The Hague: Marinus Nijhoff.

Schutz, Alfred and Thomas Luckmann. 1973. *The Structures of the Life-World* (Richard M. Zaner and H.Tristram Engelhardt, Jr, trans.). Evanston, IL: Northwestern University Press.

Sheehan, Thomas. 1981. 'Husserl's Critique of Psychologism', in Peter McCormick and F. A. Elliston, eds, *Husserl: Shorter Works.* South Bend, IN: University of Notre Dame Press, pp. 143–45.

Spencer, Herbert. 1898. *Principles of Sociology.* New York: Appleton.

Stace, W. T. 1955. *The Philosophy of Hegel.* New York: Dover Publication Inc.

Sweezy, Paul. 1946. *The Theory of Capitalist Development.* London: D. Dobson.

Timasheff, N. S. 1967. *Sociological Theory.* New York: Random House.

Turner, Jonathan H. 1974. *The Structure of Sociological Theory.* Homewood, IL: Dorsey Press.

———. 2003. *The Structure of Sociological Theory.* Belmont, CA: Wadsworth.

Wallace, Ruth and Alison Wolf. 1999. *Contemporary Sociological Theory*, 5th ed. Upper Sadle River, NJ: Prentice Hall.

Wallace, William. 1892. *The Logic of Hegel.* Humphrey Milford: Oxford University Press.

Walsh, George. 1967. 'Introduction', in Alfred Schutz, ed., *The Phenomenology of the Social World.* Evanston, IL: Northwestern University Press.

Weber, Max. 1922. *The Nature of Social Action*, in W. G. Runciman, ed. and E. Mathews trans., *Weber: Selections in Translation.* UK: Cambridge University Press.

———. 1978 [1925]. 'Economy and Society', in Guenter Roth and Claus Witch, eds. Berkeley: University of California Press.

———. 1949 [1903–17]. *The Methodology of the Social Sciences* (A. Shils and Henry A. Finch, eds and trans.). New York: Free Press.

———. 1958 [1904–05]. *The Protestant Ethic and the Spirit of Capitalism* (Talcott Parsons, trans.). New York: Charles Scribner's Sons.

———. 1964. *The Theory of Social and Economic Organization* (A. M. Henderson and Talcott Parsons, trans.). New York: Free Press.

Wolff, Kurth (ed.). 1959. *Georg Simmel, 1858–1918: A Collection of Essays, with Translations and a Bibliography.* Colombus: Ohio State University Press.

Zetterburg, Hans L. 1979 [1901]. 'Introduction', in Vilfredo Pareto, *The Rise and Fall of the Elites.* New York: Arno Press.

Index

L

M

N

O

P

R

S